Study Abroad for P1 In-Service Teachers

M000236113

By exploring the experiences of pre- and in-service teachers, as well as the design and implementation of study abroad programs developed specifically for them, this volume highlights the potential of international learning in promoting teachers' global and critical understandings of their roles as educators in an increasingly diverse and interconnected world.

Recognizing teacher study abroad as a unique strand within the wider foreign education literature, *Study Abroad for Pre- and In-Service Teachers* emphasizes how it can be conceptualized, theorized, and implemented as part of initial and continuing teacher training. Chapters consider study abroad programs and teaching practices in Europe, Asia, the Americas, and in Indigenous communities, and document the transformative learning experiences which impact the way teachers think about learning, teaching, and identity. Together, the chapters foreground the personal and professional advantages of teacher study abroad, and provide key insights to inform design and programming for sustainable, impactful teacher study abroad which supports teachers in building incultural competence and enhances their capacity to serve students of varying cultural and linguistic backgrounds.

This volume will appeal to researchers, scholars, education abroad facilitators, and teacher educators with an interest in international mobility, multicultural education, culturally responsive pedagogy and study abroad. In addition, pre- and in-service teachers will find the book of value.

Laura Baecher is Professor of TESOL at the Hunter College of Education, The City University of New York, United States.

Routledge Research in Teacher Education

The Routledge Research in Teacher Education series presents the latest research on Teacher Education and also provides a forum to discuss the latest practices and challenges in the field.

For more information about this series, please visit: https://www.routledge.com/Routledge-Research-in-Teacher-Education/book-series/RRTE

Study Abroad for Pre- and In-Service Teachers

Transformative Learning on a Global Scale

Edited by Laura Baecher

Routledge
Taylor & Francis Group

NEW YORK AND LONDON

First published 2021
by Routledge
52 Vanderbilt Avenue, New York, NY 10017

and by Routledge
2 Park Square, Milton Park, Abingdon, Oxon, OX14 4RN

Routledge is an imprint of the Taylor & Francis Group, an informa business

Library of Congress Cataloging-in-Publication Data
A catalog record for this title has been requested

ISBN: 978-0-367-43571-4 (hbk)
ISBN: 978-1-003-00438-7 (ebk)

Typeset in Bembo
by KnowledgeWorks Global Ltd.

This book is dedicated to all of the amazing teachers around the world who open their hearts, minds, and classrooms to each other with a sincere desire for learning and reflection, and to my own three intrepid study abroad companions: Zachary, Jacob, and Rianna.

Contents

List of Figures

List of Tables

About the Contributors

Laura Baecher is Professor in the Department of Curriculum and Teaching, Hunter College School of Education at The City University of New York, US.

Clara Vaz Bauler is an Associate Professor at Adelphi University, US.

Sharon Brennan is an Associate Professor and Director for the Office of Clinical Practices and School Partnerships, US.

Dr. Erik Jon Byker is the International Studies Resident Director at Kingston University in London, UK, and he is also an Associate Professor for the Cato College of Education at the University of North Carolina at Charlotte, US.

Danielle M. Carrier is a former US and international elementary school teacher, and current doctoral student in the College of Education at the University of Georgia, US.

Lynell Caya is an Early Childhood Special Education teacher at Bristol School in Bristol, Wisconsin, US.

Karena Cooper-Duffy is a Professor at Western Carolina University, US.

Nicholas Elam is the Assistant Professor of Educational Leadership at Ball State University, US.

Rachel Louise Geesa, EdD, is the Assistant Professor of Educational Leadership at Ball State University, Muncie, Indiana, US.

Andrew Gilbert is an Associate Professor at George Mason University, US.

Lucinda Heimer is an Associate Professor at the University of Wisconsin-Whitewater, US.

Shannon M. Hilliker is the Assistant Professor of TESOL at Binghamton University, US.

Ellie Holliday is a Lecturer and College of Education Coordinator of International Partnerships at the University of Kentucky, US.

Blair Izard is an Assistant Professor at the University of Northern Iowa, US.

Brandon Kawa is the Associate Director of the International Graduate Programs for Educators at SUNY Buffalo State College, US.

Linda Krakaur is an Adjunct Professor at the University of Maryland at College Park, US.

Paige Lancaster is an Early Childhood Special Educator for Walworth County Birth to Three Program, US.

Chesla Ann Lenkaitis is an Assistant Professor at Binghamton University, US.

Wei Liu is the Associate Director of International Programs of the College of Education at the University of Illinois at Urbana-Champaign, US.

Barbara Loranc- Paszylk is an Assistant Professor at University of Bielsko-Biała, Poland.

Michael Lovorn is the Director of Global Engagement and International Graduate Programs at SUNY Buffalo State, New York, US.

Silvija Marnikovic holds a Master's degree in TESOL from Eastern Michigan University, US. She is an English teacher at Marko Nuculovic school, Montenegro.

Helen Marx is a Professor at the College of Education at Southern Connecticut State University, US.

David M. Moss is an Associate Professor at the University of Connecticut, US.

Thalia Mulvihill, Ph.D. is the Professor of Higher Education & Faculty Fellow (VP for Academic Affairs) at Ball State University, US.

Carmel O'Sullivan is a Professor of Education at Trinity College Dublin, Ireland.

S. Michael Putman is a professor and department chair at the University of North Carolina, Charlotte, US.

Kathleen A. Ramos is an Associate Professor at George Mason University, US.

Gloria Romero is an Assistant Professor at Universidad de Santiago de Chile.

Amy Rose is an Assistant Professor at Western Carolina University, US.

Dr. Jared A. Russell is a Professor of Kinesiology and Director of Diversity (College of Education) at Auburn University, US.

Jon Simmons is a doctoral student at the University of Connecticut, US.

Abigail Teeters is Associate Administrator at Bishop Watterson High School in Columbus, Ohio, US.

Chippewa M. Thomas is Director (Office of Faculty Engagement, University Outreach) and Professor (Counselor Education and Supervision programs) at Auburn University, US.

Devin Thornburg is Professor at Adelphi University, New York, US

L. Octavia Tripp is Associate Professor at Auburn University, US.

Amie VanHorn-Gabel is a K-12 English Learner Teacher in Michigan at Livonia Public Schools, US.

Gene Vasilopoulos is a Ph. D Candidate and Part-time Professor at University of Ottawa, Canada.

Xiao-lei Wang is Dean and Full Professor at Adelphi University, US.

Dennis White is Faculty Member in Mathematics and Art at Lac Courte Oreilles Ojibwe College in Hayward WI, US.

Allison Witt is Director, Office of International Programs and Program Leader, International Education Administration and Leadership at the University of Illinois Urbana-Champaign, US.

Rebecca Woodland is Professor of Educational Leadership and Policy at the University of Massachusetts Amherst, US.

Elizabeth Laura Yomantas is an Assistant Professor in the department of Humanities and Teacher Education at Pepperdine University in Malibu, CA, US.

Introduction to the Volume

Teachers who participate in learning and teaching abroad enhance their intercultural competence, develop more globally-informed and critical perspectives on education, and improve their foreign language and teaching skills (Pfingsthorn & Czura, 2017). Studies of study abroad programs designed for teachers have shown they positively impact participant teachers' foreign language growth, confidence in teaching skills, adaptability, world views, intercultural awareness, and sense of independence (Kabilan, 2013). Some teacher education programs have therefore begun to offer pre-service teachers experiences abroad through placements in teaching practica in international settings. Often, these international placements are in "developing" nations with student teachers coming from "developed" nations. Major and Santoro (2016) suggest that the power differentials and the complexities of post-colonialism must be thoughtfully and carefully addressed so that teachers move from compassion to a critical stance. A critical stance in study abroad enables teachers to increase their intercultural awareness, knowledge, sensitivity, and competence, as well as their ability to understand, respect, engage with, and ultimately teach diverse cultural groups (Dunn, Dotson, Cross, Kesner, & Lundahl, 2014; Pilonieta, Medina, & Hathaway, 2017; Sharma, Rahatzad, & Phillion, 2013; Shedrow, 2017).

If an essential component of teacher development is to promote a more global, and critical understanding of schooling, one of the less common, yet potent ways to enhance teachers' empathy is through study-abroad. However, while research on study abroad points to such transformative learning (Baecher & Chung, 2020), there have, to-date, been relatively few publications on study abroad for teachers, as the bulk of study abroad literature focuses on undergraduate student experiences rather than study abroad in the teacher education context. This edited volume addressed that gap by illuminating how study abroad experiences designed specifically for teachers, both pre- and in-service, are being conceptualized, theorized, implemented, and researched.

Key objectives of this volume are:

- To develop scholarly awareness of teacher study abroad as a unique strand within the wider study abroad literature

- To support teacher educators in designing and implementing impactful study abroad that also benefits host communities
- To orient international and global education professionals toward the potential of teachers as study abroad participants
- To offer compelling evidence for the creation of teacher study abroad programming that is intentionally conscious and critical of structural inequities and their connection to schooling
- To theorize about study abroad in teacher education in ways that lead to knowledge-building in this new area of research
- To position study abroad in teacher learning experiences in ways that build teacher capacity for serving multilingual and multicultural students

This text offers perspectives from a variety of global teacher education contexts and will advance readers' understanding of teacher education and development for global understanding through study abroad. Chapters selected for inclusion in this volume are presented in three sections.

Section 1, Intentionality in the Instructional Design of Teacher Study Abroad, provides insights into the design decisions and structures for creating sustainable, impactful teacher study abroad programming. Holliday and Brennan lay out a comprehensive approach to routine inclusion of teacher study abroad across a consortia of colleges of teacher education, with many years of experience to draw upon. Putman and Byker break down their key components and help us see how they play out as they bring teacher candidates to South Africa. Witt and Liu, as well as Moss, Simmons, Izard, and Marx delve into the aspects of scaling up study abroad, from psychological measures of change to study its impact, to addressing and overcoming institutional constraints. Woodland's chapter as well as Vasilopoulos and Romero's turn the table to examine how teacher study abroad that invites teachers from Pakistan and China to the United States and Canada are designed and how those theories are made actionable.

Section 2 offers a number of cases of implementation of teacher study abroad programs. These range in sites from Fiji (Yomantas) to Botswana (Rose & Cooper-Duffy) to Malawi (Tripp, Love, Barry, Thomas, & Russell), from Ireland (O'Sullivan & Krakaur) and Germany (Geesa, Mulvihill, Elam, & Teeters), and Ecuador (Carrier) to Costa Rica (Gilbert & Ramos). Each case is unique and provides insights into the program's goals and how those were realized, while also exploring some of the limitations. The reflections of participants and faculty leading these programs create windows into the impact of these programs on the way they think about learners, teaching, and identity.

Section 3 points to innovative new directions for the future of teacher study abroad. These include four principal directions that herald the next frontier for teacher study abroad. First, Tomaš, Van Horn-Gabel, and Marniković dive deeply into what it really means to create teacher study abroad programming that lives up to the promise of service-learning and truly benefits the host community. Their work returning to Montenegro with teacher candidates has created a long-lasting positive impact on the local school, personnel, and residents. Mutual benefit and sensitivity towards "helping" versus truly partnering, especially with Global North teachers traveling to Global South contexts, is a critical future direction for programing. Second, Bauler, Wang, and Thornburg offer up a menu of possible ways to bring internationalism to the local campus. They share a variety of initiatives, from video-conferencing with teachers abroad, engaging with international students on campus, in order to expand our notions of what "study abroad" can look like. Especially in times where travel is restricted, these alternate international experiences can offer many of the benefits to teacher thinking that travel does. Next, along the same line, Hilliker, Loranc-Paszylk, and Lenkaitis describe a direct and consistent videoconferencing exchange program between teachers of English in the United States and Poland. They weave together the pedagogical skills both groups are addressing in their coursework while adding on the cultural dimension quite tangibly as teacher groups wrestle with concepts and language teaching together. Finally, Heimer, White, Caya, and Lancaster travel "abroad" within the United States by creating the opportunity for teacher candidates to live, study, and work in a nearby Indigenous sovereign nation. Such study "abroad" experiences that are domestic but can expose teachers to culturally, linguistically, ethnically, and socially diverse communities may be one of the most important new directions for this work.

Taken together, the chapters included in this volume provide clear and compelling professional development models grounded in a globalized vision for teacher learning and practice, explore the impact of study abroad on pre- and in-service teachers' beliefs, knowledge, and practices before, during, and immediately after their participation; and provide a heuristic for the design of such programs in terms of international service learning for teacher educators seeking to design a similar initiative.

References

Baecher, L. & Chung, S. (2020) Transformative professional development for in-service teachers through international service learning, *Teacher Development*, 24(1), 33–51.

Dunn, A. H., Dotson, E. K., Cross, S. B., Kesner, J., & Lundahl, B. (2014). Reconsidering the local after a transformative global experience: A comparison of two study abroad programs for preservice teachers. *Action in Teacher Education*, 36(4), 283–304.

Kabilan, M. K. (2013). A phenomenological study of an international teaching practicum: Pre-service teachers' experiences of professional development. *Teaching and Teacher Education*, 36, 198–209.

Major, J., & Santoro, N. (2016). Supervising an international teaching practicum: building partnerships in postcolonial contexts. *Oxford Review of Education*, 42(4), 460–474.

Pfingsthorn, J., & Czura, A. (2017). Student teachers' intrinsic motivation during a short-term teacher training course abroad. *Language, Culture and Curriculum*, 30(2), 107–128.

Pilonieta, P., Medina, A. L., & Hathaway, J. I. (2017). The impact of a study abroad experience on preservice teachers' dispositions and plans for teaching English language learners. *The Teacher Educator*, 52(1), 22–38.

Sharma, S., Rahatzad, J., & Phillion, J. (2013). How pre-service teachers engage in the process of (de)colonization: Findings from an international field experience in Honduras. *Interchange*, 43, 363–377.

Shedrow, S. J. (2017). Cross-cultural student teaching: Examining the meaning-making of one white, female, middle-class preservice teacher. *Journal of International Students*, 7(2), 270–290.

Section 1

Intentionality in the Instructional Design of Teacher Study Abroad

1 Building a Pathway to Prepare Globally Competent Teachers

Ellie Holliday and Sharon Brennan

Laying a Foundation for Global Competence

For some time now, education policy making groups in the United States (e.g., Council of Chief State School Officers, Partnership for 21st Century Schools) have stressed the importance of preparing P-12 school students for success in what has become an interconnected world (Longview Foundation, 2008). A recent report of the global Organisation for Economic Co-operation and Development (OECD) reinforced this point, asserting that students who cannot communicate across cultures will face immense challenges as they enter a workplace that now requires collaboration at a global level (OECD, 2016). In proposing a framework for placing a global lens on the school curriculum, Tichnor-Wagner and Manise (2019) state that enhanced technology, access to transportation, and global migration intensify the need for students to be what they call "global-ready" (p. 3).

The call to "ready" students for employment in the global community means teachers must be prepared to facilitate the process. Boix Mansilla and Jackson (2011) suggest that this involves embracing the existing diversity in P-12 classrooms and helping all students in those classrooms develop skills needed to fully "engage the world" (p. viii). Considerable evidence suggests that P-12 schools are increasingly more diverse (Digital Promise Global, 2016; US National Center for Education Statistics, 2018). Given the changing demographics in schools and increased human interaction around the world, global competence presents as an essential skill for those entering the teaching profession. Essentializing from research by others in the field (e.g., Brennan, 2017; Cushner, 2016; Jackson, 2015), we believe globally competent teaching includes two elements: skill with helping students understand and address globally and locally relevant issues as well as knowing how to help students develop cultural self-awareness and awareness of other cultural perspectives.

Our emphasis on global competence for teachers and their students is situated in a *transformative learning* theoretical perspective. Transformative learning, originally conceptualized by Mezirow (1991), addresses the notion of reality and meaning as constructs of the individual. Each individual holds a certain perspective of the world, constructed through prior experiences. Through learning, both in reflection and hands-on tasks, the learner can expand their worldview. Similarly, global citizenship can be viewed through a transformational lens. As described by Shultz (2007), transformationalist global citizens expand the perspective of globalization to include more than just the dominant Western notion of neoliberalism and competition. They see themselves as connected to others around the world and "understand their connection to all other people through a common humanity, a shared environment, and shared interests and activities" (Shultz, 2007, p. 249). Shultz' view undergirds curricular frameworks that provide ways to prepare "global-ready" students (e.g., Programme for International Student Assessment [PISA] & OECD, 2018; Tichnor-Wagner & Manise, 2019). This view also relates to *cosmopolitanism,* an ancient ideology as described by Appiah (2006). He characterizes this ideology as having two critical elements: concern for others and respect for difference (p. xv). Transformational theory espoused by Shultz and embedded in cosmopolitanism fits well within an education context given the emphasis on addressing humanitarian needs.

In this chapter, we describe our journey as faculty members and proponents of internationalization in the University of Kentucky (UK) College of Education (COE) to help candidates in the Educator Preparation Program (EPP) develop a global perspective. The initiative, which has evolved over the last four decades, emanates from a transformational, cosmopolitan perspective. From the beginning, the overarching goal has been to help teacher candidates develop a skillset associated with global competence so they, in turn, can help students they serve in P-12 schools from a wide array of backgrounds develop sufficient intercultural understanding and global awareness to thrive in today's interconnected world. The school district where UK is located serves the Lexington community, which has experienced a nearly 300% growth in the numbers of English Language Learners (ELLs) in the last decade. The number of first languages spoken by students in the local school system rose from 27 in 2005–2006 to nearly 100 in 2016–2017 according to data reported recently by the metro city government multicultural affairs coordinator (Lexington-Fayette Urban County Government, 2019). In contrast, UK's EPP enrollment data indicate that 87% of the candidates enrolled are Caucasian and 80% are female across certification programs, though we do not currently have data on the candidates' linguistic diversity (University of Kentucky, 2016). The contrast between the school and university demographics indicate a need for inclusion of cultural and global competency initiatives in the EPP curriculum. In sharing our story, we describe our conception of a Global Learning Pathway for teacher candidates and the steps that have led us there. These include study abroad programming for teacher candidates; the formation of our overseas student teaching (OST) program; and the assignments, assessments, and considerations developed to address teacher candidates' global competency.

Development of a Global Learning Pathway

International initiatives for teacher candidates in our EPP began in 1973 with the establishment of the OST program by a faculty member who served as the Director of Field Experiences for the university's EPP. Among his many responsibilities, Dr. Leland Smith conducted accreditation reviews for P-12 schools in Central and South America along with administrators from other US universities. These other US universities shared a common feature with UK: many of their teacher candidates also came from rural areas with homogeneous populations and had very limited exposure to cultural diversity. Some had never traveled outside the region where they resided. When these institutional representatives conducted accreditation visits at school sites abroad, they shared concerns about whether teacher candidates from their home institutions were equipped to address students' needs if employed by schools with diverse populations. As a result, a partnership was formed to provide opportunities for candidates to student teach in the schools they reviewed. This formal partnership was named the Consortium for Overseas Student Teaching (COST), and it still exists today as an option for teacher candidates to complete part or all of their student teaching requirements.

Despite recruitment and marketing efforts, a small percentage of teacher candidates participate in the OST program as compared to our local student teaching opportunities. In recent years, our EPP has developed a goal to increase the number of international and intercultural opportunities available to our teacher candidates. This goal stemmed, in part, from the process to craft a new 2015–2020 strategic plan in the College of Education. The plan called for support for diversity and inclusion by, among other objectives, enhancing "opportunities to infuse... international and diverse perspectives across the curriculum and the co-curriculum" (University of Kentucky College of Education, 2015, p. 4). The Curriculum and Instruction Department in which we reside created a strategic plan following the COE's example, which explicated a specific action plan for producing globally competent graduates. The department set a goal to increase global mindedness while fostering diversity and inclusiveness among faculty, staff, and students with a pledge to scaffold experiences as candidates progress through the program to help broaden their worldviews (University of Kentucky College of Education, 2015).

Prior to the strategic planning process, the UK International Center undertook several initiatives to integrate education abroad experiences more deeply into the curricula. One such initiative relates to curriculum integration. In the field of international education, "curriculum integration" refers to "a variety of institutional approaches designed to fully integrate study abroad options into the college experience and academic curricula for students in all majors" (NAFSA: Association of International Educators [NAFSA], 2016). For UK Education Abroad, this process resulted in designing a set of "Major Advising Pages" highlighting various international opportunities available for specific majors in each college. Some featured 4-year academic plans with integrated semesters abroad

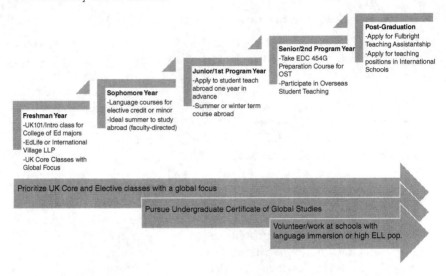

Figure 1.1 College of education global learning pathway for undergraduate students in EPPs

(NAFSA, 2016). This initiative, as well as the Curriculum and Instruction department's strategic goals related to global competency, sparked the creation of the Global Learning Pathway for teacher candidates in all EPP certification areas. See Figure 1.1 for a depiction of the Global Learning Pathway.

Opportunities to engage with people from diverse backgrounds are readily available to UK's teacher candidates, but are often difficult for candidates to discover on their own. These opportunities include but are not limited to: (a) Living Learning Programs (residential academic experiences in which students with similar majors or interests live and learn together) that offer opportunities to volunteer or work with under-represented populations; (b) courses in the UK Core and electives with a global focus; and (c) education abroad programs. The Global Learning Pathway integrates many opportunities into one single advising document, to be shared with teacher candidates by academic advisors or faculty, especially for those not yet admitted to the EPP who are seeking global or intercultural experiences. The Global Learning Pathway provides a "step-by-step" approach, laying out various opportunities on- and off-campus. The following sections will describe some of the opportunities available specifically for teacher candidates and the considerations that led to their formation.

Creating Opportunities for Education Majors to Broaden their Cultural Perspectives

While creating the content of the Global Learning Pathway advising document, we noticed a lack of relevant, affordable international opportunities for education majors between the time they entered the university as freshmen and when they began the EPP. Additionally, it appeared existing opportunities did not offer academic credit toward their major. Before beginning EPP coursework (typically in their late sophomore or early junior year), education majors are generally disconnected from the COE and its faculty members as they complete UK Core coursework and electives. To help address these issues, Ellie Holliday collaborated with another faculty member to develop a faculty-directed embedded study abroad program with travel to Belize in March 2019. It was marketed to freshmen and sophomore education majors and had a lower cost comparable to other education abroad programs marketed to education majors. The Belize program offered academic credit toward a targeted education-based elective requirement for many education majors. The course was titled *Globally Minded Teaching and Learning,* and participants in the program spent several days observing, volunteering, and collaborating with students and teachers in a rural elementary school in Corozal, Belize. The development of the program was made possible by generous support from the Curriculum and Instruction Department, COE, and the UK International Center. We intend to offer it as an academic credit-bearing program at least every 2 years.

Because the Belize program was developed with the Global Learning Pathway in mind, it can serve as a steppingstone for teacher candidates interested in increasing their global competence before formally entering the EPP. The program includes many learning objectives and assignments candidates will encounter again, at a higher level, if they choose to participate in the overseas student teaching program. These include developing a home culture "story," conversing with college-level English as a Second Language (ESL) partners, and developing globally minded instructional resources to use in classrooms.

Reflecting on skills gained during the experience, participants said the Belize program helped broaden their cultural perspectives. One noted that "observing differences in educational methods and customs at [the Belizean school] broadened my perspective on possible teaching methods, particularly ones based on values that are not prevalent in my culture." We interpreted this to mean that the participant observed and appreciated classroom practices based on values that they identified as different compared to their US cultural values. In class discussions, these differences were identified as a slower pace of life, greater community involvement and integration with the school, and greater focus on decorum from students in the classroom in Belize as compared to the United States. One white US participant reported what we interpreted as an increased awareness and respect for people of color and those from other cultural backgrounds, saying that "I was able to see a lot of people who were not like me but were just as successful and happy, and it helped me to deepen the understanding that there are multiple types of people and ways to live life, and that is more than okay."

The Belize program was designed in a way that accommodates the needs of students with financial concerns by providing a shorter and cheaper international experience than many other education abroad programs. We also implemented targeted outreach efforts to students of color and first-generation students, who are traditionally under-represented in education abroad programming (NAFSA, n.d.). Of the 10 participants in the Spring 2019 Belize cohort, one was African-American, five were first-generation college students, four were from out-of-state, and five of them had never traveled outside of the United States. Many were able to use their existing financial aid packages to pay for the program and/or earn additional need- and merit-based scholarships. The success of the Belize program has piqued the interest of several faculty members who have begun planning similar programs. We expect these programs, and those created in the future that are tailored to accommodate a broad range of needs, will help expand the pool of candidates who participate in international initiatives.

Building Global Competence for Overseas Student Teaching

After the formation of the OST program in the 1970s, Dr. Smith designed a three-credit, academic bearing course that UK COST participants were required to complete prior to student teaching. The course, entitled *Culture, Education and Teaching Abroad,* was unique within the COST network at the time because it was not required for teacher candidates from other institutions in the Consortium. It was designed to help candidates examine cultural perspectives—their own and others'—as well as learn more about education systems in countries where they would teach students. Over the years, the program has changed in several ways. One relates to placement site expansion: while placements had been limited to partner schools in Central and South America when the program began, candidates now have opportunities to teach in schools in Africa, Asia, Europe, New Zealand, and Australia. In addition, the curricular focus has changed to emphasize pedagogical practices designed to help P-12 school students thrive in the world as it exists now and in the future. Our ability to "shift gears" is largely due to guidance from resources that have become available in the last decade, such as Boix Mansilla & Jackson's (2011) report titled *Educating for global competence: Preparing our youth to engage the world* and the Council of Chief State School Officers' (2013) document titled *InTASC: Model core teaching standards and learning progressions for teachers 1.0.* When we began teaching the preparatory course together in 2017, we used the new resources to create assignments linking cultural learning with specific, globally focused pedagogical practices. In doing so, we tightened the coupling between the preparatory course and the OST experience.

Program Revisioning: Applying Global Learning to Teaching Practice

While the preparatory course we currently teach still aims to help teacher candidates participating in the OST program expand their cultural perspectives, we now spend considerable time helping course participants translate what they are learning into concrete teaching practices. See Table 1.1 for a summary of all key assignments along with their descriptions, timelines, and connected learning objectives.

Table 1.1 Key Assignments Completed Through Preparatory Course and Student Teaching

Assignment	Description	Timeline	Learning Objective
Home Culture Story	Digital presentation highlighting cultural values, traditions, traits, etc., related to their cultural identity.	Completed early in the prep course. Participants encouraged to share the story while student teaching, and have their students share their cultural stories.	To help OST participants examine their own cultural "story" before considering the cultural story of those from different backgrounds.
Project-Based Globally Focused Instructional Unit Plan	Using the "Core Domains" outlined by Boix Mansilla & Jackson (2011), OST participants create an interdisciplinary unit plan addressing a globally focused topic, such as "pollution" or "human rights".	Unit is completed at end of course and implemented while in their overseas classroom.	To help P-12 students make local-global connections for issues affecting them and others in meaningful ways.
Connecting Two Classrooms	While teaching overseas, OST participants digitally connect their overseas classroom with one in Kentucky.	Connections initiated during the preparatory course then carried out during student teaching. Unit Plans included when possible.	To facilitate cultural exchange and promote intercultural understanding.
Cultural Exchange Experience	OST participants meet with international students who are studying at the University of Kentucky several times during the preparatory course to exchange ideas about culture.	Throughout the preparatory course.	To broaden cultural perspectives.
Cultural Plunge	OST participants visit an unfamiliar place within their US community and write a reflective report about culture and overcoming challenges.	Visit and report completed mid-semester.	To experience being an outsider in an unfamiliar place.

Two assignments in particular help with building the foundation of respecting cultural differences and understanding diverse perspectives. The Cultural Exchange Experience connects teacher candidates with a UK student participating in the college-level intensive ESL program and prompts them to meet several times during the semester to discuss their cultural similarities and differences. The Cultural Plunge asks teacher candidates to experience what it is like to be a stranger in a strange place by visiting local events or locations in which the main attendees are culturally different from the candidate. While the Cultural Exchange and Cultural Plunge assignments are not directly linked to participants' teaching practice, they serve as valuable building blocks for working with students and colleagues who come from backgrounds different from their own. These experiences also provide ways to understand "culture shock." Reading Kohls' (2001) *Survival Kit for Overseas Living*, another course assignment, helps candidates understand "culture shock," which is defined as "the more pronounced reactions to the psychological disorientation most people experience when they move for an extended period into a culture markedly different from their own" (p. 91). Though most OST participants are usually only abroad for 8 weeks, the experience of working in a school overseas, especially for those who have never been abroad before, can create confusion, frustration, and homesickness brought on by culture shock. The Cultural Exchange and Cultural Plunge experiences, together with the in-class discussions about Kohls' book, help prepare them for possible cultural adaptation challenges as they begin their overseas teaching experience.

The Home Culture Story, Instructional Learning Unit Plan, and Connecting Two Classrooms assignments lay the groundwork for teacher candidates to translate what they are learning about culture into instructional resources for use in the classroom. The Home Culture Story both introduces them to their fellow teacher candidates in the preparatory course and also serves as their introduction to their overseas student teaching classroom students. It asks them to deeply consider their core values, where those values come from (such as family, community, religion, friends, etc.), and how their values affect their daily life, beliefs, goals, and practices. The Unit Plan involves formulating lesson plans and an overarching unit theme that combine project-based learning with exploration of a locally and globally focused theme such as recycling, water usage, pollution, poverty, and more. Many teacher candidates connect two classrooms by virtually linking their overseas placement with their local placement. For instance, one recent OST graduate, while student teaching at a bilingual school in Spain, conducted several sessions via Skype between her fourth-grade students in Spain and fifth-grade students in Kentucky where she had previously completed an extended practicum.

Ann (a pseudonym) established two goals for student interchange (conversations conducted in English): (a) to learn about each other's cultures and (b) to compare energy systems used in their locales. Ann foreshadowed this during her practicum placement by helping students in the classroom where she was placed examine energy sources used locally in Kentucky. When she began student teaching in Spain, she used the same approach with the class there. Prior to the first Skype session, Ann asked the students in Spain to develop questions for their Kentucky counterparts, vote to determine which questions they would ask, and consider how they would answer questions they might be asked by students in Kentucky. Questions, she explained, would first focus on cultural traditions and then proceed to discussions about energy sources.

When students in the Spanish school initially examined the topic, they began to see value in the European Union's goal to shift to renewable energy sources. At this point, students in Spain thought the approach was ideal and did not understand why anyone would have a different perspective. When Ann directed her students in Spain to examine energy sources in Kentucky including the use of coal, their initial reaction was negative. However, once the Spanish students learned about the economic impact of Kentucky's failing coal industry, they expressed concern about the potential negative effects, such as job loss, if coal was replaced by other energy sources. Expressed concerns led to conversations about how renewable energy may be better for our planet but might have negative consequences in certain areas, at least in the short term. Students in both locales started researching solutions and generating ideas about how to reduce the carbon footprint and create jobs for people who may lack employment when energy sources change. Students in both locations also shared their findings with parents and school administrators in forums as a small action step, seeking their advice about what might be done to help those who lost jobs.

The entire process was student led and all involved seemed eager to learn from students close to their age who lived in another part of the world. Connecting students in Spain with those in Kentucky helped everyone better understand the complex issues associated with conditions within and outside their immediate environment.

Guiding and Assessing Global Competence in Teaching

We use several newly created tools to guide and assess growth as OST participants progress through the preparatory course. See Table 1.2 for a summary of these tools, when they are used, and their purpose.

One tool we use to assess program impact is the *myCAP* Self-Reflection and Discussion Tool from the My Cultural Awareness Profile (myCAP) commissioned by NAFSA and developed by Marx and Moss (2016). MyCAP focuses specifically on helping teacher candidates consider their cultural perspectives. Through the survey, candidates examine their cultural perspectives and views about global issues in education. Candidates complete the Self-Reflection and Discussion Tool, consisting of 15 survey style questions and 6 short-answer prompts, early in the preparatory course. The positioning

Table 1.2 Assessment Tools to Guide Growth Regarding Global Competencies

Assessment Tool	Description	Timeline	Purpose
My Cultural Awareness Profile (*myCAP*) commissioned by NAFSA (Marx & Moss, 2016)	OST participants reflect about their cultural perspectives using *myCAP's* structured surveys to guide responses.	OST participants complete *myCAP* at several checkpoints: • Beginning of the preparatory course. • Conclusion of preparatory course. • Conclusion of their overseas teaching experience.	To promote cultural and pedagogical growth related to global competence.
Overseas Student Teaching Reflections	OST participants reflect about cultural learning including challenges with communication, culture shock, etc., throughout their overseas experience, examining growth and communicating challenges and successes with facilitators back home.	OST participants complete first reflections when they arrive overseas, second midway through their experience, and third when they prepare to return home.	Written reflections exploring their evolving cultural perspectives, coping with culture shock, and strategies promoting global competence while student teaching overseas.
NAFSA's (2015) "Global Lens" Document: *InTASC as a Framework: Viewing the InTASC Standards through a Global Preparation Lens*	The document provides a concrete way to guide and assess growth regarding globally competent teaching practice related to InTASC Standards.	Planning and evaluating instruction throughout the student teaching experience.	To guide and assess growth regarding globally competent teaching practice and provide a vehicle for reflection between student teachers and their supervisors on this domain.

of the survey when the course begins follows Bennett's (2013) assertion that "cultural self-awareness… is the necessary beginning point for any analysis of cultural interaction" (p. 58). Indeed, as students dive deeper into cross-cultural interaction and analysis throughout the course, they reflect about similarities and differences between their cultural values and those they meet from diverse backgrounds while participating in the OST program.

Results from pre- and post-course myCAP surveys have been illuminating as participants have shared their cultural learning journeys. A preliminary review of the 2018 Fall Semester course participant group's responses showed growth in several areas. When asked on a scale ranging from "strongly disagree" to "strongly agree" regarding the phrase "It is easy to find a global connection in most topics I [plan to] teach," the post-course survey average moved toward "strongly agree." When asked whether "school curriculum should encourage students to consider how their actions impact global issues," all participants "strongly agreed" in the post-course survey, whereas there was less enthusiasm in the pre-survey. Participants also indicated growth in acknowledging falsehoods inherent in the phrases such as "other people are more cultural than I am" and "the cultural background of students shouldn't impact the way you teach."

To augment myCAP and foster deep reflection during student teaching, the OST Reflections prompt teacher candidates to describe changes in their cultural perspectives as well as strategies they are using to promote global competence. We also conduct a debriefing session when they return from their overseas placement as a final reflection. During that debriefing, returning candidates often report mild homesickness and cultural adaptation challenges experienced when the overseas placements began. Once acclimated to their new surroundings, participants frequently say that they are able to examine different cultural practices in a new light and even incorporate them into their lives. One such example is the enhanced global stewardship exhibited in countries outside the United States, especially in New Zealand where there is a strong effort to care for the environment. OST participants also say the schools overseas embrace the globally focused strategies they bring to the classroom. During the debriefing, OST participants also present what we refer to as a "signature piece"—an example showing how they impacted student learning while student teaching overseas. The presentation provides a way to highlight strengths they might share with an interview committee when applying for teaching positions with an emphasis on the impact on student learning.

Student teachers' performance assessment is based on the NAFSA (2015) *InTASC as a framework: Viewing the InTASC standards through a global preparation lens* document to identify how OST participants demonstrate global competence related to the InTASC Model Core Teaching Standards (Council of Chief State School Officers [CCSSO], 2013). For example, regarding InTASC Standard 2: Learning Differences (d), we consider how OST participants infuse multiple perspectives in lessons to help students create and share their cultural stories. We also consider how participants address InTASC Standard 5: Application of Content (f) to engage their students in … "seeking inventive solutions to local and global problems …" when designing, implementing, and evaluating their unit plans (CCSSO, 2013, p. 14).

We believe the updates to the OST program and preparatory course have positively influenced participants' perceptions and practices. OST participants have consistently given high ratings to the preparatory course and to their experience student teaching overseas. While some indicated the preparatory course was more rigorous than expected, several said it transformed their thinking and practice. One comment represents the whole group's general sentiment: "discussions about becoming a global citizen and gaining new perspectives were extremely helpful." Student teachers' perception evaluation ratings were equally strong. Some expressed a desire to continue using the practices developed during the program in their teaching, especially connecting students in classrooms where they taught in Kentucky with those in their classrooms overseas.

Designing a Certificate Recognizing Global Competence in Teaching

From the Global Learning Pathway project, individual 4-year plans that weave intercultural and international opportunities together with program requirements are being developed for each EPP to advise prospective and current teacher candidates. For example, the Elementary Education Program plan offers opportunities such as: (a) joining a Living Learning Program with opportunities for freshmen to volunteer in schools and/or community agencies with diverse populations; (b) participating in faculty-directed study abroad programs (e.g., the Belize program) that include relevant credit-bearing courses; and (c) enrolling in overseas student teaching.

These comprehensive plans encourage faculty input on recommended international and intercultural experiences and allow university students to choose opportunities best fitting their academic, personal, and career goals. Ultimately, these plans will serve as advising tools for candidates interested in earning a certificate highlighting the skills they have acquired to address the needs of all P-12 students, whatever their background, to live and work in our interconnected world. The certificate will be flexible enough to allow teacher candidates to choose the opportunities best fitting their goals yet rigorous enough to ensure they have acquired the necessary skills to do the job. The certificate can serve as a tool for graduates, when applying for teaching positions, to show they bring added value to schools with their unique skillset. The certificate would be more targeted to teacher candidates than the "Undergraduate Certificate of Global Studies" currently indicated in the Global Learning Pathway in Figure 1.1.

Discussion of Initiatives Within the Theoretical Frameworks

Transformative learning asks the learner to stretch their worldview and consider perspectives beyond their own through reflection and problem solving. In asking teacher candidates to consider themselves "transformationalist global citizens," they are able to make connections to other people through an understanding of our common humanity (Shultz, 2007, p. 249). In the framework of "cosmopolitanism," Appiah (2006) articulates a need to understand others' perspectives and respect their differences.

Elements of transformative learning, through the lens of global citizenship and cosmopolitanism, are woven through the curricular and co-curricular elements of the Global Learning Pathway. The Belize program introduced multicultural perspectives to teacher candidates by having them work with Belizean teachers to develop instructional resources for the classroom that were culturally relevant. Teacher candidates enrolled in the OST preparatory class consider their own cultural perspectives through the Home Culture Story, and others' perspectives through the Cultural Plunge and Cultural Exchange project. They utilize problem solving in crafting a project-based locally and globally focused instructional learning unit plan. Throughout OST program participants' time abroad, and when they return, they are given ample time and direction to reflect on their experiences and their expanding worldview. Assessing teacher candidates throughout the process using tools such as myCap and the InTASC Global Lens allow facilitators to gauge their growth in intercultural and global competency.

Solidifying the Global Learning Pathway and Overcoming Obstacles

When it becomes an option for all teacher candidates, we believe the Global Learning Pathway project currently underway at UK will increase the pool of candidates in our EPP who have the skillset to infuse global competency into their teaching. However, we know there is more work ahead to fully realize our goal. We must involve more faculty in the process and engage more fully with our partners in local and overseas schools as well as within the communities where our schools are located. Although we have established a team with school and university partners, we must engage more stakeholders in the work.

Additionally, while current frameworks for global competence in education are considered to "encompass a broad number of other 'adjectival' educations, such as … multicultural education, anti-racism education… and others," we acknowledge that including explicit challenges to notions around race, equity, and justice is an area of growth for us as teacher educators (Suša, 2019, p. 5). We intend to collaborate with faculty colleagues involved more deeply with antiracist and social justice education work to examine ways in which we can further integrate these concepts into our assignments, discussions, and our own personal critical consciousness.

Finally, some obstacles stand in the way of effectively integrating global competency into both the EPP and K-12 curricula. Some EPP faculty may not see the value of making room in the curricula for global competency, and others do not have the resources to do so. Though scholars have expressed concern about the lack of attention to internationalizing the EPP curriculum (e.g., Brennan, 2017; Cushner, 2016; Roth & Rönnström, 2015; Quezada, 2010), resources from the Longview Foundation (2008) and NAFSA (2011) are available to address this concern. Curriculum standards imposed on P-12 schools related to student achievement understandably take priority over other interests. However, documents such as Boix Mansilla and Jackson's (2011) "Educating for Global Competence" provides a framework for integrating global competency into the existing curriculum, and NAFSA's (2015) *InTASC as a framework: Viewing the InTASC standards through a global preparation lens* document provides guidance on integrating global competency into teaching standards. Integrating global competency into the EPP curriculum through a transformative learning framework is both possible and necessary in today's interconnected world.

References

Appiah, A. (2006). *Cosmopolitanism: Ethics in a world of strangers*. W.W. Norton.

Bennett, M. J. (2013). *Basic concepts of intercultural communication: Paradigms, principles, and practices* (2nd ed.). Intercultural Press.

Boix Mansilla, V., & Jackson, A. (2011). *Educating for global competence: Preparing our youth to engage the world*. https://asiasociety.org/files/book-globalcompetence.pdf

Brennan, S. (2017, May 30). *Building teachers' global competence to reach all students* [Conference session]. NAFSA: Association of International Educators Global Learning Colloquium on Teacher Education, Los Angeles, CA, United States.

Brennan, S., & Holliday, E. (2019). Preparing globally competence teachers to address P-12 students' needs. *Global Education Review, 6*(3), 49–64.

Council of Chief State School Officers. (2013, April). *InTASC: Model core teaching standards and learning progressions for teachers 1.0*. https://ccsso.org/sites/default/files/2017-12/2013_INTASC_Learning_Progressions_for_Teachers.pdf

Cushner, K. (2016, November). *The intercultural training of teachers. What? When? How* [Paper presentation]? 7th Intercultural Forum on Intercultural Learning & Exchange, Rome, Italy.

Digital Promise Global. (2016, September). *The growing diversity in today's classroom*. http://digitalpromise.org/wp-content/uploads/2016/09/lps-growing_diversity_FINAL-1.pdf

Jackson, J. (2015). Becoming interculturally competent: Theory to practice in international education. *International Journal of Intercultural Relations, 48*, 91–107. https://doi.org/10.1016/j.ijintrel.2015.03.012

Kohls, R. L. (2001). *Survival kit for overseas living* (4 ed.). Nicholas Brealey Publishing.

Lexington-Fayette Urban County Government. (2019). LFUCG title VI plan annual report to liaisons: *Spring 2019 foreign languages in Fayette county* [Unpublished report].

Longview Foundation. (2008). *Teacher preparation for the global age: The imperative for change*. http://www.longviewfdn.org/files/44.pdf.

Marx, H. & Moss, D. (2016). *My cultural awareness profile: Self-reflection and discussion tool*. NAFSA: Association of International Educators. https://www.nafsa.org/mycap-suite-resources

Mezirow, J. (1991). *Transformative dimensions of adult learning*. Jossey-Bass.

NAFSA: Association of International Educators. (n.d.). *Trends in U.S. study abroad.* https://www.nafsa.org/policy-and-advocacy/policy-resources/trends-us-study-abroad

NAFSA: Association of Interational Educators. (2011, July 5). *Internationalizing teacher education online resources.* Retrieved June 16, 2020, from https://www.nafsa.org/professional-resources/browse-by-interest/internationalizing-teacher-education-online-resources

NAFSA: Association of International Educators. (2015). *InTASC as a framework: Viewing the InTASC standards through a global preparation lens.* https://www.nafsa.org/about/about-international-education/nafsa-global-preparation-lens

NAFSA: Association of International Educators. (2016). *Curriculum integration: Best practices.* https://www.nafsa.org/Professional_Resources/Browse_by_Interest/Education_Abroad/Network_Resources/Education_Abroad/Curriculum_Integration_Best_Practices/

Organisation for Economic Co-operation and Development. (2016). *Global competency for an inclusive world.* http://globalcitizen.nctu.edu.tw/wp-content/uploads/2016/12/2.-Global-competency-for-an-inclusive-world.pdf

Programme for International Student Assessment & Organisation for Economic Co-operation and Development. (2018). *Preparing our youth for an inclusive and sustainable world: The OECD PISA global competence framework.* https://www.oecd.org/education/Global-competency-for-an-inclusive-world.pdf

Quezda, R. L. (2010). Internationalization of teacher education: Creating global competent teachers and teacher educators for the twenty-first century. *Teaching Education, 21*(1), 1–5. https://doi.org/10.1080/10476210903466885

Roth, K., & Rönnström, N. (2015). Teacher education and the work of teachers in an age of globalization and cosmopolitization: The case in Sweden. *Policy Futures in Education, 13*(6), 705-711. https://doi.org/10.1177/1478210315595170

Shultz, L. (2007). Educating for global citizenship: Conflicting agendas and understandings. *Alberta Journal of Educational Research, 53*(3), 248-258.

Suša, R. (2019). *Global citizenship education (GCE) for unknown futures: Mapping past and current experiments and debates.* https://www.bridge47.org/sites/default/files/2019-07/bridge47_gce_for_unknown_futures_report-compressed_0.pdf

Tichnor-Wagner, A., & Manise, J. (2019). *Globally competent educational leadership: A framework for leading schools in a diverse, interconnected world.* Association for Supervision and Curriculum Development & The Longview Foundation. http://files.ascd.org/pdfs/publications/general/ascd-globally-competent-educational-leadership-report-2019.pdf

US. National Center for Education Statistics. (2018). *English language learners in public schools.* Retrieved April 29, 2019, from https://nces.ed.gov/programs/coe/indicator_cgf.asp

University of Kentucky College of Education. (2015, August 21). *College of education strategic plan.* https://education.uky.edu/wp-content/uploads/2013/12/COE-Strategic-Plan-Approved-08212015.pdf

University of Kentucky. (2016). *Enrollment and demographics.* Retrieved April 26, 2019 from https://www.uky.edu/irads/enrollment-demographics

2 Using Global Citizenship 1-2-3 and Study Abroad to Prepare Global-Ready Educators

S. Michael Putman and Erik J. Byker

Introduction

It is the last day of a month-long study abroad trip in South Africa for a group of teacher candidates. As a culminating activity, the candidates have been asked to reflect on their experience as it relates to the development of global citizenship, including the adoption of an action-oriented approach to make a difference in the world. The reflection prompt requested the candidates consider an experience during the study abroad trip where they saw someone making a difference in the world or where they were moved to take action. As part of this prompt, candidates were also asked to imagine, moving forward, how they could take action to make a difference in the world after their cross-cultural experiences in South Africa.

Several of the candidates' reflections described entrepreneurial South Africans they met who created employment opportunities for people in the townships making artwork and ornaments from recycled materials. Other candidates shared observations about the children they met in schools who spoke three or four different languages. The teacher candidates described how the children taught them about the importance of language and communication in a global society. For one teacher candidate, the experience of working in the South African schools resonated in a more personal manner. In her reflection, she described one South African teacher who came back to her community to teach in the local schools "because that is where she could make the biggest difference". The candidate wrote how she was amazed to see the dedication to education by this teacher, regardless of the conditions and what she perceived as a lack of resources. Perhaps more importantly, however, the candidate recognized her own role in changing the world. In her own words:

> I'm ready to make a difference in any way. There's a quote that I have kept thinking about throughout this study abroad trip. The quote goes something like this: "People travel to faraway places to watch the kind of people they ignore at home." This study abroad trip has taught me that I can no longer ignore the kids back home. As a global citizen, I know I can make a difference in the world no matter where I am. Now I am

more aware of the difference that I can make as a future teacher with kids who are closest to home. Sometimes you have to travel halfway around the world to have your "eyes-open" to how you can make the biggest difference in a place you know the best: home.

While many educators cannot travel across the world, this candidate's reflection underscores the powerful potential of experiential learning related to common issues and challenges in schools worldwide. It also demonstrates how making local and global connections can help an educator gain a greater sense of her role as a global citizen, spurring thoughts of actions to make the world a more equitable place. In essence, we see an example of the power of preparing someone to be a global-ready educator.

We define global ready as being equipped with the global competencies in order to actively participate in a pluralistic and culturally diverse society (Kerkhoff, 2017; Putman & Byker, 2020). Yet, how do teachers develop and grow in becoming global-ready educators? We argue that educator preparation programs (EPPs) that incorporate study abroad and international teaching opportunities have a unique role in equipping future teachers to be effective global citizens. Acknowledging this idea, the purpose of our chapter is to summarize a case study of a study abroad program to South Africa specifically designed for preparing teacher candidates to be global-ready educators. First, we provide background information on global citizenship in relation to teacher education. Second, we describe a model for the development of global citizenship, Global Citizenship 1-2-3. Third, we summarize findings from a case study of the aforementioned study abroad program.

Background

Given the increased prevalence of cultural and linguistic diversity in classrooms across the United States, there is an intense focus on preparing educators "to teach for diversity, equity and interconnectedness in the local community, nation and world" (Merryfield, 2000, p. 430). For EPPs, this means designing experiences that will ensure our future educators will possess the knowledge, skills and dispositions to work with diverse populations and to participate in a pluralistic, interconnected world (Byker & Putman, 2019; Putman & Byker, 2020). The chapter's opening vignette describes how one teacher candidate developed her understanding of her role as an educator in an interconnected world. It is important to expand opportunities for all future educators to realize they are part of a global community of citizens and, relatedly, to understand the collective responsibility they have for ensuring the next generation understands the importance of the sustainability of our planet (United Nations Education, Scientific and Cultural Organization, 2014). Indeed, one undergirding principle of global citizenship education is the notion of equipping educators to engage with the world and to be responsive to the diverse children that inhabit it.

Global Citizenship

The United Nations Education, Scientific and Cultural Organization (UNESCO) (2013) defines global citizenship as empowering individuals to "assume active roles both locally and globally to face and resolve global challenges and ultimately to become proactive contributors to a more just, peaceful, tolerant, inclusive, secure and sustainable world" (p. 3). Global citizens demonstrate respect for and value diversity, are actively engaged with the local, national and global community, are committed to sustainability and promote human rights as part of a shared common humanity (Byker, 2016; Oxfam, 2019). The importance of the development of global citizens is evident in the United Nations' (2015) Sustainable Development Goal 4: Quality Education. Specifically, Target 4.7 states:

> By 2030, ensure that all learners acquire the knowledge and skills needed to promote sustainable development, including, among others, through education for sustainable development and sustainable lifestyles, human rights, gender equality, promotion of a culture of peace and nonviolence, global citizenship and appreciation of cultural diversity and of culture's contribution to sustainable development.
>
> (United Nations, 2015, p. 21)

Acknowledging and accepting the characteristics of global citizenship and the important ideas presented by the United Nations means that both learners and educators will need to think about and take action in developing global citizens. This point is underscored with the realization that children in elementary school today will be coming into early adulthood by 2030.

Teachers play a pivotal role in the process of children's global citizenship development. Tawil (2013) explains how schools and teachers have an essential role in "preparing children and young people to deal with the challenges of todays increasingly interconnected and interdependent world" (p. 5). The Partnership for Twenty-First Century Skills (2014) sums up the important role of teachers with the following statement, "for students to be global, teachers must be global" (p. 5). Teachers should be able to model what it means to be a global citizen and have respect for the similarities and differences within a pluralist society. We argue that EPPs have a responsibility in preparing teachers who are global-ready citizens and educators.

Global Citizenship Education

Global Citizenship Education (GCED) is based on the recognition that learners need to be globally aware and prepared to participate in the global society (Byker, 2013; Freire, 1970). Broadly conceived, GCED is about investigating global issues through an engagement in collaborative work—both locally and globally—in order to develop potential actions and solutions to address these issues. UNESCO (2014) organizes GCED into three dimensions: (a) a socioemotional dimension, (b) a cognitive dimension, and (c) a behavioral dimension.

The socioemotional dimension relates to the development of empathy, communication skills and respect for diversity, including people from different backgrounds and cultures. This dimension includes the sense of belonging to a common humanity. Within the cognitive dimension, GCED is about gaining knowledge of the interconnectedness of global, national and local issues. Additionally, the cognitive dimension uses critical thinking and problem-solving skills to creatively address these issues with dispositions oriented on universal values such as justice, equality, dignity and respect. The third feature of GCED is the behavioral dimension, which references the capacity to collaborate and act responsibly toward goals associated with the collective good.

Educators play an instrumental role in global citizenship education. Thus, it is necessary to consider the preparation of teacher education candidates with respect to GCED. The extent to which this is happening is unclear (McGaha & Linder, 2014), though, and EPPs can fulfill a unique and important role in designing international curricular opportunities, including coursework and learning experiences, to equip teacher candidates to become global citizens. As the literature (see Byker & Putman, 2019; McGaha & Linder, 2014; Olmedo & Harbon, 2010) states, such opportunities (a) facilitate an understanding of the interconnectedness of global, national and local issues, (b) address the development of global perspectives, (c) build cross-cultural knowledge and (d) help candidates learn to value cultural diversity.

A Model for Global Citizenship Education

As teacher educators, we recognize our role in this process and have actively sought to develop our candidates' global perspectives as well as prepare them to be global-ready educators. We believe this is effectively accomplished through a program of study that infuses global citizenship education in the curriculum, with supporting examples of how globally competent teachers integrate these elements in PreK-12 classrooms. As a result, we created a model that would both support our teacher candidates' development of global competencies and provide a tool for them to use with PreK-12 students. The result was a GCED model we refer to as Global Citizenship 1-2-3.

Returning to the UNESCO dimensions of GCED, we acknowledge this terminology as helpful as a point of reference, but we believe the dimensions are not always relatable to future PreK-12 teachers who seek relevancy and direct applications of GCED within their practice. Retaining a focus on a common vocabulary, the Global Citizenship 1-2-3 model adopts what we view as more practical terminology in describing the dimensions of GCED. We use the term, *culturally responsive,* to describe how GCED is anchored in the socioemotional connection to empathy and the respect for diversity. As Gay (2002) explains, cultural responsiveness is the connection to "cultural characteristics, experiences and perspectives of ethnically diverse learners"

(p. 106). It represents an important component within the Global Citizenship 1-2-3 model as it provides a foundation for knowledge candidates need to be successful in educating all students. In describing the cognitive dimension, we employ the term, *global-infused content,* which captures how GCED includes global awareness and the examination of the interrelatedness of global, national and local issues. Finally, we use the term *experiential opportunities* to describe UNESCO's behavioral dimension. Experiences are critical to helping teacher candidates develop as global citizens. Notably, they can help to develop global awareness, build empathy and move learners to the recognition of interconnectedness and shared challenges. We contend that experiential opportunities have a heightened benefit when they include a study abroad component, which we will address later in the chapter.

As Figure 2.1 illustrates, Global Citizenship 1-2-3 is premised on the Learn-Think-Act cycle (Oxfam, 2019). First, culturally responsive content applicable to the setting, whether local or global, is introduced. Candidates explore (i.e., **learn** about) topics necessary for the development of culturally responsive knowledge under the guidance of an expert facilitator. The topics may include the cultural-historical context, the cultural traditions, values, ways of communication and intercultural relational patterns. As candidates gain knowledge about the culture or cultures where they are situated, the instructor provides opportunities for learners to examine, compare and reflect (i.e., **think**) about how the culture and place are globally situated. The global-infused content may focus on an examination of international issues like environmental sustainability, immigration or topics within the Sustainable Development Goals. Global Citizenship 1-2-3 seeks to move candidates to action. The learning and thinking steps are scaffolds within this process as

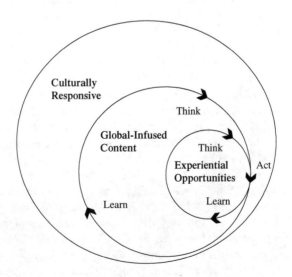

Figure 2.1 The Global Citizenship 1-2-3 theoretical model

the candidates engage in opportunities to individually and collectively take some form of action related to an issue under study. It is within this final step (i.e., **act**) where global citizenship development is most evident. It represents the culmination of knowledge gained within the learning of cultural responsiveness, supported by the reflection of globally infused content, in order to engage in experiential opportunities to see, implement and reflect upon the specific teaching strategies associated with GCED, fostering a critical consciousness of the world (Byker, 2013).

Further examining the model, the outer circle in Figure 2.1 serves to reinforce that cultural responsiveness serves as an encompassing principle for development of global citizenship. We believe that teachers cannot help students develop traits such as empathy or respect for differences without knowledge of cultural characteristics, perspectives and experiences of learners from diverse backgrounds. This is developed through a direct emphasis on integrating principles and tenets of culturally relevant teaching (see Gay, 2002) or culturally sustaining teaching (see Paris, 2012) into a program of study. The goal is to build content knowledge emphasizing various aspects of diversity (e.g., culture, race and language) as well as examine how this knowledge could be strategically implemented within instructional design and teaching practice. This will enable teaching candidates to develop more in-depth knowledge of cultural diversity, enact a curriculum that ensures ethnic and cultural diversity is represented, understand the necessity of building learning communities and effectively communicate with ethnically diverse parents and students (Gay, 2002). Teaching with these principles in mind will help candidates learn about their students' lives and cultural background and establish deeper relationships with them. It will also help the future teachers build the cultural competence and dispositional attributes necessary for cultural responsiveness, including a willingness to self-reflect, to acknowledge personal bias and to recognize societal reflections of power and privilege attributable to cultural differences, which are all hallmarks of GCED. In turn, these same candidates will develop activities that will assist the learners in their classrooms to develop similar dispositions.

While integrating tenets of globally competent teaching into the coursework may improve candidates' knowledge for enacting the signature pedagogies of GCE, we return to the importance of using experiential opportunities to help candidates gain firsthand knowledge and new insights about an issue or topic. We feel candidates need experiential opportunities, including direct cross-cultural experiences, to develop their own socioemotional skills and gain a greater understanding of diverse perspectives. Willard-Holt (2001) noted that these experiences contributed to an expanded worldview as well as the development of flexibility and compassion within teacher education candidates. This is especially true when experiences occur in contexts where preservice candidates directly engage with diverse people and communities unfamiliar to them and where candidates can link coursework that introduces the tenets of cultural competence into practice.

Beyond the traditional placement at a local school, partnerships with local nongovernment or community-based organizations provide opportunities for candidates to work with and learn about local and national conditions or issues that are impacted or aligned with those present on a global scale, including water scarcity or immigration. This could also include a number of international agencies that engage in ongoing efforts that could be presented to candidates. Whether local or global, teacher education candidates working with these organizations have an opportunity to develop greater knowledge and a more thorough understanding of the relationships between local and global challenges and, in turn, exhibit aspects of global citizenship.

It is also becoming more common for EPPs to incorporate international teaching experiences, and we are proponents of these types of experiences having led several ourselves. International experiences have been shown to offer a range of benefits for candidates, including opportunities to actively engage with people from diverse cultures and experiences, developing knowledge regarding the intersection of local and global issues, greater awareness and acceptance of cultural diversity and the development of intercultural competence (Byker, 2016; He et al., 2017). Study abroad experiences have been referred to as one of the most effective ways to prepare global teachers (Cushner & Mahon, 2002). Indeed, we have observed firsthand the many ways candidates learn and grow while abroad.

Yet, it is important to acknowledge that teaching in an international context, by itself, may not produce the aforementioned benefits for candidates (Cushner & Mahon, 2002; Vande Berg et al., 2012). Use of Global Citizenship 1-2-3 as a guiding framework, however, maximizes the opportunities for candidates' development given the combination of instruction in content, i.e., culturally responsive teaching and globally significant topics, in combination with the study abroad experience. In the following section, we explore the implementation and impact of Global Citizenship 1-2-3 as part of a study abroad experience to South Africa.

Implementation of Global Citizenship 1-2-3

As we have noted, study abroad represents an authentic experience that can be utilized to expand participants' worldview, thus enabling them to become global citizens. Since its development, Global Citizenship 1-2-3 has been an organizational facet of a short-term study abroad program to South Africa, guiding the conceptualization of the content and experiences that occur in country as well as the pre- and post-trip activities.

Background of Program

The program was conceived after the first author traveled to the Western Cape near the city of Cape Town several times to engage in humanitarian work. Upon returning from one such trip, he was informed of a partnership between the University of North Carolina Charlotte and Stellenbosch University, which is located in a city about 50 km from Cape Town. In an effort to broaden the relationship between two universities through the inclusion of education-focused programming, the respective offices for international programs facilitated communication between faculty members in education from each university to discuss and identify short-term study abroad opportunities for candidates. Initial focus was placed upon U.S. students traveling to South Africa and through a collaborative effort between the first author and two faculty members from Stellenbosch, a program was designed that would provide elementary education majors with the opportunity to compare the educational systems of the United States and South Africa and, in turn, explore manifestations of power, privilege and multicultural perspectives relative to the United States and South Africa, broadly as well as specific to educational institutions. Subsequently, the program also incorporated additional opportunities to explore the culture and history of the country through content presented in coursework and in-country experiences, which are detailed later.

In its current form, the study abroad program encompasses 4 weeks in South Africa. The participants reside in a guest house a short distance from the university for the duration of the program. One or both of the authors travel with the students, developing the schedule in partnership with faculty and staff from Stellenbosch and serving as a co-instructor/facilitator within coursework. Participants can elect to enroll in up to 6 credit hours, taking 1–2 courses while abroad. The primary course for all participants focuses on topics associated with diversity, equity and inclusion within schools and educational contexts. Candidates explore these concepts through literature, direct experiences and joint lectures from the faculty from both universities. The second course was only recently added and is focused on community engagement, with candidates seeking to explore NGOs or other community-based organizations in South Africa that support schools and students within the broader municipal area and the historically segregated township that is a few miles from the university. Notably, the program includes direct opportunities for candidates to observe and teach in local elementary schools over the final 3 weeks in South Africa. These visits are facilitated by the faculty at Stellenbosch University as they identify and work directly with the schools to schedule these opportunities. In doing so, they seek to provide 2–3 different school sites that are visited by all candidates to enable them to experience the diversity inherent within the South African educational system.

Participants

Given the broader focus on education as well as the teaching and observations that occur within elementary schools, which are described within the recruiting efforts, the program is comprised of participants who are primarily undergraduate candidates majoring in elementary education. Consistent with the demographics of the major and profession, most participants are Caucasian females between 18 and 22 years old. However, in recent years, participation has been expanded to undergraduate students who have a specific interest in education. As a result, the program has drawn participants from other majors, including public health and computer science. The outcome of this expansion has been a diversification of the participants. On average, the program attracts between seven and nine participants each year.

Culturally Responsive Content

Given the importance of developing foundational knowledge associated with South African culture prior to departure, the culturally responsive aspects of the program begin 1–2 months before departure within orientation sessions facilitated by the faculty member leading the program. Most program participants have very limited knowledge of South Africa before attending the orientation sessions, thus focus is on the introduction of the history and socio-cultural aspects of South Africa. For example, few participants know about South Africa's multilingual society where there are 12 official languages, including sign language, so we introduce them to basic greetings in isiXhosa, which is one of the languages spoken in the South African elementary schools they visit.

Prior to the study abroad program, the participants also read Nelson Mandela's autobiography, *Long Walk to Freedom*. We use this book as a foundational text for debrief discussions that occur over the 4 weeks in South Africa. Throughout the program, candidates read other texts about diversity, equity and inclusion. They also attend presentations about the South African education system and the legacies of apartheid inherent in the education system. Excursions to Robben Island, the prison where Nelson Mandela was held, and the District Six Museum, which documents the forced relocation of a community near Cape Town, further demonstrate aspects of apartheid and the history of the country.

Global-Infused Content

As part of the content introduced within coursework, the faculty member leading the trip is tasked with determining content that has both local and global significance and integrating it within the overall experience. Given the applicability to the locale, global-infused content within prior trips has focused on poverty, quality education, language, and sustainable cities and communities. When possible, we coordinate with South African peers to identify university personnel or local residents with expertise in the content. During our 2018 study abroad program, for example, Cape Town was facing the threat of "Day Zero", when the city would run out of water entirely. Given this situation, the participants engaged in an investigation of Sustainable Development Goal #6: Clean Water and Sanitation. This engagement included a day-long field investigation with a local professor who showed the teacher candidates the impact of water, sanitation and health (WASH) issues and the accessibility of clean water to residents who live in townships, which includes the children who attend the schools where candidates are placed.

Experiential Opportunities

The experiential opportunities within the program offer dual-level benefits. First, the cultural immersion associated with going abroad and living in South Africa creates a sense of cognitive dissonance as participants experience constant "feelings of being an outsider" (Willard-Holt, 2001, p. 515). Second, the participants engage in more than 40 hours of observation and teaching at local elementary schools. These field experiences are divided among schools designated at different levels within the school classification system within South Africa. For example, during one trip, one school was classified in the second quintile, which means there are no school fees; while the second school was in the fifth quintile, which meant student fees were substantially higher to attend this school. The schools were selected by faculty at the South African university based upon the authors' wishes to create experiences in schools with varying resources and diverse student populations. We held daily debrief sessions about connecting the international teaching experiences with the study abroad program readings.

Findings

To assess the impact of Global Citizenship 1-2-3 on participant outcomes, during each study abroad program, we have engaged in data collection in several forms, including administration of instruments such as My Cultural Awareness Profile (myCAP) (Marx & Moss, 2011), collection of participant reflections and the development of a final project that synthesizes all related elements from the experience, which is submitted at the conclusion of or shortly after the program. Examinations of these data sources revealed that participants have demonstrated a greater willingness to self-reflect, increased capacity to recognize and accept cultural diversity, and a greater likelihood to acknowledge the necessity of including content that reflects cultural and linguistic diversity in the curriculum (see Byker & Putman, 2019; Putman, 2017). Examining each of these in turn, participants appeared more willing to acknowledge that culture represents an important influence on their own behaviors. This personal self-awareness contributed to the realization of the importance of acknowledging, learning about and appreciating the cultures of students and families.

Extending this, participants constructed meaning about the importance of building relationships as part of what it means to be a global citizen. Participants referenced the process of getting to know students and their backgrounds (e.g., developing culture-specific information), and developing an appreciation of cultural differences as a mechanism for building relationships. Participants further noted that they should acknowledge differences between home and school and take the appropriate steps for building relationships, including those with parents, to overcome these differences. It was also common to read reflections about how the study abroad opened participants' eyes to making a difference as future teachers both globally and locally. On a global level, a number of the preservice teachers expressed the desire to pursue international teaching positions or join the Peace Corps upon their graduation. At the same time, many preservice teachers gained a deeper commitment to teaching at a local level to ensure they could make a difference within their local communities.

There was also a pervasive theme relating to participants' feeling culturally different and linguistically deficient in nearly all situations. Notably, this would not likely have occurred if participants could return to the relative "safety" of the university or a familiar locale. At the local level, participants discussed their feelings of being an outsider as analogous to what an English Language Learner may feel when entering a U.S. classroom and are unable to understand instruction or comprehend ongoing conversations among classmates. They became more deeply aware and empathetic of the experiences of learners from linguistically diverse backgrounds. As their cross-cultural sensitivity was heightened, participants constructed their understanding of empathy and recognized their role in advocating for the acknowledgement of the plurality of languages in schools. This led one candidate to return to South Africa to conduct research on how language learners were supported in schools, especially when the child's primary language was not one of the languages historically privileged in schools, i.e., Afrikaans or English.

Our integration of Global Citizen 1-2-3 as part of the study abroad program to South Africa represented one step in examining how to help preservice candidates develop "a meaningful understanding of other cultures as well as one's own place in an interconnected world" (Cushner, 2007, p. 37). Our intent moving forward is to expand the use of the model to different study abroad opportunities with different lengths and structures, including those that are integrated within a traditional academic semester. Furthermore, the intent of Global Citizenship 1-2-3 is to guide teacher candidate learning as well as to prepare them to enact similar principles within a PreK-12 classroom (see Putman & Byker, 2020). Because of this, another aspect of our research of the model will focus on following former participants into the classroom and examining how the study abroad experiences impacted educators' professional practice and their perceptions of what it means to be a global educator.

Relatedly, we would like to explore the applicability and impact of Global Citizenship 1-2-3 in developing opportunities for teacher education candidates from South Africa to come to the United States. While the original intent was to create short-term study abroad experiences at each institution, it has not proven economically feasible for students from South Africa to travel to the United States. Thus, though the authors have engaged in scholarly collaborations with their peers from Stellenbosch University and have hosted one student and one faculty member in Charlotte, we have not been able to fully explore how the tenets of the model help prepare global-ready South African teachers. It is our intent to do so in the future. We believe this is an issue of equity related to access to international teaching experiences and student mobility opportunities in the Global South compared with the Global North. We continue to build on the dialogue and collaboration with Stellenbosch University to address these challenges and provide greater access to South African teacher candidates for student mobility experiences.

Conclusion

Developing teacher candidates to be global citizens may not truly be as easy as 1-2-3, but we believe that our Global Citizenship 1-2-3 model provides a framework for supporting the development of global citizen educators who (a) learn in culturally responsive ways, (b) think and reflect on globally infused content, and (c) act in socially just ways. When delivered as part of a study abroad program, we feel the benefits are magnified as concepts are manifest in the reality of being in an unfamiliar locale and seeing the reality of global challenges. In the end, we feel Global Citizen 1-2-3 will help prepare teachers who "think deeply about their actions…and discover other ways to become active and responsible global citizens" (Martin et al., 2012, p. 163).

References

Byker, E. J. (2013). Critical cosmopolitanism: Engaging students in global citizenship competencies. *English in Texas Journal, 43*(2), 18–22.

Byker, E. J. (2016). Developing global citizenship consciousness: Case studies of critical cosmopolitan theory. *Journal of Research in Curriculum Instruction, 20*(3), 264–275.

Byker, E. J., & Putman, S. M. (2019). Catalyzing cultural and global competencies: Engaging preservice teachers in study abroad to expand the agency of citizenship. *Journal of Studies in International Education, 23*, 84–105. https://doi.org/10.1177/1028315318814559

Cushner, K. (2007). The role of experience in the making of internationally-minded teachers. *Teacher Education Quarterly, 34*(1), 27–39.

Cushner, K., & Mahon, J. (2002). Overseas student teaching: Affecting personal, professional, and global competencies in an age of globalization. *Journal of Studies in International Education, 6*(1), 44–58. https://doi.org/10.1177/1028315302006001004

Freire, P. (1970). *Pedagogy of the oppressed.* Herder and Herder.

Gay, G. (2002). Preparing for culturally responsive teaching. *Journal of Teacher Education, 53*(1), 106–116. https://doi.org/10.1177/0022487102053002003

He, Y., Lundgren, K., & Pynes, P. (2017). Impact of short-term study abroad program: Inservice teachers' development of intercultural competence and pedagogical beliefs. *Teaching and Teacher Education, 66*, 147–157. https://doi.org/10.1016/j.tate.2017.04.012

Kerkhoff, S. (2017). Designing global futures: A mixed methods study to develop and validate the teaching for global readiness scale. *Teaching and Teacher Education, 65*, 91–106. https://doi.org/10.1016/j.tate.2017.03.011

Martin, L. A., Smolen, L. A., Oswald, R. A., & Milam, J. L. (2012). Preparing students for global citizenship in the twenty-first century: Integrating social justice through global literature. *The Social Studies*, *103*(4), 158–164. https://doi.org/10.1080/00377996.2011.601358

Marx, H. A., & Moss, D. M. (2011). *My cultural awareness profile (myCAP)*. NAFSA: Association of International Educators.

McGaha, J. M., & Linder, S. M. (2014). Determining teacher candidates' attitudes toward global-mindedness. *Action in Teacher Education*, *36*(4), 305–321. https://doi.org/10.1080/01626620.2014.948225

Merryfield, M. M. (2000). Why aren't teachers being prepared to teach for diversity, equity, and global interconnectedness? A study of lived experiences in the making of multicultural and global educators. *Teaching and Teacher Education*, *16*(4), 429–443. https://doi.org/10.1016/S0742-051X(00)00004-4

Olmedo, I., & Harbon, L. (2010). Broadening our sights: Internationalizing teacher education for a global arena. *Teaching Education*, *21*(1), 75–88. https://doi.org/10.1080/10476210903466992

Oxfam. (2019). *The Sustainable Development Goals: A guide for teachers*. https://www.oxfam.org.uk/education/resources/the-sustainable-development-goals

Paris, D. (2012). Culturally sustaining pedagogy: A needed change in stance, terminology, and practice. *Educational Researcher*, *41*(3), 93–97. https://doi.org/10.3102/0013189X12441244

Partnership for Twenty-First Century Skills. (2014). *Framework for state action on global education*. Retrieved from http://p21.org/storage/documents/Global_Education/P21_State_Framework_on_Global_Education_New_Logo.pdf

Putman, S. M. (2017). Teacher candidates in international contexts: Examining the impact on beliefs about teaching culturally and linguistically diverse learners. In H. An (Ed.), *Efficacy and Implementation of Study Abroad Programs for P-12 Teachers* (pp. 295–321). IGI Global.

Putman, S. M., & Byker, E. J. (2020). Global Citizenship 1-2-3: Learn, Think, and Act. *Kappa Delta Pi Record*, *56*(1), 16–21. https://doi.org/10.1080/00228958.2020.1696088

Tawil, S. (2013). *Education for 'Global Citizenship': A framework for discussion* (ERF Working Papers Series No. 7). UNESCO. https://unesdoc.unesco.org/ark:/48223/pf0000223784

United Nations Education, Scientific and Cultural Organization (UNESCO). (2013). *Global citizenship education: An emerging perspective*. https://unesdoc.unesco.org/ark:/48223/pf0000224115

United Nations Education, Scientific and Cultural Organization (UNESCO). (2014). *Global citizenship education: Preparing learners for the challenges of the 21st century*. https://unesdoc.unesco.org/ark:/48223/pf0000227729

United Nations (2015). *Transforming our world: The 2030 agenda for sustainable development*. A/RES/70/1. https://sustainabledevelopment.un.org/post2015/transformingourworld

Vande Berg, M., Paige, R. M., & Lou, K. H. (2012). Student learning abroad: Paradigms and assumptions. In M. Vande Berg, R. M. Paige, & K. H. Lou (Eds.), *Student learning abroad: What our students are learning, what they're not, and what we can do about it* (pp. 3–28). Stylus.

Willard-Holt, C. (2001). The impact of a short-term international experience for preservice teachers. *Teaching and Teacher Education*, *17*(4), 505–517. https://doi.org/10.1016/S0742-051X(01)00009-9

3 Transforming Teacher Preparation for Global Readiness

Scaling Up Education Abroad

Allison Witt and Wei Liu

Introduction

It is widely accepted that teachers need global competencies in order for them to in turn, prepare future students to be globally ready (Cushner & Brennan, 2007). Similarly, a growing body of literature credits study abroad with instilling global and intercultural competencies in teachers (Boix Mansilla & Jackson, 2011; Cushner & Mahon, 2002; Morley et al., 2019; Pilonieta et al., 2017).

Despite these ongoing developments in teacher education, preservice teacher participation in study abroad remains low. According to the Institute of International Education (2019), from 2007 to 2018, only 3–4% of undergraduate study abroad participants were education students. A review of teacher education programs finds most institutions have between one and two specific offerings, mostly short-term, faculty led, with only one or two faculty within departments clearly committed to providing study abroad (Grey et al., 2019). Part of the issue may be that like other disciplines within academia, study abroad development is not typically included in promotion and tenure review of faculty (Peterson, 2006). According to the survey conducted by the American Council on Education (2012), only eight percent of the faculty respondents reported that international work or experience might be considered in the faculty promotion and tenure process at their institution. Without significant reform or innovation, the dearth of study abroad in teacher education seems poised to continue.

It was in this context that the College of Education at the University of Illinois Urbana-Champaign strove to dramatically increase participation in study abroad among teacher education undergraduate and graduate students. College leadership recognized that prioritizing study abroad could be an important way to provide teachers with the competencies needed for our increasingly globally connected world. At the end of 2014, the College of Education set the goal of giving every student the opportunity to study abroad as a part of teacher education and dedicated staff and scholarship funds toward this objective. The college also partnered with the campus' four Title VI National Resource Centers in global and area studies for expertise and funding to support program development.

For context, the College of Education is situated within a public land-grant university that maintains enormous representation in global linkages, partnerships, international students, study abroad programming and research partnerships. According to the 2016–2017 Open Doors report, Illinois had the second highest number of international students enrolled on its campus (Institute of International Education, 2019). In addition, the campus maintains over 300 partnerships with institutions outside the United States.

Yet, as is typical for most teacher training programs, our College of Education lagged behind the more internationalized departments of campus. For example, when the campus achieved its highest rate of undergraduate study abroad in 2014 (40%), the College of Education's rate was only 26% (University of Illinois at Urbana-Champaign, 2020). This lag is primarily due to the fact that teacher licensing is a very local and rigorous process with specific requirements determined by each state. This course of study does not leave much flexibility for preservice teachers to study abroad. On the contrary, study abroad might delay education students, making it even more difficult for preservice teachers to complete their state's license-required courses on time (Cushner & Mahon, 2002). This deficit has an exponential impact since, taking the long view, the graduates of teacher training ultimately prepare the students that will enter all other disciplines. Education, then, is the beginning point for sustaining all international efforts for the rest of higher education and ultimately, society. Simply put, globally competent engineers, scientists, or business leaders, begin in K12 schooling with teachers that can develop global readiness in all students as a part of the overall academic preparation. Taking this perspective, our College of Education leadership felt that our efforts at study abroad for educators were urgent. Perhaps even more importantly, when we considered the land grant mission of our university that prioritizes engagement with the local community, we could see no better way to provide global readiness to the region than by preparing globally conscious teachers who can prepare their students with skills and competencies for a globalized future.

If teacher education is to broadly incorporate study abroad as integral to teacher preparation, programs must first increase opportunities of education-focused study abroad. Given the myriad other challenges facing teacher education, it seems unlikely that most programs will be able to add multiple faculty or staff to meet this goal. Instead, the challenge will be for programs to find ways to harness existing staff and resources toward this outcome. Until now, most study abroad designed for education students has been developed in an ad hoc manner driven by faculty who commit significant time outside of their traditional research, teaching and service workloads. Planning study abroad programs can be difficult and challenging for faculty (Koernig, 2007). Faculty might not be familiar with scheduling or booking local cultural activities (Brokaw, 1996), or selecting airlines or hotels for groups of students (Gordon & Smith, 1992). While leading study abroad, faculty have to play many other roles than a teacher, such as a manager, counselor, liaison, administrator, and a friend (Keese & O'Brien, 2011). Such models are often successful, but not likely scalable. The case at hand describes the intentional development of study abroad specifically designed to be scalable to reach more students and provide more global programming for preservice teachers.

Methods

The narrative case study presented here lays out the process of scaling up study abroad for education students. Narrative case study is "used for the in-depth study of ... stages or phases in processes, and to investigate a phenomenon within its environmental context" (Gilgun, 1994). Here, we attempt to portray this process in the context of our study. Preskill (1998) contends that narrative stories are valuable ingredients that could help those striving to improve the quality of teacher education. Weber (1993) similarly finds that storytelling is an underestimated and important aspect of teaching and research. She applies narrative case study to higher education, stating that narrative research reconceptualizes professional knowledge, providing detailed examinations of the individual's experiences within a specific context. It is this examination of our processes that we provide here, sharing a chronological retelling of our reflections to encourage analysis and discussion regarding the process of scaling up study abroad within teacher education.

First Steps

With the goal of scaling up study abroad, we first tried to understand why in the College of Education study abroad did not already exist on par with the rest of campus. While much of the literature cites the low numbers of teacher education students participating in study abroad (Cushner, 2009; Institute of International Education, 2019), there is little theorizing about why. Of course, on the one hand, teacher education is locally constructed, with licensure requirements tied to the state level. Such requirements tend to be lock step, with little time for exploration in the degree program so we might not be surprised to find students locally bound. Yet on the other hand, most US teacher training requires time away from the university campus, with teacher education students placed directly in schools as a critical part of their training. A great deal of research has considered the process of taking students across the boundary of the university context into the local school context and the resulting translation of practice that must occur (Harrison, 2018; Smith & Lev-Ari, 2005). We considered this body of literature as a foundation for building study abroad programming for our teacher education students that could be situated squarely within our long-term practices in the teacher preparation discipline.

In 2014–2015, when we began this expansion endeavor, our own education-focused international programming looked like most of the programming found in teacher education, with one or two faculty-led options offered per academic year, augmented by worldwide programming available through campus, though none of those campus programs especially targeted education majors. The short-term programs we offered were led by charismatic, enthusiastic faculty leaders who managed all the preparation, logistics, and course supervision themselves. We speculated that their extraordinary efforts may have inadvertently made the process seem daunting to other faculty who may have otherwise considered developing study abroad. Our numbers of participants hovered at around the national average, which is low compared to all other degree tracks on our campus. When asked informally, students cited the cost as well as the schedule as major impediments and claimed less interest in taking time away from campus for general study abroad not directly related to their major. Our college established both need- and merit-based scholarships to augment other study abroad funding to offset the costs, but it was clear that if we wanted to increase the numbers of education students participating in study abroad, we must first greatly increase the number of affordable education-focused programs.

With time constraints identified as a major remaining barrier, we recognized the need to develop programming that would fit within the tight structure of the teacher preparation program. While our campus already fostered multiple suitable semester or year length study abroad programs, our education students were not only constrained from leaving campus by courses to meet licensure requirements, but this group of students also tends to participate in multiple activities on campus, in local schools, and community. We were loath to disrupt such connections and commitments, believing that these experiences were also critical to teacher preparation. While there is literature that cautions about the lack of impact from shorter experiences (Medina-López-Portillo, 2004), we looked at significant and growing bodies of research that showed impact can be achieved if the experience is set within a context of pre and post departure instruction and reflection (DiFrancesco et al., 2019; Kissock & Richardson, 2010; Newton et al., 2020; Pence & Macgillivray, 2008; Whatley et al., 2020; Willard-Holt, 2001). We considered study abroad literature as well as research coming specifically from education that argued for the benefits of short-term programs with well-planned activities and experiences designed to promote perspective taking, empathy and reflection (Banks, 2008; van Driel et al., 2016). Following this research, we developed multiple short-term programs coinciding with winter, spring, and summer break, each set within a 6-week course that would provide both pre-departure and post program instruction.

As we reflect on the manner in which we approached this task, we can identify steps in our process and roles that correspond to Grey's et al. identification of program *architects*, *champions*, and *linchpins* (2019). Rather than focusing on systematic planning, we were forced to adapt the evolution or accretion model to meet our expansion goals, where the three types of individuals (architects, champions, and linchpins) were "drivers and sustainers" of programs (Grey et al., 2019). Architects are those who initiate and design the program, while champions being those who join to strengthen and expand the program, and linchpins being those who work behind the scenes to maintain the program (Grey et al., 2019). We strived to use data and research to design our programs, but we were also conscious of the need to move quickly in order to provide opportunities for as many students as possible. With the world and even our own campus rapidly globalizing around us, we felt increasing pressure to provide preservice teachers with international opportunities meeting the needs of their profession before they stepped into our communities as teachers in need of global competencies. We could not wait for new faculty to be hired, for example, knowing that such positions take time to develop and to fill. Instead, we needed to work with existing faculty, staff and systems while scaling up study abroad participation.

We turned to the literature, considering studies of study abroad more broadly, then focusing on teacher education as a specific strand within the wider study abroad literature. Next, we considered those studies within the context of teacher education research and the long traditions of research on school placements. Bringing these bodies of literature together, we set out to design multiple programs simultaneously that would include the key components of meaningful programs identified in the research while avoiding or minimizing the often-cited barriers. Our review of the teacher education-based literature confirmed our sense that rather than continue to rely on general study abroad programming, we would need to develop education specific study abroad experiences.

Key Components in Instructional Design

Drawing from the teacher education and study abroad literature, as well as best practices in student teaching, we identified four key components that were foundational to our program design. We developed a template for a short-term education program that includes (a) guided observation in classrooms abroad observing, presenting, or teaching; (b) opportunities to meet or work with preservice and practicing teachers on location; (c) an emphasis on reflection, and (b) homestays with local families when possible (Stachowski & Sparks, 2007; Stachowski & Mahan, 1998; He et al., 2017; Mikulec, 2019; Searle & Ward, 1990; Ward & Kennedy, 1993, 1994; Ward & Searle, 1991). The model is modified to fit local circumstances, but working from these broad strokes, we were able to flesh out programming of equal quality in each site.

At this early stage, the initial step was to choose locations for the programming. First, we considered the local context of Illinois where our students become licensed to teach. We considered what cultures are significantly represented in Illinois. We researched the current demographics and diversity in order to understand the cultural backgrounds that our preservice teachers will encounter in their classrooms and communities. Of course, we recognize that such demographics can shift dramatically. As an example, our own campus community is home to an increasing number of immigrants from the Democratic

Republic of the Congo. As a response, the schools local to our university are displaying many adaptations, including a dual French language program in several elementary schools. Current safety concerns meant we could not do a program in the DRC at this time. Yet, this example taught us that we could not look only to the current demographics, but need to prepare teachers to be flexible in the face of global events that may suddenly and dramatically shift the needs of local communities. Moreover, teachers need to be poised to maximize the benefits and opportunities for education that diverse cultures afford.

In addition to programs specific to our populations within Illinois, we wanted to develop programs in multiple sites around the globe, working from the assumption that increased exposure to diverse cultures would develop competencies that could be deployed in all cross-cultural encounters. Therefore, we used three additional factors to help us choose sites: destinations that are famous for education achievement such as Finland, Japan and Hong Kong; destinations that are popular for US students such as France, Spain and Australia; and destinations where our college or campus has strong partnerships already in place such as China, Tanzania, Italy, and Morocco. Our underlying assumption was that good teaching occurs everywhere in the world. Our goal would be to identify teachers in places where we could arrange for partnerships, and at the same time, where we could most readily convince our students to go. Working to find overlap between our students' vacation periods, and times when our hosts would be in school session at suitable times for us to visit the host site, we arranged a 3-year calendar of programming including approximately 14 programs per year. With each program targeting 10–15 students, it was clear that our number of participants would dramatically increase with up to 200 to 300 students participating each year through this new programming.

Perhaps as notable as what factors we did consider in choosing locations is also what we did not. We did not focus on language learning as a primary goal of our programs. First, our university already has robust language learning programs abroad. Moreover, our programs are short-term, so not as suitable for significant language study. We did target places where students' language skills could be used, but we were not specifically focusing on developing language abilities.

In this model, designed to be scalable, our college international office developed the program logistics in each site working with international partners of our college or our campus, or with alumni stationed in, or from, the target site. Our alumni serve as teachers and professors all over the world, providing an obvious link to classrooms and universities. For instance, we have arranged students to meet with alumni and visit their classrooms. In addition, we also have programs such as our Hong Kong program, which is built around three prestigious universities in Hong Kong and Macau, where many alumni are faculty members in education departments.

Even though our programming would need to be short-term—ranging from 1 week to 3 weeks—we aimed to include all four of the key components of sound design that we had identified in the literature in each program and location. First, research convinced us that our students would need time in schools similar to the local placements we already do in teacher training (Phillion et al., 2008; Stachowski & Mahan, 1995). As might be expected, this is difficult to arrange since each country and location has specific requirements to enter schools, and administrators and teachers are understandably protective of their own academic calendars and agendas. Obviously, educators do not want their school treated as a tourist destination, and the resistance to academic tourism is justified (Breen, 2012).

We found that working through teacher education programs, and in particular, those where we have alumni, provided the best avenue to develop partnerships with host destination schools. Teacher education institutions were able to select school partners and help us to identify ways that we could collaboratively approach the planning of our visit. Depending on the local circumstances, some schools were interested in having our students prepare short lessons, while other host institutions would allow us to observe quietly. We tried to respectfully honor these expectations. We aim to develop the same trust-based, long standing relationships with these host schools as we have with our local schools that collaborate locally in our teacher training program.

Another primary goal of our program was to learn from educators at the host site. Rather than impose our US perspectives and judgments defining quality education, we wanted to learn how education is constructed and taught at the host site. Coaching our students not to judge education practices according to US norms, we encouraged students to learn what education practice is in the host country and gain firsthand exposure to the ideas that determine how it functions. To that end, we wanted to learn directly from the teaching faculty on location. We have structured this exchange of ideas in multiple ways depending on the requests from the host site. We have attended education classes at the host site, joined in mini-conferences with both sides sharing ideas, or had faculty from the host site present specifically to our group. In each of these ways, we strive to respectfully engage with the host location education faculty, learning from their expertise and from their perspective. We also have found that when faculty on location have knowledge about US education or have studied in the US themselves, they are especially effective at transforming the learning in a more efficient and meaningful way for the students. Those faculty seem to serve what researchers have identified as the necessary "intercultural guide" who can help students to "see the culture" through their insights (Marx & Moss, 2017).

Another key component of our program is for students to meet teacher candidates in the host location. This idea was drawn less from the literature and more from our own hunch that our students would value the opportunity to meet direct peers. One of our main goals was to provide students an opportunity to develop their own global network of teachers. To that end, we wanted them to not only meet teacher education students in the host country, but also spend time with them both in structured activities and as in social programming. Some examples have included attending education classes at the host university, accompanying local teacher education students to their placements in host schools, informal conversations around the design and lived experience of teacher preparation, and arranged social outings where host students introduce our students to the local student culture. In each example, we are pleased to see our students include host country peers in social media and maintain connections well beyond the program's duration.

Supporting Coursework

Once key components were identified and the locations were selected, we then turned to the development of the course, which would provide the pre-departure orientation and preparation, travel-congruent activities, and post-program reports and debriefing. Research shows that short-term programs can be impactful if they are used as opportunities for growth and reflection (Kissock & Richardson, 2010; Pence & Macgillivray, 2008; Willard-Holt, 2001). Of course, the additional challenge of hosting multiple short-term faculty-led programs is recruiting enough faculty with the expertise, time and inclination to lead students on study abroad. Our college did have some faculty who were interested in developing more programs, but not enough faculty who could immediately step in, particularly in the context of ongoing research projects and current course loads. Here, we strayed from the traditional model of faculty led experiences in order to develop what we call faculty-accompanied programming.

Rather than relying only on faculty members to develop each course, we again structured a model designed to be scalable to larger participation. We developed a template for an online course to surround our study abroad that included standard pre-departure orientation materials, information about travel resources, as well as health and safety information. We developed a comprehensive syllabus of readings and activities that define and outline the value of cultural competencies for teachers and explore concepts related to teaching in a global context. Drawing upon recommendations from faculty in the College of Education, Area Studies experts from Title VI Centers, and faculty from across campus with relevant expertise, we developed reading lists for each destination. The readings not only are centered on education but also emphasize culture and history. In addition, we curated a list of additional materials that include potential lesson plans of interest to future teachers, films, music, and literature from or relevant to the destination. All resources are augmented with recorded lectures and assignments specific to education in the host destination. Our Education and Area Studies Librarians compiled supplemental resources about education policy and practice in each destination as well as bibliographic guides to library resources.

In addition to the educational context, we strive to encourage critical reflection. Broadly, we believe the privilege of travel combined with the privilege of US universities globally, necessitates discussions of students' own positionality as well as an awareness of the hosts' perceptions. As a part of the online course, we introduce students to post-colonial theory and provide opportunities to critically reflect on the study abroad experience. We share critical readings and engage in online discussions about what it means to travel to view education outside of one's own culture. In particular, we consider what it means to cross borders between the global north and global south. Because of the structure of programs we have developed, students will encounter pockets of the global south even within our programming in the global north. We draw from sources that help researchers to prepare for fieldwork abroad, and encourage students to consider their own program as fieldwork related to the school placements that they will do throughout their preservice program.

The online course is constructed so that students have 4 weeks of preparation before the program, approximately 2 weeks of travel, followed by 2 weeks of course work after the program. During the 4 weeks of the pre-departure course, students use the wealth of resources provided in the online course to develop a group project in which they create a narrative describing education in the local host context. They revisit this narrative upon return in the final 2 weeks of the course to augment, correct, and adapt the narrative based on what they learned abroad. Early iterations of this project taught us that we needed students to build a corresponding narrative about education in the US context. While abroad, students are frequently asked to describe various facets of US education to host teachers, students and university faculty they meet. We learned that without preparation, students might only refer to their own experience within US schools rather than providing our hosts with accurate information that reflected the US education context more broadly. When students return, they revisit these narratives, adding or changing information based on what they learned. Our findings show that most students develop more-informed narratives after they return, which move beyond the stereotypes and their initial cultural assumptions of the host country. This assignment provides an opportunity for students to identify what specifically was shared or different across the locations before departure and again upon return, further facilitating post-program reflection. It is interesting to note that information about the US context is also learned while abroad, proving again that study abroad brings one's own context into view more clearly (Cushner & Mahon, 2002). These revised narratives form the basis of presentations made with other education students in the College of Education and are shared with future participants as background preparation for their own journey abroad.

Faculty, Student and Staff Support

Once we had developed a general template of this course, we recruited graduate students pursuing research on study abroad or related fields to serve as teaching assistants. We specifically selected graduate students with expertise, heritage or research interests in particular regions. In addition to assisting with the course, graduate students then serve as program leaders during the travel portion of the class. They finalize itineraries, coordinate with host teachers and families, and manage other details while serving as teaching assistants in the study abroad class. While traveling, they manage the detailed day to day logistics of the program, working closely with partners to support the program. This arrangement has provided a rare professional development opportunity for graduate students, developing the next generation of faculty with expertise in providing study abroad. This role not only trains graduate students to develop and run education abroad programming, but also has the benefit of developing other international opportunities more broadly. For example, several graduate students have used this opportunity to establish their own global professional network, building relationships that become valuable research or career placement connections.

In addition to the graduate student program leaders, faculty are recruited to accompany the program, serving to provide depth, further expertise, and act as the official representative of the university when greeting and thanking host universities, schools, and families. While traveling with the group, faculty often gives talks or provides professional development on site, adding another layer of exchange with host institutions. While it is still a significant time commitment for faculty to travel with students, by eliminating the necessity of developing the course and managing logistics, we are able to recruit professors of all ranks to join the program. Freed from the burdens often associated with such programs, faculty are able to bring their rich experience and learned perspective to the program. Upon return, faculty become champions of study abroad (Grey et al., 2019), sharing their experience with colleagues and students and encouraging further participation. Some faculty have joined programs multiple times in vastly different locations. This enables professors to then offer comparative perspectives, reaching across programs to provide exceptional and rare insights.

As our new programs rolled out, we quickly found that demand for study abroad increased accordingly among our students. Of course, once we began to admit larger numbers of students, our previous administrative process became quickly overwhelmed. Individualized systems that worked for admitting 25 students were not effective when we were suddenly enrolling 150 students per year. Here, our college staff served as linchpins (Grey et al., 2019), working with colleagues across campus to scale up our administrative process to match our academic goals. By working creatively and collaboratively, staff were able to adapt to the larger numbers and create new systems to accommodate our expanded practice.

Conclusion

This narrative case study depicts reflections from one institution's first steps in intentionally scaling up study abroad for greater participation from students in teacher education. Since this process began, the college's study abroad participation rate moved from 18% in 2015–2016 in our first year to 38% in 2018–19, surpassing the current campus average of 30% of students studying abroad. While these data capture one outcome, the narrative case study provides a more fulsome depiction of the process including the research, resources, and support provided from international partners, university colleagues, and from within the college.

Though teacher education continues to lag in study abroad participation despite the continued research arguing its many benefits, the case presented here demonstrates that increased participation is possible and can be developed in scalable models. Teacher education has always relied on school placement as a part of teacher training. The narrative case demonstrates one institution's efforts to extend the longstanding practice on a global scale.

This case presents the first steps in a process. Next steps include sustained research on the outcomes of the programs as well as a longitudinal look at impacts as the students become teachers themselves. In addition, we are studying the impact on assistant graduate students who may become program developers and leaders in their own careers. Finally, by following a similar model in locations around the world, we are able to collect data on outcomes in a systematic and longitudinal manner. Future research will analyze the lasting impact on teachers both at the home and host destinations.

References

American Council on Education (2012). *Mapping Internationalization on U.S. Campuses: 2012 Edition.* Washington, DC: American Council on Education. https://www.acenet. edu/news-room/Documents/Mapping-Internationalizationon-US-Campuses-2012-full.pdf.

Banks, J. A. (2008). Diversity, group identity, and citizenship education in a global age. *Educational Researcher, 37*(3), 129–139.

Breen, M. (2012). Privileged migration: American undergraduates, study abroad, academic tourism. *Critical Arts, 26*(1), 82–102. http://doi.org/10.1080/02560046.2012. 663163

Brokaw, S. C. (1996). Planning, organizing, and executing short term international exposures for U.S. students of marketing and business: An alternative method. *Marketing Education Review, 6*(3), 87–93.

Boix Mansilla, V. & Jackson, A. (2011). *Educating for global competence: preparing our youth to engage the world.* New York: Asia Society.

Cushner, K. (2009). The role of study abroad in preparing globally competent teachers. In R. Lewin (Ed.), *The handbook of practice and research in study abroad* (pp. 151–169). New York: Taylor & Francis.

Cushner, K., & Brennan, S. (2007). The value of learning to teach in another culture. In K. Cushner & S. Brennan (Eds.), *Intercultural student teaching: A bridge to global competence* (pp. 1–12). Lanham, MD: Rowman & Littlefield Education.

Cushner, K., & Mahon, J. (2002). Overseas student teaching: Affecting personal, professional, and global competencies in an age of globalization. *Journal of Studies in International Education, 6*(1), 44–58.

DiFrancesco, D., Nguyen, L. K., Spurlin, D., Dutt, A., Furst-Holloway, S., & Rogers, N. (2019). The effects of short-term study abroad on expanding students' culture perception and identity. *Journal of Higher Education Theory and Practice, 19*(7), 22–28. https://doi.org/10.33423/jhetp.v19i7.2528

Gilgun, J. (1994). A case for case studies in social work research. *Social Work, 39,* 371–380.

Gordon, P., & Smith, D. K. (1992). Planning, organizing, and executing short term international exposures for U.S. students of marketing and business. *Marketing Education Review, 2*(1), 47–54.

Grey, C., Kristmanson, P., Landine, J., Sears, A., Hirschkorn, M., Ingersoll, M., & Kawtharani-Chami, L. (2019). From Canada to the World: Initial teacher education and attention to international teaching in Atlantic Canadian universities. In J. Mueller & J. Nickel (Eds.), *Globalization and diversity in education: What does it mean for Canadian teacher education* (pp. 444–474). Ottawa, ON: Canadian Association for Teacher Education.

Harrison, C. (2018). Boundary crossing during pre-service teacher training: Empowering or hampering professional growth? *Cultural Studies of Science Education,* 1129–1133. Canadian Association for Teacher Education.

He, Y., Lundgren, K., & Pynes, P. (2017). Impact of short-term study abroad program: Inservice teachers' development of intercultural competence and pedagogical beliefs. *Teaching and teacher education, 66,* 147–157.

Institute of International Education. (2019). *Fields of Study of U.S. Study Abroad Students, 2005/6-2017/18 Open Doors Reports on International Educational Exchange.* http://www.iie.org/opedoors

Kissock, C. & Richardson, P. (2010). Calling for action within the teaching profession: It is time to internationalize teacher education. *Teaching Education, 21* (1), 89–102.

Keese, J. R. & O'Brien, J. (2011). Learn by going: Critical issues for faculty-led study-abroad programs. *Journal of California Geographical Society, 51,* 91–113.

Kissock, C., Richardson, P. (2010). Calling for action within the teaching profession: It is time to internationalize teacher education. *Teaching Education, 21,* 89–101.

Koernig, S. K. (2007). Planning, organizing, and conducting a 2-week study abroad trip for undergraduate students: Guidelines for first-time faculty. *Journal of Marketing Education, 29*(3), 210–217.

Marx, H. & Moss, D. M. (2017). It takes a global village: The design of an internship-based teacher education study abroad program. In C. Schlein & B. Garri (Eds.), *A reader of narrative and critical lenses on intercultural teaching and learning* (pp. 53–72). Charlotte, NC: Information Age Publishing.

Medina-López-Portillo, A. (2004). Intercultural learning assessment: The link between program duration and the development of intercultural sensitivity. *Frontiers: The International Journal of Study Abroad, 10,* 179–200.

Mikulec, E. (2019). Short-term study abroad for pre-service teachers: Personal and professional growth in Brighton, England. *International Journal for the Scholarship of Teaching and Learning, 13*(1), 11.

Morley, A., Braun, A. M. B., Rohrer, L., & Lamb, D. (2019). Study abroad for preservice teachers: A critical literature review with considerations for research and practice. *Global Education Review, 6*(3), 4–29.

Newton, J., Oudghiri, S., Obenchain, K., & Phillion, J. (2020). Preservice teachers' understandings of social justice within the context of study abroad programs. *Theory Into Practice, 59*(3), 259–268. http://doi.org/10.1080/00405841.2020.1739956

Pence, H. M., & Macgillivray, I. K. (2008). The impact of an international field experience on preservice teachers. *Teaching and Teacher Education, 24,* 14–25.

Peterson, N. J. (2006). Still missing the boat: Faculty involvement in study abroad. In M. Tillman (Ed.), *Study Abroad: A 21st Century Perspective*. Stamford, CY: AIFS Foundation.

Phillion, J., Malewski, E., Rodriguez, E., Shirley, V., Kulago, H., & Bulington, J. (2008). Promise and perils of study abroad: White privilege revival. In T. Huber (Ed.), *Teaching and learning diversity: International perspectives on social justice and human rights* (pp. 365–382). Greenwich, CT: Information Age.

Pilonieta, P., A. L. Medina & Hathaway, J. I. (2017). The impact of a study abroad experience on preservice teachers' dispositions and plans for teaching English language learners. *The Teacher Educator, 52* (1), 22–38.

Preskill, S. (1998). Narratives of teaching and the quest for the second self. *Journal of Teacher Education, 49*, 344–357.

Searle, W., & Ward, C. (1990). The prediction of psychological and sociocultural adjustment during cross-cultural transition. *International Journal of Intercultural Relations, 14*, 449–464.

Smith, K., & Lev-Ari, L. (2005). The place of the practicum in pre-service teacher education: The voice of the students. *Asia-Pacific Journal of Teacher Education, 33*(3), 289–302.

Stachowski, L. L., & Mahan, A. L. (1995). Learning from international field Experiences. In G. A. Slick (Ed.), *Emerging trends in teacher education: The future of field experiences* (pp. 99–107). Thousand Oaks, CA: Corwin Press.

Stachowski, L. L., & Mahan, J. M. (1998). Cross-cultural field placements: Student teachers learning from schools and communities. *Theory into practice, 37*(2), 155–162.

Stachowski, L. L., & Sparks, T. (2007). Thirty years and 2,000 student teachers later: An overseas student teaching project that is popular, successful, and replicable. *Teacher Education Quarterly, 34*(1), 115–132.

University of Illinois at Urbana-Champaign Division of Management Information. (2020). *2019–2020 Campus Profile*. https://dmi.illinois.edu/cp/strategic.aspx

van Driel, B., Darmody, M., & Kerzil, J. (2016). Education policies and practices to foster tolerance, respect for diversity and civic responsibility in children and young people in the EU. *Examining the evidence*. Luxembourg: European Union. http://doi.org/10.2766/46172

Ward, C., & Kennedy, A. (1993). Psychological and sociocultural adjustment during cross-cultural transitions: A comparison of secondary students at home and abroad. *International Journal of Psychology, 28*, 129–147.

Ward, C., & Kennedy, A. (1994). Acculturation strategies, psychological adjustment, and sociocultural competence during cross-cultural transitions. *International Journal of Intercultural Relations, 18*, 329–343.

Ward, C., & Searle, W. (1991). The impact of value discrepancies and cultural identity on psychological and sociocultural adjustment of sojourners. *International Journal of Intercultural Relations, 15*, 209–224.

Weber, S. (1993). The narrative anecdote in teacher education. *Journal of Education for Teaching, 19*, 71–82. https://doi.org/10.1080/0260747930190107

Whatley, M., Landon, A. C., Tarrant, M. A., & Tarrant, D. R. (2020). Program design and the development of students' global perspectives in faculty-led short-term study abroad. *Journal of Studies in International Education*. http://doi.org/10.1177/1028315320906156

Willard-Holt, C. (2001). The impact of a short-term international experience for preservice teachers. *Teaching and Teacher Education, 17*, 505–517.

4 Going Global in Teacher Education

Lessons Learned from Scaling Up

David M. Moss, Jon Simmons, Blair Izard, and Helen Marx

Introduction

This chapter discusses a portfolio of university-based teacher education study abroad programs that aim to promote global and intercultural competence in ways that directly foster culturally responsive teaching practices. The inaugural education abroad program at the Neag School of Education at the University of Connecticut took place over 20 years ago. This program placed a cohort of approximately a half dozen teaching interns in London, England for a semester-long post student teaching internship. Over time, this initial program has grown into a more comprehensive international experience, including pre-departure and re-entry coursework. This initial program has also served as a model for the development of multiple education abroad international sites, including Cape Town, South Africa; Cusco, Peru; and two distinct content-area focused programs in Nottingham, England—one in Secondary Social Studies and the other in Mathematics Education. Presently, nearly 50 preservice teachers participate in these various programs, representing almost half of the students in the master's year of our Integrated Bachelor's/Master's program.

As one considers international programs across higher education, colleges of teacher education face significant challenges in designing and maintaining education abroad programs, and as a result, preservice teachers are an under-represented population in study abroad. According to a comprehensive report on study abroad trends (Open Doors, 2019), only about 3% of all students studying abroad from the United States are education majors. Thus, there are limited programmatic-level models upon which to draw guidance as one considers scaling up to fully integrate international experiences, including study abroad, into university-based teacher preparation programs. Despite the challenges of designing and maintaining education abroad programs, including issues underpinning requirements of licensure, there remains a need to prepare teachers who are on the path to an ethnorelative and intercultural worldview (Marx & Moss, 2011). At our institution, the development of a portfolio of programs is meeting this need, and as such we will address the challenges and successes we encountered in the scaling up of these study abroad international programs and offer a clear conceptual frame for moving in this direction.

Grounding the Programs in a Theoretical Framework

Prior to our discussion of our current study abroad offerings, it is necessary to address the origin of our education abroad programs that have served as the model for the development of subsequent international offerings, and articulate the theoretical frames that have guided our work. Participants in our semester-long teaching internship programs are matriculated in an Integrated Bachelor's/Master's teacher preparation program. Eligible participants are from all of our certification tracks, including elementary (certification for grades 1–6), the secondary disciplines of mathematics, English, social studies and science, and the K-12 certification areas of special education and music education. Although the participants are abroad for a single semester, programmatically our international offerings are essentially a year-long experience, including the predeparture course work, semester abroad, and a re-entry semester seminar. Prior to the international experience, students have completed the bachelor's portion of our integrated program, which includes four semesters of practice teaching (including a full semester student teaching experience) and the associated course work common to many university-based teacher preparation programs, such as a suite of methods courses, foundational coursework, and assessment classes. The international track features a summer course prior to going abroad, two semesters of school-based post-student teaching internships (one abroad and one home-based) and graduate-level classes (30 post-graduate credits).

In the early years, the school offered only one program—the London Program—which served only about 5–6 education participants, and was offered through the larger context of the University of Connecticut (UConn) Study Abroad in London program. Courses included those that offered perspectives on British history, London geography and other survey-type experiences designed to provide context and a sense-of-place for living and studying in London. Within just a few short years, primarily through discussions in the re-entry semester, it became apparent that issues of intercultural learning within the program were merely *implicit* in the experiences of students. With the desire to more explicitly attend to intercultural learning, and as the number of participants quickly grew to surpass a dozen, there emerged a critical mass that allowed us to spin the education program off from the core university London program, resulting in a process of curriculum design with the explicit intent of developing culturally responsive teachers. London was chosen as the inaugural international site for this program because it afforded opportunities for the teaching interns to engage in multiracial, multinational and urban cultural contexts, while being able to swiftly overcome many linguistic barriers, an essential necessity for our participants as they are almost exclusively speakers of English. The majority of our teacher education candidates are monolingual, white, middle class suburban individuals. Partner schools in London have been purposefully selected for performing at the high levels of academic excellence and achievement as documented by the Office of Standards in Education (Ofsted) in the United Kingdom. Thus, within their international internships, participants experience many best practices of education in a culturally complex urban setting. Making the study of culture *explicit*, with a clear focus on unpacking deep cultural differences and not steering away from the dissonance and challenges associated with immersive experiences is the key to such programs. The program elements and notions underpinning how we have made cultural learning explicit have been the key to our participants' growth and successfully scaling up our program offerings and this will be the focus of the balance of this chapter.

Across our education abroad programs, the unifying conceptual frame for considering intercultural competence is the Developmental Model of Intercultural Sensitivity (DMIS) that articulates a continuum of perspectives from ethnocentric to ethnorelative, and can be probed by exploring one's orientation to cultural difference (Hammer & Bennett, 2003). Bennett (2004) refers to an ethnorelative worldview as one that allows for "the experience of one's own beliefs and behaviors as just one organization of reality among many viable possibilities" (p. 62). As such, the ethnorelative developmental stages are "ways of *seeking cultural difference*, either by accepting its importance, by adapting perspective to take it into account, or by integrating the whole concept into a definition of identity" (p. 63, italics in original). Being mindful of the ways culture and cultural differences impact our professional endeavors is at the heart of what Bennett (1993) has described as an ethnorelative worldview and that, we contend, is a key prerequisite for engaging in culturally responsive teaching practices (Gay, 2000).

In contrast, Bennett (2004) defines an ethnocentric worldview as "the experience of one's own culture as 'central to reality'" and where "the beliefs and behaviors that people receive in their primary socialization are unquestioned: they are experienced as 'just the way things are'" (p. 62). Advocates for internationalizing teacher education via study abroad experiences propose that living and teaching in international contexts beyond one's home culture offers the opportunity to uncover and impact preservice teachers' ethnocentric worldviews and start them on a journey toward intercultural competence (Cushner & Brennan, 2007). It is important to note that simply experiencing a different culture does not automatically lead to ethnorelative worldviews. Thus, the various program components are designed to scaffold reflections and discourse that promote such growth. According to Cushner (2011), studies show that many preservice and in-service teachers are typically "on the ethnocentric side of this scale and may not have the requisite disposition to be effective intercultural educators nor possess the skills necessary to guide young people to develop intercultural competence" (p. 605). Although acknowledging the many challenges of fostering ethnorelative perspectives, we have in fact demonstrated considerable progress of our preservice teachers in their intercultural learning and development toward ethnorelative and intercultural mindsets. Hammer & Bennett (2003) state such progress demands a significant shift in thinking and strategies and, in this chapter, we propose that purposefully planned international teaching programs are an effective means to rise to the challenge.

Program Components

The original London Internship Program included key components that are cited as important underpinnings of study abroad program design: (a) experiential learning opportunities that provide a context for intensive immersion into the local culture, (b) credit-bearing coursework grounded in cross-cultural issues, and (c) support for guided cultural reflection (Engle & Engle, 2004). It is important to note that the participants complete their student teaching prior to the initiation of their international experiences. Our global experiences follow the completion of student teaching in part because our state certification requirements for licensure made it challenging to establish and support student teaching experiences abroad, which is even more complex today with additional accountability elements mandated by the state. Moving conceptually beyond those logistical challenges, the graduate year of our integrated program is thematically focused on developing the teacher as leader. Building upon the foundation of effective instruction established in student teaching, our participants engage in post-graduate internship work in schools that may include curriculum development, support of students with specific learning needs (emergent bilinguals, etc.), after-school community projects and other leadership-focused efforts beyond whole class instruction. Although the cornerstone of the London program is a 15-week internship in state funded primary and secondary London schools where participants engage in approximately 20-hour-per-week internships, the internship does not stand alone. Course work and an inquiry project with an international focus are also designed to provide participants with purposeful opportunities to reflect upon schooling and their roles as educators. The London Program is classified as an "island program" (Norris & Dwyer, 2005), where students stay together as a cohort for classes and living accommodation while abroad, and are not affiliated with a host-country institution. In the London Program, teacher candidates remain together as a cohort through the initial summer class, their study abroad in London, and during the seminar in the re-entry spring semester back on their home campus. Our experiences in coordinating and teaching in the program over the years have taught us that the program components, such as pre-departure and re-entry seminars, that bracket the international experience semester are equally as important to participants' intercultural learning as their time abroad. Research has found that pre-departure and re-entry experiences provide students with the support they need to enter into a challenging international experience and to make sense of international experience in ways that support their intercultural learning (Martin & Harrell, 2004; Wilson & Flournoy, 2007). Thus, intentionally planning for cultural learning across all the three phases of any international experience—pre-departure, international experience, and re-entry—is essential.

Pre-Departure

The program kicks off each cycle at the conclusion of the spring semester with a half-day meeting and celebration where the outgoing group meets with the newly admitted cohort. The outgoing cohort formally presents their inquiry project research to the new group and shares information and advice about navigating many of the cultural aspects of the program, including living, interning, and studying in London. This handoff meeting has proven to be an important event for both groups, helping the outgoing group bring closure to their year of graduate work and allowing the new cohort of students to begin to see themselves as advanced students, successful researchers and intercultural learners. The inquiry project is essentially a master's-level thesis where students explore aspects of schooling through the lens of novice educational researchers. This past year, the London cohort explored teacher perspectives on the multi-faceted impact of Brexit on pupils and schooling. The purpose of the inquiry project is to build capacities as teacher leaders through the development of research skills designed to encourage these emerging practitioners to perhaps one day initiate their own investigations of school policies and/or practices. It also serves as an additional lens on professional policies and practice in the United Kingdom, affording a deep dive into facets of schools and schooling that might not otherwise be readily facilitated without this requirement.

Following this transition, the new cohort of participants officially begin their course of study in the London Program as they engage in their *Seminar in International Education* course, which spans the entire summer as a hybrid offering (both in-person and remotely). The first element of the course comprises a multiday workshop where students engage in activities and discussions related to the construct of culture and theories of intercultural development (Bennett, 2004; Gay, 2000). Through presentations, readings, and videos, they explore aspects of the English school system as a comparative context for reflection. The new cohort also begin the process of developing a focus for their collaborative inquiry project, which will be a key element of their cooperative group work that takes place across the balance of the summer. This program requirement encourages them to dig deeply into the literature and generate a group product addressing the context of their pending research project. The group reconvenes on campus for a 2-day workshop at the end of the summer term and immediately prior to departing for London where students continue their intercultural learning with a focus on exploring ethnographic methods of inquiry that will support both their inquiry project and promote cultural learning in their pending semester abroad. This prede-parture meeting also affords us the opportunity to facilitate the requisite risk and safety orientation, and address other logistical aspects of their semester away from campus.

At present, we teach multiple sections of this summer course as we have scaled up to various international sites—each course section focuses on a single site as the cultural preparation work differs between places like London and Cape Town. Yet, as noted, the Developmental Model of Intercultural Sensitivity (Hammer & Bennett, 2003) serves as a conceptual common denominator providing a thread of commonality across programs. But before addressing our approach to assessing the various programs leveraging this conceptual frame, we address the balance of the program model, including the abroad and re-entry semesters.

International Experience

Once abroad, the internships in schools are one of the central features of this program. Participants are placed in schools throughout the city in small groups, typically 2–4 teaching interns per site. Having multiple teaching interns at school is important, as it provides interns with a peer to reflect upon and discuss what they are experiencing on an ongoing basis. All placements are facilitated by the program director, who in essence also serves as the Professional Development School (PDS) coordinator for the international site. As within domestic placements developing and nurturing relationships with these partner schools is critical. The work is both time intensive and challenging in its own right, and it is important to note here that from the outset of the London program over 20 years ago these responsibilities were considered core aspects of the faculty work load engaged in this program. As such, the teaching, advising, partner school engagement, and scholarly efforts by faculty were documented, reported, and considered for both annual performance and promotion and tenure reviews. We ardently recommend that faculty who innovate and work in this area, including the development and implementation of international study abroad programs, not be obliged to engage in this work as merely an overload to other core responsibilities that must be attended to. Scaling up would simply not have been possible without a collaborative culture of commitment and support by all faculty and administrative stakeholders who view this work as intellectually challenging and important, with great promise to advance the work and impact of teacher education.

The notion of participants' exploring their various identities, especially as Americans, is central to all of our international programs. During the semester abroad, the London program curriculum presently consists of a seminar in intercultural learning grounded in the professional context of British schooling where students and the instructor journal weekly. In addition, there is a historical and contemporary British education course offering participants a context for the school-based experiences. The Nottingham Social Studies program has several goals specific to preservice social studies teachers that include preparing social studies teachers with increased intercultural competence. Participants in this program are asked to be both historians and teachers from a global perspective. Studying world cultures and history is already a part of the social studies curriculum, and the shift we ask preservice teachers to make as part of this program is to consider culture and history explicitly from the point of view of non-American cultures. In Cape Town, our school partners are in the Townships outside the city center, in Cusco the participants are placed in homestays for housing, and such culturally complex contexts offer our participants an opportunity to consider aspects of their own identities in ways that are explicit and authentic. Previous research on the London program suggests that planned cultural dissonance within the immersion internship experience combined with strategic support for reflection is the key to intercultural learning in the international immersive experience (Marx & Moss, 2011). In the design of our programs, we do not seek to make students' work within the internships or their lives abroad culturally "easy" and do not seek to reduce what is often referred to as culture shock. Rather, we intentionally leverage the situations that cause students cultural dissonance as learning opportunities, framing them as intercultural puzzles and problems to be understood. These puzzles are formidable for these preservice teachers and due to the intense nature of the programs as briefly described here, we have found that students need substantial and purposeful opportunities to reflect upon their experiences beyond the courses and seminars offered during their term abroad. These opportunities for reflection can serve as a catalyst for change in a participant's worldview (Anderson & Fees, 2018). As a critical component, reflection must continue even after the international experience ends, thus every participant enrolls in a seminar in the re-entry semester immediately following their time abroad.

Re-entry

In some ways, the re-entry process kicks off in the last weeks of the students' time abroad as they begin to plan for returning home and engaging in their next semester teaching internships in US schools. Students return home in late December, and return to campus in January eager for their final semester of the Integrated Bachelor's/Master's program. Historically, the London cohort has remained together in a seminar during the re-entry semester. However, with our scaling up efforts we have also begun to combine participants from different international sites. Although this was initially a logistical necessity grounded in course minimum enrollment thresholds, instructors have noted that affording students an opportunity to reflect through the lenses of multiple sites and perspectives has yielded interesting class discourse. At the time of the writing of this chapter we have both single program and combined seminars underway and will programmatically consider the benefits and challenges of both models following the conclusion of the semester. Both program specific and conjoined seminars provide a dedicated space during the re-entry semester for the various cohorts to reflect upon and make sense of their international experience. It also encourages them to engage in cultural learning opportunities within their internship in a US school as a vehicle for comparative thinking (Marx & Moss, 2011). They begin the spring semester already having completed a draft of the inquiry project. During their semester abroad, they had refined their research questions, honed their research methodology, and collected and analyzed data. In the spring, they finish writing and consider the implications of their research for their own practice and for policies and practices underpinning teaching and learning. In the re-entry seminar, then, they once again leverage their post student teaching school based internships and inquiry projects to engage in critical reflection and intercultural learning, building upon ideas developed while abroad. This work is supported in seminar and other coursework by readings related to issues of culture, race, social justice, and equity.

To complete the annual cycle, the cohort ends the re-entry semester by presenting their inquiry project to the newly admitted incoming program cohort. This handoff meeting, as stated previously, is an important point of closure for the group. The cohort participants take this opportunity very seriously and have extended discussions about what they should present to the new cohort, clearly considering the process of intercultural learning through education abroad and how they, as more experienced intercultural learners, might best facilitate the outset of the process for others. By the conclusion of the program, each cohort has been engaged in explicit intercultural learning for a full calendar year. While it is the international experience itself often receives the most attention from many researchers, we contend that equal consideration must be paid to the design and research of learning experiences within the pre-departure and re-entry phases of a program as these phases are vital to the success of the overall program and should not be overlooked. The importance of the sustained attention to intercultural learning and development—spanning predeparture and re-entry—best allows for participants to leverage their international experiences toward growth in their professional and personal lives (Martin & Harrell, 2004; Wilson & Flournoy, 2007). Such a longer term proposition than merely considering the single term abroad has huge implications for scaling up programmatically as will be discussed in the final section of this chapter. In this section, we addressed the core organizational and curricular model of our education abroad program(s) (predeparture, semester abroad, and re-entry) and in the following section we will address a key aspect of our data-driven assessment. Finally, we will conclude this chapter by making summative recommendations for teacher education programs looking to scale up their international offerings.

Assessing and Supporting Student Growth

The Intercultural Development Inventory (IDI) is a means to assess aspects of intercultural perspectives (Hammer, 2012), specifically one's orientation to cultural difference, and historically is grounded in the Developmental

Model of Intercultural Sensitivity (DMIS) as described by Milton Bennett (1993). The DMIS delineates six stages of intercultural sensitivity development including three ethnocentric stages (denial, defense, and minimization) and three ethnorelative stages (acceptance, adaptation, and integration). Underpinning the current version of IDI, still echoing much of the DMIS, the instrument is framed around a continuum of monocultural to intercultural perspectives across five stages (denial, polarization, minimization, acceptance, and adaptation). From a programmatic perspective, the Intercultural Development Inventory (IDI) has proved to be an extremely valuable tool in both promoting and documenting intercultural learning for our preservice teachers. The lead author on this chapter is a qualified administrator of the instrument, and the IDI is given prepost to participants in each education abroad cohort. The resulting IDI Profile Report for each student is generated via an online platform and presents information about how one makes sense of and responds to cultural differences and commonalities.

The Developmental Orientation (DO) score presented in the report indicates one's primary orientation toward cultural differences and commonalities along the continuum as assessed by the IDI. The DO score can be within Denial, Polarization (Defense/Reversal), Minimization, Acceptance or Adaptation. Scores can also be reported for an entire cohort. As an example, the mean Developmental Orientation (DO) score for the most recent London cohort ($n = 17$) prior to the start of the program was 89.41 with a standard deviation of 9.56 (the range of score for Minimization is 85–115), indicating that the group's primary orientation toward cultural differences is within the Minimization stage of the Intercultural Development Continuum, reflecting a tendency to highlight commonalities across cultures that can mask important cultural differences in values, perceptions and behaviors. Following the semester abroad in London, the group's mean DO was reported as 118.86 with a standard deviation of 12.51 (the range of score for Acceptance is 115–130), indicating that the group's primary orientation toward cultural differences is now within Acceptance, reflecting an orientation that recognizes and appreciates patterns of cultural difference in one's own and other cultures in values, perceptions and behaviors. The mean score increased by approximately 29 points, which is a remarkable gain at the cohort-level given that as Cushner (2011) notes educators are often "stuck on the ethnocentric side of this scale" (p. 605). It is important to note that although each individual participant showed prepost gains, several of them remained in the transitional minimization stage following their international experiences even though the mean placed the entire cohort in Acceptance. Given that each participant gained in this measure, regardless of where they scored prior to outset of the program, is one confirmatory point of data suggesting the program is meeting its aim of fostering perspectives underpinning intercultural competencies.

Taken holistically, along with extensive use of journal prompts and other written assignments as elements of our core teacher education curriculum, the IDI pre- and post-measures corroborate the impact of thoughtfully scaffolded intercultural learning opportunities. Although no single measure can reveal a complete portrait regarding the growth of a preservice teacher, we are confident given data from the IDI that we are on the right track to helping preservice teachers carefully consider issues of culture and identity as they develop as professional educators. The IDI, a validated and widely utilized instrument offers an opportunity to consider data at the programmatic level.

Our various international sites approach various aspects of program implementation and student assessment through the unique cultural lens of each site. For example, the course work in Peru differs from that of Cape Town as we aim to leverage the local contextual elements that are, in fact, the core of the experiences for our students and should serve as the basis of the curriculum. It is important to note here that the selection of additional sites beyond London resulted from a combination of expressed student interest identified through surveys administered to enrolled teacher education candidates and faculty profiles. Ultimately, it was a matching process of identifying international sites that were of interest to our students while pairing that to faculty expertise. As Director of Global Education for the Neag School of Education, the lead author of this chapter worked closely with faculty to conceptualize each new program, including course work, teaching internships, and student recruitment plans to develop, approve, and launch the various programs over a coordinated timeline in recent years.

Beyond the Developmental Orientation (DO) score, the IDI offers additional data points and interpretation for our students along with an associated Intercultural Development Plan (IDP). The plan is designed to promote and scaffold intercultural learning opportunities. Across all sites we have incorporated, the plan into the experiential curriculum and activities of our program. In the predeparture course, students consider their options for cultural engagement while abroad. During their semester abroad, the plan is utilized to guide students' activities and reflection as they immerse themselves in learning opportunities. Upon re-entry the post-IDI report and plan, in reference to the initial ones, serve as a touchstone for growth and identifying learning still yet to be done as they transition from our program to their induction years as a practicing teacher. Working together, the DMIS conceptual frame and IDI instrument set the stage for a coherent model of curriculum and assessment that has enabled us to consider scaling up from the initial London program in an informed and data-driven way. In the final section for this chapter, we will address lessons learned as we have scaled up our international offerings for our teacher education candidates.

Lessons Learned from Scaling Up

At the University of Connecticut Neag School of Education faculty have over recent years purposely engaged in internationalization efforts by scaling up from a single teacher education study abroad program to multiple programs that at present serve approximately one-half of our cohort in the graduate year of our Integrated Bachelor's/Master's program. These international programs have school-based immersion experiences in non-US schools that go beyond student teaching and are crafted as an innovative way to impact preservice teachers' intercultural development and prepare them for teaching with culturally diverse student populations. In our experience of developing and sustaining such programs we have found the key for effective policies and strategies supporting the scale up of the internationalization of teacher education to be multifaceted. Such approaches include extensive collaboration within and beyond university-based education faculty, the institutionalization of programs to work effectively within both the conceptual and logistic frames of one's unique setting, and the attention to an arc of experiential curricula that goes beyond the semester abroad and includes predeparture and re-entry course work.

Collaboration for the impactful implementation of international efforts is essential on a variety of scales and contexts. On the home front, reciprocal and ongoing communication between the faculty in our teacher education academic unit and the professional staff in Education Abroad located in the Office of Global Affairs is vital for both the development and maintenance of such international programs. Within this collaborative model, the rigor of the curriculum along with the design, supervision and quality of school placements are key responsibilities of faculty. Risk management, travel, and other logistics fall under the purview of Education Abroad. Equally as essential, such close collaboration must also exist between institutional members domestically and their international counterparts. In fact, fundamentally it must be understood that success of any study abroad program rests on the quality and engagement of the international partners who bring it to life on a day-to-day basis. For example, within the London program our international instructors who teach in the program serve as intercultural guides or ambassadors beyond merely delivering the content of each course, and help our participants consider professional teaching practices—and living abroad in general—through an ethnorelative lens. These instructors historically have held multiyear teaching appointments in service of the program. Our university-based faculty, serving as PDS coordinators, work closely with their international instructor counterparts to deliver the program in a coordinated way.

In support of this process in the London program, home campus faculty has extensively collaborated with our British counterparts. This ongoing and reciprocal professional learning often takes place when UConn faculty travel to the United Kingdom when the program is not in session for the explicit purpose of engaging in this collaborative effort focused on developing the role of mentor and guide. This demands a commitment in terms of resources, time and intellectual effort. In practice, these commitments result in the UK-based instructor routinely being able to offer factual information and perspectives to contextualize observations and/or address misconceptions of participants who are immersed in living, teaching, and learning abroad. However, the host country instructor not only supplies information about British culture, but also additionally models the key skills of nonjudgmental observation, reflection, and information gathering. While, initially, many program participants find it difficult to describe UK culture without comparing it to US culture (often negatively), the instructor, serving as cultural guide, models the comparative process at a metacognitive level to question such assumptions. Such intensive and enduring collaboration demands resources and commitment that can only be achieved through the second element necessary for effective policies that support the scaling up of the internationalization of teacher education—program institutionalization.

The institutionalization of our international teacher education programs is essential for their success. Such institutionalization is about commitment. To scale up from our single London program to include Nottingham, Cape Town, and Cusco (in addition to shorter term programs not addressed in this chapter including Costa Rica, Puerto Rico, and Iceland), commitment by faculty, commitment of resources, and administrative commitment to global education were all required. Since the inception of our urban education full semester program in London about 20 years ago, the faculty effort required to facilitate such a program has been substantial. Support from the departmental and school-level leadership regarding the preparation of globally and culturally competent teachers has been expressed in many ways, but as noted previously perhaps none more so than in assigning the supervision and teaching in this intensive program as part of the standard faculty work load. It is understood and appreciated that the faculty effort to lead a cohort of students through such an international program is substantial, and administrators have recognized and acknowledged this effort when considering policies used to assign faculty teaching, committee and advising responsibilities. The faculty serves as instructor, registrar (admitting and managing student enrollment), advisor, professional development school coordinator, and mentor along with a host of other academic and logistical roles. Unfortunately, all too often the internationalization of programs is a mere add-on to existing commitments, and as a direct result faculty effort is often above and beyond their assigned duties diminishing the potential for long-term sustainability and success. Stated unambiguously, the international effort of faculty should not be considered an *add-on* but a valued aspect of any university with a global mission and reach. Given such a commitment to institutionalization efforts of these programs, faculty has leveraged their programmatic and teaching roles to engage in scholarship in the field of education abroad as well as have been awarded extramural grants to support international initiatives (see Marx & Moss, 2011; Marx & Moss, 2016; Moss & Marcus, 2015). When such faculty-driven internationalization is valued as central to the mission and work of an institution everybody benefits. The model that has so well served the London program over the past two decades continues to be the exemplar as new faculty takes on such work at other international partnership sites.

The final essential element underpinning successful efforts to build and maintain international teacher education programs relates to the notion of curricular alignment and an arc of connectedness that goes beyond the single semester abroad to include the predeparture and re-entry semesters. Best practices within education abroad program development tell us the predeparture, the experience abroad, and re-entry phases of such programs are all essential for participant success (Martin & Harrell, 2004; Wilson & Flournoy, 2007). As such, it is important to consider not only the full scope of the international experience, but also its relationship to the core sequence of experience and courses within teacher education. Larger scale thinking must work within course sequences and program requirements in ways that do not penalize student participation by delaying graduation or creating other academic issues that are often significant deterrents for participation. At UConn, such a coordinated and thematic course of study involves a three-semester, full-calendar year program as we believe this model has the best opportunity for adding significant value in terms of promoting intercultural competence given the time necessary for both meaningful experiences and reflection.

Conclusion

Teacher education programs seeking to scale up from one-off or limited international efforts must adopt a workable model that suits both their conceptual and logistical realities such that "going global" is a sustainable effort that can best serve their developing teachers for years to come. Perhaps one the most fundamental implications from the work described in this chapter is the need for ongoing support of critical cultural reflection as the cornerstone for any international immersion experience. Critical cultural reflection does not come easily, and most certainly does not happen spontaneously or even inevitably when someone travels abroad from one's own home country. Students are being asked to explore and often reconsider deeply held understandings and beliefs, to be critical of existing systems within which they live, and to struggle with the notion that there may be multiple ways of understanding and making sense of an experience. Such discourse and reflection take time and must be facilitated as a core element of any successful program by committed, collaborative and supported faculty who are eager to prepare the next generation of teachers for our K-12 schools.

References

Anderson, H., & Fees, B. S. (2018). Reflecting on international educative experiences: Developing cultural competence in preservice early childhood educators. *Journal of Early Childhood Teacher Education*, 39(4), 364–381.

Bennett, M. J. (1993). Towards ethnorelativism: A developmental model of intercultural sensitivity. In M. Paige (Ed.), *Education for intercultural experience* (pp. 21–72). Intercultural Press.

Bennett, M. J. (2004). Becoming interculturally competent. In J. Wurzel (Ed.), *Toward multiculturalism: A reader in multicultural education* (pp. 62–77). Intercultural Resource Corporation.

Cushner, K. (2011). Intercultural research in teacher education: An essential intersection in the preparation of globally competent teachers, *Action in Teacher Education, 33,* 5-6, 601–614.

Cushner, K., & Brennan, S. (2007). The value of learning to teach in another culture. In K. Cushner, & S. Brennan (Eds.), *Intercultural student teaching: A bridge to global competence* (pp. 1–12). Rowman & Littlefield Education.

Engle, L., & Engle, J. (2004). Assessing language acquisition and intercultural sensitivity development in relation to study abroad program design. *Frontiers: The Interdisciplinary Journal of Study Abroad, 10,* 219–236.

Gay, G. (2000). *Culturally responsive teaching: Theory, research, and practice.* Teachers College Press.

Hammer, M. (2012). The Intercultural Development Inventory: A new frontier in assessment and development of intercultural competence. In M. Vande Berg, R.M. Paige, & K.H. Lou (Eds.), *Student learning abroad* (Ch. 5, pp. 115–136). Stylus Publishing.

Hammer, M. R., & Bennett, M. J. (2003). Measuring intercultural sensitivity: The Intercultural Development Inventory. *International Journal of Intercultural Relations, 27*(4), 403–419.

Martin, J. N., & Harrell, T. (2004). Intercultural reentry of students and professionals: Theory and practice. In D. Landis, J. M. Bennett & M. J. Bennett (Eds.), *Handbook of intercultural training,* 3rd ed. (pp. 309). Sage Publications.

Marx, H. & Moss D. M. (2011). Please mind the culture gap: Intercultural development during a teacher education study abroad program. *Journal of Teacher Education, 62*(1) 35–47.

Marx, H. & Moss D. M. (2016). Coming home: Continuing intercultural learning during the re-entry semester following a study abroad experience. *Journal of International Social Studies, (5)*2, 38–53.

Moss, D.M. & Marcus, A.S. (2015). Over there: Exploring a WWII themed short-duration study abroad program for preservice teachers. In D. Schwarzer & B.L. Bridglall (Eds.) *Promoting global competence and social justice in teacher education* (pp. 45–70). Lexington Books.

Norris, E. & Dwyer, M. (2005). Testing Assumptions: The impact of two study abroad program models. *Frontiers: The Interdisciplinary Journal of Study Abroad. 11,* 121–142.

Open Doors. (2019). *Open Doors 2019 Fast Facts.* New York, NY: Institute for International Education.

Wilson, A., & Flournoy, M. A., (2007). Preparatory courses for student teaching abroad. In K. Cushner, & S. Brennan (Eds.), *Intercultural student teaching: A bridge to global competence* (pp. 34–56). Rowman & Littlefield Education.

5 An International Graduate Program for Educators

Transformative Professional Development for In-Service Teachers in International Schools

Michael Lovorn and Brandon Kawa

Introduction

We are living in an era of unprecedented social and educational globalization marked by ever-evolving means of communication, cultural diffusion, and sharing of ideas. Technological advancements continue to have a tremendous impact on how we perceive ourselves, where we go, what we study, and the careers and lifestyles we pursue. As members of a truly global community, the time is now for young people of all backgrounds to develop global competencies including curiosity and openness about other cultures and peaceable resolution to conflict (Participate Global Educators [PGE], 2017). Certainly, teachers must do the same.

Today's teachers must enter the profession with skills to individualize instruction and assessment, promote inquiry-based learning, and imbue students with sustainable conceptions of equity, equality, and collective humanity (Lovorn et al., 2017). Naturally, such an important and timely focus requires teacher educators to continue global competencies training and development (Deardorff, 2015). Over the past decade, many US teacher education programs have developed short-term travel and other exchange opportunities for their teacher candidates to work toward these goals (Kasun & Saavedra, 2016). This is an advancement of note, as teacher education programs have lagged behind other college majors in presenting their students with study abroad options (Altun, 2017; Wooldridge et al., 2018).

Of course, in-service teachers need professional development in these imperative areas as well, and for this reason, in 1999, Buffalo State College—State University of New York (known regionally as "Buffalo State") launched the International Graduate Program for Educators (IGPE). Now in its 21st year of operation, IGPE continues to offer timely professional development for in-service teachers in international schools with the overall intent of advancing their teaching practice through enhanced global competency. IGPE courses and workshops are designed to enhance teachers' analytical and critical thinking skills, promote their openness and respect toward other cultures, and inform and enrich their interactions with their peers, students, and parents. To this end, IGPE instructors seek to deepen teachers' knowledge and understanding of education in global contexts by engaging them in research on global-mindedness and intercultural understanding, and advancing their development of professional empathy, flexibility, and self-awareness.

This chapter will provide a brief history of IGPE's important role in graduate studies in international education, orient the reader to IGPE's professional development design and curriculum, discuss program challenges, propose a list of essential attributes for any university seeking to launch such a program, and elaborate on how IGPE's facilitation of relationships between PK-12 international schools and the university promotes concepts of global competence.

Recent Graduate Studies in International K-12 Schools and IGPE's Emergence

International schools are largely privately funded institutions that have historically served the families of American and Canadian diplomats and international businesspersons. For many years, these institutions tended to open anywhere embassies or consulates were found around the world. As such, they have historically offered most, if not all, instruction in English, which has also made their curricula attractive to locals who aspire to send their children to universities in the English-speaking world (it should be noted there are also many French-, German-, Italian-, and Chinese-speaking international schools around the world).

In 1999, there were an estimated 2000 recognized and reputable PK-12 international schools in operation on six continents. Today, there are over 10,000 dotting those six continents. Of course, geographic diversity is only part of this 20-year proliferation. Private international schools have always served families of plutocracy and the ruling elite; however, many have now evolved to accommodate children from across various societal spectra and backgrounds, including those from bi- and tri-lingual households, those who have tested (and yet to be tested) gifted and talented, those with special needs, and those designated high-needs/high-risks. Studies attribute this exponential growth in services to a boom in global business and industry as well as demands for higher quality schools by more parents from more places (ISC Research, 2018).

As more international schools opened in cities and towns around the world during the early 2000s, competition among them increased. This competition for students and families created several positive byproducts, among them, competitive tuition pricing, rigorous curricula, and aggressive teacher hiring practices. One additional byproduct was the need for school administrators to ensure their teaching faculty remains at the forefront of theory and practice in the field. Such organic quality control led many directors to maximize their professional development reserves by adopting school-wide training goals and initiatives.

International education experts at Buffalo State took note of this growing need—and market—and in 1999, launched the International Graduate Program for Educators (IGPE) over the past 20 years, IGPE has offered Middle States-accredited, graduate credit-bearing, advanced education coursework and professional development for teachers and administrators in over 60 international schools in more than 30 countries around the world. To date, IGPE has over 3000 alumni worldwide, many of whom have risen to school directorships themselves, and who, based on their experience, have launched their own partnerships with the program.

IGPE's Contributions to Best Practices

IGPE has a special arrangement with SUNY and Middle States to facilitate a Master of Science degree in Multidisciplinary Studies with an emphasis (programmatic theme) in International Education. Our program is open exclusively to teachers, qualifying teacher assistants, and administrators who are actively engaged and employed by English medium or English bilingual private American-, Canadian-, and/or European-style schools. It is important to note that while many US scholars understandably avoid the term "American" in describing programs or entities of US origin, the international PK-12 schools market generally does not subscribe to or follow this practice. Many of our partner schools, agencies, and associations incorporate the phrase "American School" in their formal names. In fact, for most, their use of the term "American" or "Canadian" as a school descriptor is generally one of their greatest selling points. We use this term here as an acknowledgement of this nomenclatural distinction.

Courses are selected from various Buffalo State department and program catalogs, including a balance of educational theory and practice, curriculum development, educational leadership, special education, English as a second language, educational technology, creativity studies, social foundations, and educational research. Once selected, courses are delivered to students in cohorts of ten or more. These cohorts are typically made up of educators from a single school, but occasionally include teachers by fully vetted adjunct instructors. Our instructor pool is made up of both Buffalo State-affiliated and local (onsite) experts. We should also note that while the IGPE-facilitated degree does not lead to New York teacher certification; our clientele of largely autonomous private schools are at liberty to set thresholds for the values, preparations and credentials of their teachers.

Most new hires from the United States and Canada do typically hold a teacher certificate from an accredited state or provincial program, and many of our partner schools perceive our credit-bearing graduate coursework as an affordable continuing education or professional development option for their teachers. Additionally, if and when teachers of United States or Canadian origin return home to continue their careers, our courses are regularly accepted by various state and provincial teacher certification offices and applied toward certificate applications.

Partner feedback and program exit surveys indicate IGPE's greatest strengths are found in its (a) faculty, many of whom are former or current international school administrators and all of whom are experts in international education; (b) truly globalized approach and techniques; (c) coursework and workshops that are tailored and contextualized specifically for teachers in international schools; and (d) flexibility to contour course offerings and requirements of the 30-credit master's degree to fit each site's professional development goals. This balance of content quality, timeliness, relevance, and design flexibility invites school administrators to help develop the program, and integrate teachers' research, scholarship, and professional growth into their strategic plans and academic designs immediately upon completion.

This concept hastens the transition of theory into practice and has yielded partnerships with PK-12 international schools on five continents. Today's geographically diverse list of prestigious partners includes the Escola das Nações (Brasilia, Brazil), the Carol Morgan School (Santo Domingo, Dominican Republic), the Shanghai Community International School (China), the English Modern School (Doha, Qatar), Quality Schools International (Kiev, Ukraine), the Hisar School (Istanbul, Turkey), and the Lusaka American International School (Zambia).

The IGPE Design

The 30-credit graduate program is designed exclusively for international educators. In fact, our agreement with SUNY and Middle States prohibits us from offering the program to teachers or administrators in domestic schools. Our active student body typically numbers about 500 worldwide. About 50% of these students hail from the United States, Canada and Europe. The other 50% are locally hired teachers who are fluent in English. Most cohorts schedule to complete the degree in 2–3 years. Again, programs are tailored to the needs of each partner site, and exit survey results indicate alumni are most appreciative of the program flexibility, rigorous and highly contextualized coursework, and responsivity of the IGPE staff. This reputation has led to many repeat partnerships, including an uninterrupted 20-year partnership with the original partner site, the Columbus School in Medellín, Colombia.

Making Connections

IGPE staff promotes the program by attending accredited regional international educational conferences. Historically, the program has maintained active membership in the Association for the Advancement of International Education, the Association of American Schools in South America, the Association of International Schools in Africa, the Central and Eastern European Schools Association, the East Asia Regional Council of Schools, the Mediterranean Association of International Schools, the Near East Schools Association, and Tri-Association of American Schools. It is at these functions where we (IGPE staff) meet with interested school administrators to introduce the unique program design and flexibility.

Tailoring the Program to Site Goals

Upon initial interest, we draft a nonbinding memorandum of understanding between Buffalo State and the host site. This MoU outlines stakeholder roles and all services to be provided throughout the partnership. The MoU is considered "non-binding," meaning the host site may opt out of the partnership at any time. With this understanding, the new partner site agrees to host the ten-course master's degree.

School heads considering new partnerships regularly cite the importance of program flexibility. Site directors and coordinators work with the IGPE administrators to select courses from the IGPE course catalog to be offered for the degree program. This collaborative process is intended to support the school's professional development initiatives and course participants' needs while adhering to all SUNY and Middle States rules, guidelines, policies, and procedures. Expert instructors then make content relevant across grade levels and developmental levels in international schools. Of the 30 semester credit hours required to complete this degree, at least half of them (five courses) must be 600-level or higher. The only required courses are *Methods and Techniques of Educational Research* and the *Master's Project*.

Accepting Applicants and Vetting Instructors

We accept master's degree-seeking, pre-major, and non-degree-seeking students. Regardless of category, each applicant must hold a bachelor's degree from an accredited university with a minimum cumulative grade point average of 2.5 (4.0 scale), or an equivalent degree as deemed by the SUNY Graduate School. IGPE does not require TOEFL scores for non-US applicants. In lieu of this cost-prohibitive and delimiting measure, SUNY and Middle States have enabled IGPE to utilize a formal English proficiency statement; a declaration signed by a school head or human resources director confirming each applicant's ability to communicate, complete coursework, meet program expectations in English.

IGPE instructors are vetted by content chairs and deans. Many IGPE instructors are faculty in the Buffalo State School of Education. Others are experts met at regional conferences or popular and academically accomplished locals suggested to us by partner school administrators. Most are veteran PK-12 international school teachers and administrators, and many are noted researchers in their respective fields.

Designing Elective Opportunities and Accommodations

As an added element of flexibility, each IGPE student may earn up to six credits toward their degree by attending an IGPE-approved professional development workshop or conference and completing a comprehensive, reflective assignment. This standard assignment is made up of preconference preparation, during-conference networking, and post-conference interaction with the instructor appropriate for the number of credits being sought (15 hours for one credit, 30 hours for two credit, and 45 hours for three credits). Workshops and conference attendance are credited as elective special topics courses.

We are attuned to the international school market and the needs of teachers in this field. Considering teachers in international schools typically sign 2- to 3-year contracts, there is an inherent degree of teacher turnover. Program participants who take new employment or move prior to completing the program as part of their original cohort may either join the active cohort at their new school or may opt to finish their degree via independently completed online courses.

Course Curriculum and Workshop Content

Most IGPE course numbers and descriptions align with the Buffalo State graduate catalog listings in educational theory and practice, curriculum development, educational leadership, special education, English as a second language, educational technology, creativity studies, social foundations, and educational research. It should be noted, however, that while these descriptions remain intact on IGPE syllabi, each course is further contextualized to meet programmatic competencies and student learning objectives. These contextualizations are typically proposed by instructors, and then reviewed and approved by the director in consultation with school heads or site coordinators.

For example, one popular course among international school heads is *Seminar in Educational Change* (Educational Leadership 704). When offered to the graduate students on the Buffalo State campus, this course examines largely local, state, and national processes of change, educational change over the last decade, qualities and processes that enhance or inhibit change, and personal and systemic change in the educational setting. In an international school, this course remains true to the course description; however, the foci are shifted to processes of change among affiliated international schools, and how US-produced curricula affect systemic change in other parts of the world.

Like this course, all IGPE offerings are grounded in the promotion of theoretical and practical global competence. The program has adopted the ten-part global competency rubric of nonprofit teacher training agent *Participate Global Educators* (2017), accessible at: https://app.participate.com/products/teaching-and-assessing-global-competencies/37266fd7-86b040c9-b2c1-718 8e0b5dd02, to ensure all program participants develop and demonstrate the knowledge, skills, and attitudes necessary to be a global citizen.

Participate Global Educators recognize ten distinct global competencies.

(a) analytical and critical thinking; (b) respectful, appropriate, effective interactions; (c) empathy; (d) flexibility; (e) knowledge and understanding of global issues; (f) intercultural knowledge and understanding; (g) curiosity and openness toward other cultures; (h) respect for other cultures; (i) global-mindedness and connection; and (j) self-awareness. These competencies provide a framework through which teachers may not only be trained, but also demonstrate measurable growth in their schools and classrooms. Upon being vetted to instruct for IGPE, each new adjunct is presented with these global competencies and asked to incorporate them into their syllabi.

Course activities are also crafted to meet one or more of six institutional student learning objectives (SLOs) for the Master of Science in Multidisciplinary Studies degree. They make up components of the graduate school assessment plan and are embedded in various courses. SLO 1 is to demonstrate effective and appropriate communication skills through coherent and well-organized written presentations. SLO 2 is to demonstrate effective and appropriate communication skills through coherent and well-organized oral and visual presentations SLOs 1 and 2 are addressed in all IGPE courses.

SLO 3 is to demonstrate the ability to creatively use information, concepts, analytical approaches, and critical thinking skills in one or more disciplines; and competency in making connections that will synthesize and transfer learning to new and complex situations. SLO 4 is to ethically identify, access, critically evaluate, and apply information throughout collections of work. SLO 5 is to demonstrate a basic knowledge of research design, methodology, and measurement strategies that address a problem in the field. SLO 6 is to demonstrate analytical skills through self-reflection to access individual performances of collections of work, and to show evidence of personal, professional, and civic engagement.

SLOs 3, 4, 5 and 6 are embedded in final two courses: *Methods and Techniques of Educational Research* and the *Master's Project*, and each is evaluated by applicable rubrics for written communication, oral communication, critical thinking, ethical reasoning, and integrative learning. Along with the global competencies, the SLOs are used to guide students' in-program growth. Many or all of these concepts are demonstrated in students' action research projects in the final two courses: *Methods and Techniques of Educational Research* and the *Master's Project*.

Challenges

IGPE has been confronted with systematic challenges that have occasionally thwarted the program mission. During a recent analysis of program strengths, weaknesses, opportunities and challenges (commonly referred to as a "SWOC analysis"), we identified three immediate and substantive program challenges: (a) confusion among SUNY administrators about new site approval processes; (b) prohibitive graduate admissions requirements; and (c) steady increases in market competitors and teachers who enter international education with a master's degree in hand. We assert that while, left unattended, any of these mounting challenges could create significant operational problems for IGPE, there is a concise and uncomplicated path to removing obstacles, overcoming each challenge, leading to unprecedented success and program growth.

Confusion About New Site Approval Processes

IGPE generates new revenue in two ways: by reactivating dormant partnerships and launching new site partnerships. The reactivation of dormant partnerships can sustain IGPE for a year or two, but longitudinal program growth depends on development of thriving new partnerships. With delays and system-level confusion over new site approval processes, IGPE has been hampered in providing timely information about new programs, particularly as it relates to launch dates.

This uncertainty about required forms and petitions has contributed to lengthy delays in the approval process and in launching new cohorts. The approval process for new IGPE sites should be clear, concise, and efficient; however, these avoidable dilemmas have resulted in diminished revenue intake and have the potential to negatively impact IGPE's market reputation.

Prohibitive Admissions Requirements

Current Buffalo State graduate admissions policy restricts the manner in which IGPE serves teachers from many other educational backgrounds and academic cultures. Many well-regarded teacher certification programs around the world culminate in a 3-year degree; however, the graduate school currently only accepts applicants who have earned the equivalent of a US 4-year bachelor's degree. Recently, an applicant with a 3-year degree was denied admission to the Buffalo State Graduate School despite having 15 years of professional teaching experience. This admission denial was counterintuitive on several levels.

We argue that prohibitive admissions requirements set in the Buffalo State Graduate School should be reviewed and, when possible, reinterpreted to reflect a more comprehensive institutional understanding of international applicants' backgrounds and records. It is our belief that professional teachers in PK-12 international schools, particularly those with multiple years of experience, should not be penalized simply due to differences in credentialing requirements in other countries. Likewise, IGPE should be accessible to those who have earned 3-year bachelor's degrees from accredited universities, as is common across Europe, India, and other parts of the world.

Increases in Market Competition and In-Hand Master's Degrees

We have observed an increase in competitors in the international program marketspace. There are a variety of new programs; some university-led, some not; some accredited, some not, that advertise credit for teachers. To date, no other program can match IGPE's price point; however, it seems only a matter of time before competing providers garner the support to develop and launch comparably priced offerings.

Additionally, due to the growth of fifth-year programs being offered across the US, the international education market is experiencing a dramatic increase in the number of teachers entering the profession with master's degrees in hand. Obviously, for a program offering only a master's degree, this trend could prove fatal in the long run. As counterbalance, IGPE administrators seek to modify admissions requirements to make the program more accessible to partner sites' local hires, most of whom are still entering the field with only a bachelor's degree. Administrators are also exploring capacity to propose an IGPE-facilitated doctoral degree.

Attributes for Success in International In-Service Teacher Education

IGPE thrives on a deep sense of trust and transparency with stakeholders. Buffalo State administrators trust the IGPE director to maintain a healthy presence in the market, to build long-lasting partnerships, and to semiautonomously manage the annual budget. School heads and site coordinators trust IGPE instructors to deliver high-quality and program-aligned coursework, and IGPE trusts school heads and site coordinators to communicate with transparency and regularity. In addition to stellar trust relationships and the programmatic promotion of the aforementioned global competencies, IGPE's successes are derived from program flexibility, highly contextualized instruction and student supports, and vision for collaborative program growth.

Program Flexibility

The master's degree is made up of ten courses, only two of which are program requirements. The preceding eight courses may be selected in a manner so as to tailor coursework and professional development to each host site's particular goals or needs. IGPE administrators have the authority to invite school heads and directors into planning phases of their cohort's course set. Many partners are International Baccalaureate schools, and thus prefer a more holistic curriculum. Others are interested in creating an in-house educational leadership pipeline. Still others are interested in revamping their English as a Second Language programs.

Once host site administrators make their professional development goals known, IGPE administrators suggest courses to address and support them. Recently, IGPE instituted a series of targeted microcredentials to address popular foci, including educational leadership, ESL, and special education. SUNY microcredentials, which must be approved at the college level, are made up of between two and five courses, and intended to outline and accomplish a minicourse of study. While the microcredential bears no formal (SUNY or Middle States-recognized) certification value, IGPE partner schools, all of which are private, generally recognize the microcredentials as valued courses of study that meet various programmatic needs.

Context-Savvy Instructors

IGPE faculty possesses expertise in teacher education in international contexts and has demonstrated track records of instructional and scholarly activities. Our program relies on a core of about 20 veteran adjunct instructors to deliver most courses, and more than 100 additional experts who instruct courses or lead workshops in ala carte fashion upon request. Most IGPE adjunct instructors have years of teaching and/or administration experience in PK-12 international schools, and many are well-known in the international schools arena. With the understanding that context is of paramount importance in all teaching endeavors, we assign instructors to meet partner sites' articulated strategic needs. As an example, Chinese partner site the Shanghai Community International School recently expressed an interest in boosting their teachers' training in International Baccalaureate curriculum and delivery techniques. IGPE administrators assigned renowned Australian I.B. expert Dr Meredith Harbord to teach the course. Dr Harbord contoured her course to fit highlight and focus on their needs.

Similarly, the English Modern School in Doha, Qatar expressed an interest in developing their teacher–leader and leadership pipeline programs. IGPE administrators assigned International School of Yangon director Greg Hedger and leadership expert Sandy Sheppard to lead micro-credential-type courses in accomplishment of this goal. Dr Hedger and Dr Sheppard are well known for not only delivering educational leadership deep dives for the East Asia Regional Council of Schools and Near East Schools Association, but also effective leadership program implementation at their own schools.

IGPE instructors are also attuned to the program's commitment to student service and satisfaction. They promote the IGPE model, and attend to students' particular needs with great care and personalized attention before, during, and after courses. One example of these accommodations is observable in the regular practice of evoking IGPE's liberal and student-centered policy on granting assignment extensions and requests for incompletes. As professional teachers, many of whom are getting adjusted to new living and working arrangements, IGPE students are always very busy. The IGPE director usually supports adjunct instructors' requests for students' extensions and incompletes as needed, at no additional cost to the student.

Additionally, most IGPE adjunct instructors emerge from careers in international schools and are well-prepared to make additional accommodations for teachers from various backgrounds and levels of English proficiency. Like many international programs, IGPE cohorts have minimum operational thresholds. As mentioned, we generally feel a cohort remains viable if it has at least ten active students. For schools with low numbers, it is important to offer courses designed to accommodate participants from various levels and departments. For these reasons, IGPE faculty craft syllabi with open-ended or adaptable assignments.

Also, IGPE faculty recognizes that conversational language fluency does not always translate to research-level language fluency. For these reasons, they accept the responsibility to implement language learner strategies, particularly those related to more individualized assistance and accommodation, for students as needed. School heads also assist in this capacity by working with instructors to share elements or structure of accelerated or remedial English programming they are utilizing at the school (often for both students and faculty). These collaborative efforts enable the instructor to gain important site-specific insights into the school's procedure for increasing English proficiency prior to arrival.

Vision for Collaborative Program Growth

Sustainable programs are those that devise and pursue plans to remain self-sufficient, relevant and collaborative, and consistently forward-thinking. A recent and active strategic goal of the IGPE director has been to diversify program enterprises and commitments to partner with on-campus and local organizations. One such example of a successful innovation in teacher education is the award-winning International Professional Development Schools (IPDS) consortium at Buffalo State (National Association of Foreign Student Advisers [NAFSA], 2019).

The IPDS consortium was founded in 2012 with the intent to develop teacher candidates' skillset in intercultural and international contexts. They devised a means by which teacher candidates could develop global competencies through first-hand experiences and interactions with their peers in various countries though short-term exchange. The overall goal of IPDS was and is to ensure teacher candidates are adept at serving diverse student populations at home and abroad (Garas-York et al, 2017). Prior to the collaboration with IGPE, the IPDS consortium operated exchange programs in more than ten countries.

In 2019, the Columbus School in Medellín, Colombia consulted IGPE experts about a new school-wide initiative to enhance professional development offerings in bilingual education. IGPE administrators helped establish a newly conceptualized IPDS site at the Columbus School. IPDS has historically served only teacher candidates; however, this initiative is designed to focus on in-service teacher development, especially targeting their cultural knowledge and perspective-based learning opportunities.

In fall 2019, four in-service teachers from the Columbus School journeyed to Buffalo, New York to visit local public schools and college classrooms, present at the annual Professional Development School conference, and attend Buffalo State's Anne Frank Project (AFP) Social Justice Festival. In spring 2020, a team of Buffalo State IGPE and IPDS representatives reciprocated by leading a group of five in-service public school teachers on a tour of Medellín and Cartagena for similar school visits and cultural activities (https://buffalostateipdscolombia.weebly.com/blogs.html). IGPE is actively coordinating similar IPDS programs at partner schools in Brazil and Qatar.

Conclusion

The Buffalo State International Graduate Program for Educators facilitates accredited graduate coursework and professional development for teachers and administrators in PK-12 international schools. As exemplified by more than 20 active international cohorts and developing collaborations with the IPDS consortium, program staff and instructors advance international education by promoting global competencies and fostering global collaboration. All IGPE endeavors are developed and implemented with the interwoven goals of making positive contributions to teaching and learning processes, and in doing so, making the world a better place through education.

In working to achieve our mission to promote international educators' intellectual, scholarly, and professional growth, and to promote global competencies and education, we are always seeking fresh and innovative approaches to improve professional development for teachers in international PK-12 schools. As demonstrated, this unique program is not without challenges; however, we are committed to actively seeking to facilitating student-centered programs that promote diversity, foster inquiry-based learning opportunities, maximize intercultural collaboration for the advancement of society, and provide cutting-edge in-service teacher education across a wide variety of international and intercultural settings.

As the model continues to evolve, we are taking steps to offer new and attractive in-service teacher education products and services. We have proposed several new site-based microcredentials, petitioned Buffalo State administrators to amend admissions criteria for international applicants, and made promising new contacts with the directors of no less than ten PK-12 international schools. Throughout this evolution, we continue to credit global competency-driven strategic planning, self-sufficiency, and vision for these ongoing developments.

References

Altun, M. (2017). The effects of study abroad on teacher competencies. *International Journal of Social Sciences & Educational Studies, 3*(4), 219–222.

Deardorff, D. K. (2015). *Demystifying outcomes assessment for international educators: A practical approach.* Stylus Publishing.

Garas-York, K., del Prado Hill, P., Day, L., Keller-Mathers, S., & Truesdell, K. (Eds.). (2017). *Doing PDS: Stories and strategies from successful clinically rich practice.* Information Age Publishing.

Kasun, G. & Saavedra, C. (2016). Disrupting ELL teacher candidates' identities: Indigenizing teacher education in one study abroad program. *TESOL Quarterly, 50*(3), 684–707.

Lovorn, M., Manning, P., & Warsh, M. (2017). Entering a new era in world history education. In M. Lovorn (Ed.), *New, critical, and re-envisioned approaches to teaching world history,* a special edition of *The History Teacher, 50*(1), 321–329.

National Association of Foreign Student Advisers [NAFSA]. (2019). *2019–2020 Senator Paul Simon Award for Campus Internationalization.* NAFSA Awards. https://www.nafsa.org/about/about-nafsa/senator-paul-simon-award-campus-internationalization

Participate Global Educators (PGE). (2017). *Teaching and assessing global competencies.* Participate Global Competencies. https://app.participate.com/products/teaching-and-assessing-global-competencies/37266fd7-86b040c9-b2c1-7188e0b5dd02

Wooldridge, D., Peet, S., & Meyer, L. (2018). Transforming professionals through short-term study-abroad experiences. *Delta Kappa Gamma Bulletin, 84*(4), 31–63. http://search.proquest.com/docview/2068462178/

ISC Research. (2018). *International schools market sees growth and new opportunities this year.* ISC News. https://www.iscresearch.com/news-and-events/isc-news/isc-news-details/~post/international-schools-market-sees-growth-and-new-oppotunities-this-year-20180117

6   Design Principles for International Teacher Study Abroad Programs

The Case of the Instructional Leadership Institute for Pakistani Educators (ILIPE)

Rebecca H. Woodland

Introduction

I vividly remember the moment, in June 2014, when 20 educators from Pakistan sat jet-lagged in a big circle in the large "70s-era" conference room on the university campus where I work in the northeast region of the United States. They had arrived from Islamabad 24 hours prior and were now attending the opening session of the Instructional Leadership Institute for Pakistan Educators (ILIPE) an intensive study abroad program funded by the United States Department of State. These men and women, all middle or high school educators representing a range of subject areas including reading, mathematics, English, social studies, science, physics, and Islamic studies, had traveled roughly 7000 miles to participate in 5+ intensive weeks of training about learner-centered education (Schwiesfurth, 2013) and learner-centered approaches to curriculum and instruction (Tomlinson, 2014). One by one, as I stood facing them in front of the room, each teacher, strangers to one another, went around and briefly shared about themselves and the school context in which they worked. They taught in government, madrassa, and private schools. They came from across Pakistan, including urban centers like Islamabad, Karachi, and Lahore as well as isolated areas such as Chitral and Gilgit-Baltistan. Some had virtually no access to texts or modern technology, while others used state of the art resources. Class sizes and demographics ranged from 150+ students of multiple ages and linguistic and cultural backgrounds in one class, to classes with a handful of single sex, same age students. Some were required to teach a mandated or scripted curriculum, while others had no written curriculum at all to work with. Many lived in, and were teaching students who also lived in, severe poverty and/or risking their lives to attend school, some taught wealthy students in schools fortified with armed private security forces. I felt dazed. I had been a public school teacher, university director of teacher education, and actively worked in partnership with principals and superintendents to design, deliver, and evaluate teacher professional development programming across the United States. Yet, as I stood in front of this group of weary but excited educators, instead of the normal butterflies, I felt trepidation. *What kind of study abroad training had my partners and I envisioned and created? Would the curriculum be of value and work for Pakistani teachers? How could we possibly meet their needs? What skills do they actually want to develop, what do they really need to learn and know how to do? What happens after they leave the United States and return to their own classrooms back in Pakistan? Will the PD we've designed do them justice? Will it make any difference in the lives of their students?*

There have now been three iterations of the ILIPE program (2014, 2016 and 2018). To date, more than 60 Pakistani teachers and administrators, who serve upwards of 45,000 Pakistani students, have come to the United States to participate in the summer portion of ILIPE. In addition, approximately 30 trainers from the United States have gone to Pakistan to immerse in the culture and to engage in school and classroom visits and workshops. Curriculum facilitators are made up of university-based instructors and public-school teachers and administrators, and ILIPE program staff, who make sure that study abroad participants get safely to and from ILIPE events are university undergraduate students. I serve as ILIPE Academic Director and work closely with the ILIPE Academic Coordinator, a former public-school teacher and current Ph.D. student to design and deliver the ILIPE curriculum. There is an extensive ILIPE recruitment and selection process. In the 2018 iteration of ILIPE, approximately 2,500 educators from across Pakistan applied to participate. Ultimately, twenty individuals (ten men and ten women) are selected to participate in the ILIPE study abroad program. The selected participants travel to the United States in the summer and live on the University of Massachusetts Amherst campus. The curriculum entails 4–6 hours of daily instruction, about 120 hours in total that focuses on the tenets of learned-centered education, including the principles of constructivist learning theory and the stages of backward curriculum design. Pakistani teachers are matched with a local Usonian middle or high school teacher, and spend several days with this educator in their classroom. Homework and readings are assigned most evenings, and capstone projects consisting of an oral presentation, written unit plan, and a professional poster presentation that is open to the public is required of each study abroad participant. The two foundational texts of the Institute are: *Understanding By Design* (Wiggins & McTighe, 2005) and *In Search of Understanding: The Case for Constructivist Classrooms* (Brooks & Brooks, 1999) and participants receive copies of each book. Teachers are also provided iPads and electronic access to numerous articles and resources related to the content of the Institute. A primary goal of ILIPE is to increase teachers' ability to carry out an array of high-leverage instructional methods that support the achievement of a diverse student population. And, as a study abroad program, ILIPE also had the dual aims to build Pakistani teacher understanding and appreciation for their host's culture, and Usonian trainer understanding and appreciation of Pakistani culture. Hence, in addition to the formal academic component, study abroad participants spend 2 weeks in social activities. They explore the region and experience Usonian culture by visiting museums, shops, restaurants, and government buildings, as well having dinners at the homes of local families. Participants, 100% of whom are Muslim, also have the option to visit places of worship, including Catholic Church services, a Jewish synagogue, a Quaker meeting house, and a Buddhist temple.

After the conclusion of the summer program, study abroad participants return home to Pakistan and engage in 1x/monthly ILIPE trainer facilitated study groups online. In these collaborative study groups, Pakistani educators stay connected with one another and ILIPE facilitators. They discuss success and challenges related to the implementation of the curricular materials they created in the summer institute, and receive and offer personalized support to each other. Approximately 6 months following the summer institute, ILIPE facilitators (about 10 people) make follow-up trips of 1–2 weeks in length to Pakistan. We reconnect in person with ILIPE participants, visit their schools, classrooms and meet their pupils and administrators. During these visits to Pakistan, ILIPE trainers conduct multiday professional development workshops for ILIPE study abroad participants, and immerse themselves in the culture (i.e., we dine in people's homes, meet participant family members, go shopping, hiking, visit the mosques, tour museums, etc.)

A primary goal of ILIPE is to increase teachers' ability to carry out an array of high-leverage instructional methods that support the achievement of a diverse student population. And, as a study abroad program, ILIPE also had the dual aims to build Pakistani teacher understanding and appreciation for their host's culture, and Usonian trainer understanding and appreciation of Pakistani culture. A summative evaluation of ILIPE 2014 concluded that ILIPE teacher study abroad participants.

> "Experienced marked increases in their level of knowledge and skills, notable positive changes in self-efficacy related to their ability to enact new approaches to curriculum and instruction, and demonstrated an ability to apply new knowledge and skills to their own teaching practice."
>
> (Mazur & Woodland, 2017)

ILIPE participants expressed that they found the principles and practices of learner-centered education, backward design, and differentiated instruction to be culturally relevant. Study abroad participants shared how as a result of participating in ILIPE they acquired a more profound appreciation for their own country, as well as new appreciation for the people and culture of the United States. Graduates of ILIPE have gone on to form nationwide teacher professional development support networks in Pakistan. For example, after completing ILIPE, Umair Quereshi, a physics teacher in Islamabad formed the inaugural chapter of Pakistan ASCD that now includes student chapters at 37 universities. ILIPE graduate Aqdus Aslam, an English teacher from Lahore, went on to found TEACH Education HRD, a professional development network that connects and serves teachers across Pakistan and beyond.

Characteristics of Effective Teacher Study Abroad Programs

In the field of teacher education, teacher professional development is widely understood as "any activity that is intended partly or primarily to prepare paid staff members for improved performance in present or future roles in the school" (Moore & Hyde, 1981, p. 9). The OECD (2009) embraces a similar broad definition of professional development, whose member nations define teacher PD as "activities that develop an individual's skills, knowledge, expertise and other characteristics as a teacher" (p. 49). These all-encompassing conceptualizations of teacher professional development recognize that PD can be structured in an almost unlimited number of formal and informal ways in both preservice and in-service settings. An important but less frequently used strategy for teacher training is teacher study abroad programming.

ILIPE has been successful because it attends to human dimensions that uniquely affect learning and the quality of study abroad programming. Specifically, ILIPE seeks to (a) embody an ethic of care and cultural appreciation; (b) ensure participants advance their knowledge in LCE (not just traditional "content"); (c) ensure participants construct curriculum and leave with products and materials for direct use in their home context and classrooms; and (e) foster long-term professional support networks for study abroad participants.

> *Promotes an ethic of care and cultural appreciation.* In traditional PD trainer/instructors are often seen as the "experts," their role is to transmit trustworthy knowledge and to maintain clear and hierarchical lines of relationship. On the other hand, more democratically oriented teacher PD is intended to engender trusting, egalitarian, mutually respectful relationships between teachers and their trainers, teacher and their colleagues, and teachers and their students. In ILIPE, the instructors and staff take great care to position the participant as expert, look to facilitate teacher construction of new knowledge and meaning making, and convey the worldview that "we're all teachers and we're all learners here." ILIPE seeks to advance both teacher learning and teacher rights, and to engender emancipation and empowerment by promoting an ethic of care and mutual cultural appreciation. ILIPE instructors and participants make and share meals together, sing songs together, dance together, share religious experiences together (i.e., honor Ramadan), and attend cultural events together (i.e. July 4th Firework celebrations). In addition, an ethic of care and cultural appreciation had the desired effect of blurring lines between "expert" and "novice." Hosts and visitors have become friends and colleagues; everyone teaching together, everyone learning together. Programs designed with an ethic of care and appreciation may be more likely to engender meaningful learning

for all stakeholders and powerful transformations for both visiting teachers and hosting faculty. I have experienced this transformation personally and know that I am different (better) teacher and human being as a result of ILIPE and the new life-long colleagues and friendships that ILIPE has afforded me the opportunity to make. I have come to more deeply understand the principles and practices of learner-centered education, I am more skilled at differentiating instruction, and I am more knowledgeable and appreciative of cultures different that my own.

Ensure participants advance their knowledge in learner-centered education (LCE). Most teacher PD, if it adheres to predominant standards of effectiveness (e.g., King, 2014) will have a very strong focus on teacher acquisition of content/subject matter knowledge. In ILIPE, content acquisition is important, but not the only driving focus. The heart of the ILIPE curriculum are the principles, practices, and purposes of LCE. The phrase *learner-centered education* (Schwiesfurth, 2015) connotes and communicates a philosophical and methodological approach to classroom instruction that stands in stark contrast to pervasive, traditional classroom pedagogy that is didactic, transmissive, and authoritarian in nature. LCE is seen as an antidote to a distressed world-wide education system in which 60% of the world's children are not minimally proficient in reading and math, and 103 million youth (mostly girls) lack basic literacy skills (UNDP, 2019). As Schweisfurth (2013) attests,

> Tragic is the number of children who are in school but are learning little, or who are studying a curriculum irrelevant to their current lives and future needs, and who are experiencing schooling largely as a combination of boredom, fear and wishful thinking. These are factors which contribute to poor learning outcomes, dropout and school refusal, and so hinder both personal and national development. There are many who believe that so-called LCE has the power to change this (p. 1).

An increased emphasis on LCE is as urgent in the Global North as it is in the Global South. Studies indicate that the percentage of US-based classroom instruction that employ extensive lecturing in which students are passive learners averages at least 60% of the time across all disciplines and has persisted in this fashion for over a decade (Hurtado, et al., 2012). As ILIPE instructors, we worked to keep the tendency to lecture in check. We began most daily sessions with open-ended writing prompts or small group conversations. Direct instruction was used minimally, typically only to offer clarification and to address participant questions that could not be addressed otherwise. Guest speakers/presenters were asked to keep their lectures to a minimum (under 20 minutes at a stretch) and to integrate hands-on, turn and talk, and collaborative Q&A into their presentations. At the end of each day, we ask study abroad participants to reflect on the quality of our facilitation and to quantify how much time they perceived having spent passively listening, engaged in dialogue with others, working independently, or in a cooperative project. We compared their perceptions to our own and made corrections to our instructional approaches as a result.

ILIPE, with a primary focus on the principles, purposes, and practices of LCE, seeks to enable study abroad participants with the skills they need to deliver a learner-centered curriculum. As such, a major focus of ILIPE is exploring the practice of *differentiated instruction*. The primary culminating performance task in ILIPE is the creation of differentiated unit of study with multiple lesson plans; study abroad participants could choose to do the unit in any curricular area, for any grade level, and for any length of time. As part of the performance task, many study-abroad participants chose to adapt their existing (undifferentiated) lessons. One history teacher worked to ensure that his pupils had far more choice in how they demonstrated their knowledge and understanding of Pakistani independence. Instead of expecting every one of his pupils to write a 5-paragraph essay on the causes and results of Pakistani independence as a sovereign state, they were given the option to demonstrate their knowledge by giving a speech, writing and performing a song, or acting out a skit. This History teacher, and nearly all the study abroad participants, had very strong preconceived notions that it is preferable and expected for teachers to require all their pupils to do the same thing, in the same way, at the same pace. They were fearful that differentiation would require them to create *individualized* lessons for every pupil. We worked to communicate and demonstrate how differentiation means designing ways for pupils to *personalize* their learning/the curriculum. We set up World Café stations (World Café Community Foundation, 2015) through which study abroad participants explored the fundamental elements of differentiation, shared their specific concerns, and acquired resources for use in their own curriculum. Study abroad participants have consistently expressed to ILIPE trainers and each other an area of greatest growth and transformation occurred in coming to see differentiation as a liberating pedagogy for both themselves and their pupils.

As a result of participating in ILIPE, I too came to more fully realize the primacy of learner-centered relationships over the delivery of program "content" in my own practice. I whole-heartedly believe that it is paramount for visiting teachers to be taught by democratically inclined hosts who ensure they are seen and valued as a human beings and that they complete the program feeling empowered, rather than be taught by didactic instructors most concerned with coverage of a predetermined set of knowledge and skills.

> *Participants construct curriculum and leave with products.* Most teacher study abroad participants may be assured of exposure to new ideas, tools, and texts (for future undetermined application); receiving trainer-made, trainer-determined materials and resources, and earning a certificate of completion. In ILIPE, study abroad participants are also

expected (and scaffolded) to produce curriculum and products for direct application and use in Pakistan. In addition to receiving the coveted certificate of completion, ILIPE participants leave the program with content-based units of study, daily lesson plans, learning activities, formative assessments, summative assessments, and dialogue protocols in hand (and on a thumb drive) for use in their school, at their grade level, in their content area with their particular students. Participants report that going home with a multitude of well-designed curricula, assessments, and activities for use in their own classrooms is one of the most important aspects of their ILIPE experience.

Foster and sustain professional support networks. Without formal and explicit mechanisms for the continuation of connections and support for participants after the conclusion of a study abroad program, it is unlikely that teacher learning will be sustained. An important feature of teacher education at all stages but most significant at the continuing PD stage is that it promotes collaborative learning among teachers through building networks of learning (Woodland & Mazur, 2015). Teachers need to work collegially through shared networks that connect institutions and individuals (Halai, 2013). Social support, defined as information leading a person to believe he or she is cared for, valued, and belongs to a group, is what helps to protect teachers against stress, builds their self-efficacy and their belief that that they are able to make a difference with students. Individual teachers who travel long distances, and alone, to acquire new and novel instructional skills through a study abroad program out of their own school and country, are in particular need of support upon returning home to serve children in their own cultural context. ILIPE has mechanisms for sustaining a professional support network among Pakistani teachers. We use web-based platforms for real-time communication and information sharing (e.g., WhatsApp and Facebook), convene ILIPE graduates and Usonian ILIPE trainers in regional follow-up workshops in Pakistan, and host synchronous collaboration meetings through web-based conferencing service, e.g., Zoom and Google hangouts.

Effective Teacher Study Abroad Programming—Seven Principles of Design

ILIPE facilitators believe that to be effective, study abroad programs must promote an ethic of care, be LCE focused, be relevant, entail active learning, produce curriculum, be of significant intensity and duration, and build a professional network. These seven principles, summarized below, have proven invaluable in the creation, implementation, and evaluation of ILIPE. I believe widespread use of these design principles could foster a shared vision and mission among the wide array of actors engaged in the design and delivery of international study abroad programming.

Seven Design Principles for Teacher Study Abroad Programming

(1) Ethic of Care	An effective study abroad program should purposefully engender mutual respect, egalitarianism, and trainer–teacher and teacher–teacher relationships characterized by an ethic of care and cultural appreciation.
(2) LCE Focused	In addition to traditional content, an effective study abroad program is intentionally designed to facilitate an increase in teacher knowledge and skills in the justificatory narratives and classroom applications of learner-centered education (LCE).
(3) Relevance	An effective study abroad program is connected and relevant to teachers' work lives and perceived future needs; teachers are provided opportunities to see LCE in action in their host country and to apply what they learn to their own context and curricula.
(4) Active Learning	An effective study abroad program is dialogic, collaborative, and active. Teacher learning is facilitated through ongoing individual and collaborative teacher inquiry, reflection, demonstration, presentation, writing, and meaning making. Lecture and other didactic approaches are used are selectively, and rarely, employed.
(5) Produces Curriculum	In an effective study abroad program, participants complete the program with curriculum in hand. Teachers produce and return home with content-based units of study, daily lesson plans, learning activities, formative assessments, summative assessments, etc., for use in their content area with their particular students.
(6) Intensity and Duration	An effective study abroad program is of significant duration and intensity. There is preprogram trainer engagement with participants, the program lasts more than a few weeks, and there is meaningful postprogram teacher–trainer, and teacher–teacher follow-up.
(7) Professional Network	An effective study abroad program builds a support network among participants and employs multiple and meaningful mechanisms to sustain professional support networks beyond the formal study abroad program.

Challenges to the Effective Design of Teacher Study Abroad Programming

At the core, the design and delivery of study abroad programming rest in the minds, hearts, and hands of individual actors—the faculty and organizations that deliver the training, and who fund and facilitate teacher study abroad experiences. It can be challenging to deliver high-quality teacher study abroad programs that enable active learning, teacher construction of highly useful and applicable curricula, the promulgation of a professional network, and an ethic of care and cultural appreciation. One reason it is so challenging is because many of us who design and or teach within study abroad programs, i.e., higher education faculty, trainers, and funders, have not been exposed to or taught how to implement learner-centered approaches to education. The dominant instructional approach of institutions of higher education and the programs they offer around the world, including my own, rely on the didactic transfer of information from instructor to student. As asserted by Hudson (2017), "Despite exhortations and abundant demonstrations of effectiveness, student-centered, active learning teaching practices are not the norm...the lecture remains that oldest and still the most widely used teaching method in universities throughout the world" (p. 18). Traditional teacher professional development, which includes an array of study abroad programs, are rarely oriented toward the promulgation of learner-centered education and can inadvertently create and perpetuate authoritarian teaching and learning environments. Vast numbers of teachers have been trained through didactic and transmissive professional development programs that socialized them to embrace power-distant relationships with children and value content delivery over student learning (Schweisfurth, 2013). It is my belief that international study abroad programs may be one of the highest leverage strategies for advancing teacher capacity for learner-centered education worldwide.

Conclusion

The seven design principles described in this chapter serve as anchor and lighthouse as my colleagues and I seek to advance the Instructional Leadership Institute for Pakistani Educators (ILIPE) teacher study abroad program. There is no question that participation in ILIPE has transformed me as a person and as a professional in profound ways. As a result of the real friendships and caring relationships that are engendered through the program, visitors and hosts have stayed in direct, reciprocal communication with one another over the long-term. ILIPE alumni email, text, and call program staff and instructors to share personal and professional achievements, to solicit advice and resources, or to share news of personal importance (including engagements to be married or the marriage of their children, births of grandchildren, or the deaths of family members). And hosts do the same. I reach out to ILIPE alumni via email and social networking sites to share and celebrate accomplishments, and to seek professional advice and perspective. ILIPE graduates are now an integrated part my work and friendship networks. However, it was not always the case that I thought postprogram host–participant friendships were appropriate. The old voice in my head used to say, "Rebecca, you are the professor, they are the students, be sure to draw the emotional line between you and them." But that's one of the beautiful things about study abroad programming—it is transformative. I now deeply appreciate and rely upon the natural, vital, and supportive postprogram connections that I have with the educators who have participated in ILIPE. Each connection, each person, enriches my life long after the program ends. When I address the next group of Pakistani teachers who have left their homes and traveled almost 7000 miles to participate in ILIPE, the voice in my head—the same one that once issued messages of doubt and uncertainty—will say, "Yes! the PD we've designed will do these teachers justice and will make a difference in the lives of their students. I am so excited for what I am about to teach, and for what I am about to learn from my new colleagues."

References

Halai, A. (2013). *Implementing curriculum change: Small steps towards a big change.* In L. Tikly & A. Barrett (Eds.), Education Quality and Social Justice in the Global South. New York: Routledge. pp. 168–180.

Hudson, K. (2017). Faculty development in developing countries: introduction and overview. In Smith and Hudson (Eds). *Faculty Development in Development Countries: Improving teaching Quality in Higher Education.* Routledge, New York and London.

Hurtado, S., Eagan, M. K., Pryor, J. H., Whang, H., & Tran, S. (2012). *Undergraduate teaching faculty: The 2010–2011 HERI Faculty Survey.* Los Angeles: Higher Education Research Institute, UCLA.

King, F. (2014). Evaluating the impact of teacher professional development: an evidence-based framework. *Professional Development in Education, 40* (1), 89–111.

Mazur, R. & Woodland, R. (2017). Evaluation of a cross-cultural training program for Pakistani educators: Lessons learned and implications for program planning. *Evaluation and Program Planning, 62,* 25-34. http://dx.doi.org/10.1016/j.evalprogplan.2017.02.011

Moore & Hyde. (1981). *Making sense of staff development: An analysis of staff develop programs and their cost in three urban school districts.* Chicago, Design for Change.

OECD. (2009). *Creating effective teaching and learning environments: First results from TALIS.* ISBN 978-92-64-05605-3 87Paris: OECD.

Schwiesfurth, M. (2013). *Learner-centered Education in International Perspective: Whose Pedagogy for Whose Development.* Routledge, NY.

Schwiesfurth, M. (2015). Learner-centred pedagogy: Towards a post-2015 agenda for teaching and learning. *International Journal of Educational Development,* 40, 259–266.

Tomlinson, C. (2014). *Differentiated classroom: responding to the needs of all learners,* 2nd ed. Alexandria, VA: ASCD.

UNDP (2019). *Sustainable development goals: 4 Quality Education.* https://www.un.org/sustainabledevelopment/education/

Woodland, R. & Mazur, R. (2015). Beyond hammers vs. hugs: Leveraging educator evaluation and professional learning communities into job-embedded professional development. *NASSP Bulletin, 1–21.* http://journals.sagepub.com/doi/abs/10.1177/0192636515571934

World Café Community Foundation (2015). A quick reference guide for hosting world café. Creative commons attribution. www.theworldcafe.com

7 Post-Method Design for an English Language Teacher-Training Study Abroad Program

From Western China to Canada

Gene Vasilopoulos and Gloria Romero

Introduction

Over the past two decades, the Chinese government has been actively reforming and modernizing its national curriculum especially in relation to English language teaching (ELT). Reforms in the early 2000's called for a shift in ELT pedagogy from a grammar-focused traditional teacher-centered model to a student-centered communicative approach with the belief that improved methods would lead to improved learning (Li & Edwards, 2013). More recent reforms in the New Curriculum Standards for Teacher Education (2011) have moved away from prescribed ELT methods and instead call for curricular innovation from the bottom-up with teachers driving the development and implementation of novel instructional approaches aimed at reinvigorating traditional language teaching practices (Wang et al., 2019). To prepare English teachers to innovate curricular change, the Chinese government has partnered with universities in the UK, US, Canada, Australia, and New Zealand to send thousands of teachers overseas for professional development (PD) and language training (Xiong, 2015 as cited in Wang, et al., 2019). The objective of such overseas ELT-PD programs is to provide a cross-cultural immersion experience while improving in-service teachers' English language proficiency and knowledge of second language pedagogy (Wang, 2014). This chapter reports on one such study abroad (SA) program, the West China Program (WCP), hosted at a Canadian university in the summer months of May–August over the course of 4 years (2015–2018).

The West China Program

From 2015 to 2018, the West China Program (WCP) hosted 243 visiting teachers from the western Chinese provinces of Yunnan and Gansu. Participating teachers were primarily in-service teachers at the elementary and secondary level either currently teaching English (Table 7.1).

A unique feature of the WCP was the ethnolinguistic diversity among participants, many of whom identified local languages as the primary language of their home and community. For these teachers, as well as their students,

Table 7.1 Demographics of Program Participants

Cohort/Province	Number of Participant	Years of Teaching Experience	Age/Gender	Ethnolinguistic Background/Home Language
2015 Yunnan	37	5–10	30–45 years 30 Females 7 Males	Dali; Lijiang; Puer;Yao; Weishan; Lingcang; Binchuan; Midu; Yongren; Han
2016 Yunnan	34	3–18	24–44 years 27 Females 7 Males	Lisu; Jingpo; Di; Hani;Yi; Han
2017 Yunnan	73	3–20	26–44 years 58 Females 15 Males	Dai; Yi; Bai; Wa; Han
2018 Yunnan, Gansu	105	5–25	28–50 years 79 Females 26 Males	Han; Hui Bai; Dai; Hani;Yi; Lisu

Putonghua (Mandarin), the official language of China was a second language, and English a third or fourth language. In rural communities, removed from the economic growth of Eastern and urban coastal regions, additional challenges to ELT included limited resources, especially with technology, overcrowded classes, a centralized curriculum, annual standardized testing that exceeded the skills and knowledge of their students, and a deep-rooted traditional of teacher-centered methods based on grammar and memorization. These constraints were amplified by low interest in English and higher education and multilingual diversity whereby many students were still learning Putonghua, that national language.

Throughout the 4 years of the program, we, the two authors, acted as program manager (author 2), curriculum designers (both) and lead instructor for methodology (author 1) at the host university in Canada. To this program, we brought our extensive experience as ELT trainers in South Korea (author 1) and Chile (author 2), and given the linguistic-cultural-socio complexity of ELT in Western China, the belief that language teaching is not apolitical, especially in global ELT where an imbalance of knowledge production persists between Anglophone institutions and members (center) as experts in ELT and English as a Foreign Language (EFL) countries (periphery), as recipients of Western-based knowledge (e.g., Kachru, 1992, Phillipson, 1992). We bear in mind that for decades, ELT pedagogy has

> roll(ed) out of Western universities and through Western publishing houses to spread out all over the world. On each occasion, teachers in other cultures have been assured that this one is the correct one, and that their role is to adapt it to their learners, or their learners to it
>
> (Kumaravadivelu, 2006, p. 20)

The expectation that in order to improve EFL learning, teachers must embrace the pedagogies of the West and diligently apply these principles with the utmost fidelity needs to be reconsidered.

This chapter focuses on designing the WCP program curriculum to redress the traditional unidirectional transmission of knowledge from theorizers to practitioners and to create space for a socioculturally responsive ELT training curriculum that contends with the impact of Global English "on the formation of individual identities of English language learners, teachers, and teacher educators around the world" (Kumaravadivelu, 2012a, p. 9). Beginning with the premise that no single method of language teaching could bring ultimate success in foreign language teaching (Brown, 2002), a post-method approach problematizes the direct application of centered-created methods to the periphery (i.e., the audiolingual method of language acquisition which privileges native-speaker ideals; the direct-method conducted exclusively in the target language; and communicative language teaching (CLT) that presumes authentic interaction in the target language). Through the principles of *particularity*, *practicality*, and *possibility,* a post-methods approach attunes to the local enactments of language teaching and learning by encouraging the local construction of classroom-orientated theories of practice. We envisioned a PD-SA program that enables visiting teachers to create language teaching strategies that meet the unique needs of their local ELT context. In this chapter, we outline the relevance of Kumaravadivelu's (2012b) post-method framework and how Kumaravadivelu's integrative model of KARDS (*knowing, analyzing, recognizing, doing* and *seeing*) was used to operationalize the concepts of *particularity, practicality,* and *possibility* for transformation in teacher PD-SA. Before doing so, we briefly review the recent literature on ELT-PD-SA to situate our program within this expanding field.

A Post-Method Approach to ELT SA Professional Development

Study abroad teacher education programs that send teachers overseas have become an increasingly popular means to prepare educators for culturally responsive globally minded teaching. These programs provide opportunities for cultural immersion, practice in teaching cultural and linguistically diverse groups, local language learning, personal and professional reflection, and international collaboration (He et al., 2017). Of particular relevance to this chapter is how these general teacher-education SA programs differ from language focused SA programs that bring teachers to the target language community with the fundamental objective of improving target language proficiency as well as developing deeper understanding of the target culture in order to improve language instruction once they return home (Wang, 2014; Zhao & Mantero, 2018).

Oversea teacher PD programs designed for EFL teachers (where English is not an official language) in collaboration with a host institution in the target language community is a growing field. Li and Edwards (2017) estimate that over 3000 English teachers from China have studied at UK universities from 2000 to 2010 in either existing graduate courses or customized short-term programs. Moreover, state-sponsored ELT-PD SA programs also differ from exchange programs where participants (either preservice or in-service teachers) travel individually or in small-groups to take pre-existing courses and experience language immersions in the target community. In the former, participants are often selected based on their professional standing within the local school board and the PD-SA curriculum is designed in collaboration with the sponsoring agencies and customized to local requirements.

To date, the sparse empirical research on state-sponsored ELT-PD-SA with Anglophone universities is promising but is not without challenges (Li & Edwards, 2017). One area of concern is the effectiveness of large-group language training and limited opportunities for participants to engage with host community members when participating in large-scale SA programs (Vargas, 2017) Furthermore, while participants report gains in linguistic outcome, low entry level language proficiency, especially in the beginning of the program, impedes participants' ability to engage in theoretical and methodological components of the training course (Vargas, 2017). Another concern is the misalignment between the ideologies, curricula, and pedagogical practices of the host community and those of the visiting teachers. On this point, scholars have called attention to cultural assumptions embedded in ELT-PD SA programs and the dominance of Western-centric models of teaching that cannot be transferred when back home into local English as a foreign language contexts (Li & Edwards, 2014; Pawan & Hong, 2014; Zhao & Mantero, 2018). As alluded to above, teachers from the remote less-developed regions of Western provinces of China (such as Yunnan and Gansu) face unique challenges in terms of limited resources and institutional and community support impeding the implementation of prescribed language teaching approaches (Zhang, 2014). Failure to account for the global diversity in language teaching can lead to ineffective curriculum and program design, yet ELT-PD-SA training programs lack a comprehensive theoretical model that privileges the local and encourages visiting teachers to act pragmatically and creatively to transform prescribed methods and pedagogies for their language teaching context.

Integrating a Post-Method Orientation into the WCP Curriculum

Five months before the arrival of the visiting teachers, we began designing the program jointly with the China Scholarship Council (CSC), the Beijing Language and Culture University (BLCU), and the Embassy of China in Ottawa. The agreed upon program objectives were loosely framed to cover three domains: (a) ELT methodology; (b) English language proficiency training; and (c) Cultural exchange. The SA portion of the program extended over 14 weeks with the visiting teachers residing together at a university dormitory near campus. The program was comprised of six components listed below chronologically:

1 *Orientation and School Visits.* Early in the program, visits to local P-12 level public schools to observe classes and (a) connect the visiting teachers to the host community; (b) give teachers an opportunity to observe and interact with local educators in institutional contexts; (c) contextualize the language learning context of the host community; and (d) offer a platform for the visiting teachers to begin reflecting on their own beliefs and preconceptions of how languages can be taught and learned.

2 *Technology Training.* A technology-centered module was incorporated into the curriculum and delivered in the second week of the program to familiarize teachers with the essential software and digital tools that would be used throughout the program such as Microsoft word and Edmodo, the learning management platform on which all course materials were shared. From the earlier needs analysis, we were aware that the teachers utilized different platforms and tools in their own institutions, and that they may be unfamiliar with the tools, search engines, and databases available in Canada. Additional learning objectives of the technology module included the integration of technology into lesson plans, theoretical principles to guide technological integration with pedagogic alignment, and creative and disruptive functions of technology in computer-assisted language learning.

3 *Lectures on Theory and Research.* Each morning, lectures and discussion groups on theoretical topics were held in a large auditorium. This format of instruction was requested by the CSC and was considered a fundamental component to developing the teachers' technical and principled understanding of language pedagogy. Lectures were delivered by a large team of guest speakers and topics focused on ESL/EFL theory including critical and post-colonial approaches in education. Each lecture was followed by a 30-minute small group-discussion period and a concluded with a question/answer feedback session.

4 *Intensive English Language Training.* An intensive language training course of approximately 7.5 hours per week was held after the morning lecture. The objective of the language training was to improve oral English language proficiency through task based and communicative activities. Topic covered everyday communicative needs, socio-cultural oriented themes, as well as a range of in-class activities that fostered collaboration and increased learner engagement.

5 *Language Methodology Workshops.* Language methods and pedagogy training was scheduled for 15 hours/week designed to link the language learning and education theories to teaching practice. Here, students experimented with new teaching strategies and techniques and

considered its potential application to their own classrooms. Workshop instructors encouraged students to engage in reflective teaching practices by maintaining a portfolio of self and collaboratively designed course materials that could be adapted to their home context. Participants were also encouraged to document their SA learning experience in a reflective English teaching/learning journal. Like the language course, the methodology curriculum was largely task-based with weekly teaching demonstrations and presentations of lesson plans to showcase the integration of novel pedagogy to their own local curriculum. Participants worked collaboratively offering peer feedback through pair, group, and class discussion. Modules in the methodology workshops covered issues in classroom management, material design, teaching core skills, grammar and vocabulary instruction, and assessment.

6 *Final Lesson Plan Task.* The last week of the program was devoted to summative assessment. Teachers were required to select a unit from their state-mandated curriculum and integrate the knowledge and content from the methodology workshop into a 90-minute task-based lesson plan. Teachers shared their lesson plan with their colleagues through a formal 20-minute power point presentation and 20-minute teaching demonstration, both of which were video recorded. Video recordings and copies of their lesson plans and PowerPoint presentations were also shared with the CSC program administrators.

Operationalizing a Post-Method Approach in Teacher SA: PPP and KARDS

Particularity, Practicality, and Possibility (PPP) in Teacher Education

In line with Kumaravadivelu's (2012b) post-method approach to language teacher education, we encouraged teachers to experiment with the content and materials introduced in the program and appropriate it as they saw fit. Kumaravadivelu described this approach as attending to the *particularity, practicality,* and *possibility* in global language education. *Particularity* addresses the relevance of "the local individual, institutional, social, and cultural contexts in which learning and teaching take place" (2012b, p.13). *Practicality* reinforces the idea that pedagogic knowledge emerges from everyday teaching in local situations and that effective teacher education is constructed from the knowledge base that language teachers bring (Glasgow & Hale, 2018). *Possibility* stresses critical awareness in order to transform teacher practices. The next section explains we how Kumaravadivelu's principles of PPP were operationalized to center the needs of the visiting teachers and guide the appropriation of established Western theory and SLA methods to their local teaching realities.

KARDS: An Integrative Model for a Study Abroad Program Design

KARDS (Kumaravadivelu, 2012b) is a framework based on five "cyclical, interactive, and integrative" components (p. 17–18): Knowing, Analyzing, Recognizing, Doing, and Seeing. In Kumaravadivelu (2012b, p. 125), he provides a visual model for language teacher education, emphasizing how KARDS shifts the learning experience from transmission of expert knowledge to the transformation of teaching practice. KARDS was woven into our curricular design and the implementation of the program as described below.

Knowing

Knowing, rather than knowledge, is defined as the "amalgamation of personal reflection and action which results in a deeper understanding of what might constitute teacher knowledge" (Kumaravadivelu, 2012b, p. 21). Language teacher knowing encompasses professional knowledge, procedural knowledge and personal knowledge. Knowing in the WCP unfolded in two ways. First, we as a team did not have specific knowledge of the classroom realities and needs of the Western China teachers who visited Canada. To customize our curriculum, we conducted an online needs analysis survey with each cohort prior to their arrival. From the survey, we recognized the diversity between and within cohorts. For example, the 2016 cohort included a larger percentage of senior instructors (10 plus years of teaching) teaching in rural communities and from ethnic and linguistic diverse groups. Conversely, the 2017 was composed of significantly younger teachers, recruited from rural communities but currently working in urban schools, and entered the SA program with stronger English language and technological proficiency. As such, the technology module created for the 2016 cohort was substantially adapted to match the advanced proficiency of the 2017 group. The 2018 cohort, the largest yet, drew from two distinct provinces in Western China representing both extreme-rural, and to a smaller extent, metropolitan contexts. Moreover, there were fundamental curricular differences between the provinces: Gansu province did not require the teaching of English listening skills at the elementary level. In this case, the Gansu and Yunnan teachers had separate methodology classes to reflect their curricular specifications. These nuances were vital in the preparation of WCP materials and learning objectives.

Knowing also relates to the principle of practicality. The starting point of professional development was based on the expertise that the visiting teachers brought with them. For instance, in the language methodology workshops, before beginning a module on "How to Teach Listening," we asked the teachers, how they were currently teaching listening skills to their students, what materials they were using, what challenges they faced, what strategies were particularly effective, and what they would like to improve the most. In these discussions, participants generously shared their experiences and thoughtfully engaged with each other through peer-learning. By beginning with the realities of local context, the instructional team was able to "add" to what the teachers were already practicing rather than negating the years of professional experience and knowledge the teachers brought with them. Furthermore, entering each module from a local perspective allowed the instructors to customize their materials to bridge Western language education theory with real-life contextualized practice. From the end-of-program surveys, we learned that many of the visiting teachers valued the opportunity to learn from their colleagues' professional experiences, and not just from the course instructors. Moreover, the detailed and systematic consideration of local conditions, priorities, and constraints allowed the participants to critically interrogate the utility of the theoretical concepts and approaches introduced in the morning lectures. Most often, the utility of any particular approach came to light in the modeling and demonstration of associated strategies in the language and methodology workshops. Only after experiencing, as a teacher and learner, how theoretically informed strategies could be integrated into the classroom were the participants able to decide for themselves if the new content would be feasible and effective in enhancing their students' learning.

Analyzing

Successful language teachers should develop the capacity to "analyze and understand learner needs, learner motivation, and learner autonomy" (Kumaravadivelu, 2012b, p. 37). Throughout the program, the teachers were reminded to reflect on their own teaching and learning conditions. Individual and group reflection tasks were designed to connect the SA curriculum to their realities back home, that is to analyze their own routines, strategies, and philosophies and to consider how the content and activities of the program could enhance (or not) their classroom practices back home. Part of the SA program included visits to local primary and secondary schools for lesson observations, and opportunities to interact with principals, teachers, and students. Subsequent debriefing sessions were held to unpack the potential relevance of Canadian educational norms and practices to that of their home communities. Participants drew attention to the resources offered in Canadian schools such as educational assistants in each class for special needs learners, as well as class sizes, classroom facilities, and classroom management approaches. Pedagogies valued in Canadian schools such as outdoor learning observed in a kindergarten class held in the school yard where the children fed insects small pieces of fruit resonated with the visiting teachers. Teachers commented on how such an activity would be impossible in their local context due to security concerns, limited facilities, or simply the belief that unstructured outside of class learning is not considered as valuable as in-class textbook based learning. Issues of classroom management and student autonomy were raised and teachers were encouraged to consider their own pedagogical orientations, their own capabilities and tendencies as a teacher, their structural and institutional conditions, as well as their learners' needs in deciding what is appropriate and worth appropriating.

Recognizing

For teacher transformation to occur, teacher training programs must provide teachers with opportunities to reflect and question who they are, what they do, what they believe in and what they value (Kumaravadivelu, 2012b). As already mentioned, ongoing professional and personal self-reflection was a dominant theme in our SA program. Morning lectures directly incorporated group reflection activities on the socio-cultural-political issues of ELT in China. These discussions lead teachers to question their own convictions on contentious issues such and their responsibility to motivate and prepare students for high-stake state-wide standardized language tests for university admission, a practice that many of the teachers supported albeit for different reasons. In encouraging teachers to recognize their own values, beliefs and identities, it was imperative for us as trainers to refrain from judging that which does not align with our own pedagogical philosophy. For example, although it was difficult to share the teachers' enthusiasm for teaching-for-test approach to language learning, we affirmed the particularity and practicality of their context.

Doing

The doing of teachers must be geared to developing and maximizing "learning potential" (Kumaravadivelu, 2012b, p. 79). Teacher education programs, and in the case of the WCP, teacher PD must empower teachers with skills and knowledge to "design appropriate curricula and classroom activities that facilitate pedagogical interactions" (p. 82) that considers the cultural and social background as well as the "lived experiences that teachers and students bring with them to the classroom" (p. 82). In our program, doing was operationalized through the principles of particularity and practicality. For instance, much of the theory and approaches introduced in the morning lectures and methodology workshops were directly applied to the course textbooks and content from the teachers' home context. At the beginning of the program, PDF copies of all the ELT material mandated at the primary and secondary level of the Chinese public education system were shared with the instructional team. The teachers then selected chapters in the textbooks for which they would create new lesson plans. These lesson plans were uploaded to Edmodo creating a repository of readymade complete lessons that could be easily accessed when they returned home.

Another key component of teaching, theorizing, and dialogizing were the video-recorded teaching demonstrations that teachers completed at the end of each module. In whole class and small group discussions, the teachers rewatched their recorded demonstrations to microanalyze how it could be modified, adapted, improved, or replicated depending on the needs of the teachers/learners. Detailed peer feedback, as well as instant recall through recorded video, allowed the participants the opportunity to engage in the final dimensions of KARDS–seeing.

Seeing

Seeing is directly connected to the professional development of teachers. It implies stopping and critically observing the life inside their classrooms through the lens of the learner, the teacher, and the observer (Kumaravadivelu, 2012b). While the systematic practice of analyzing video-recorded teaching demonstrations offered an observer perspective, perhaps the most apparent manifestations of seeing occurred through the participants experience as learners. To maximize opportunities for seeing, we devised a rotation system where instructors switched classes every 2 weeks so that the visiting teachers could experience different teaching styles. Faculty members were also invited as guest lecturers to further widen teacher's exposure to diverse perspectives and pedagogical approaches. Post-program feedback confirmed that the visiting teachers found increased opportunity to see different possibilities as valuable and inspirational; there was no one perfect way to teach any given lesson, and teachers can draw on their unique characteristics and abilities (i.e., humor, creativity, artistic, digital etc.) to make their lesson work.

Post Program Outcomes

Various data collection instruments were employed from the outset of the program to document the participants experience (see Table 7.2).

The post-program data revealed the effectiveness of the curriculum in meeting the PD-SA learning objectives namely, ELT methodology, language proficiency training, and increased cultural awareness. In terms of ELT methods, participants were eager to return home and implement the teaching strategies, techniques and resources modeled in the language, and methodology workshops, especially the communicative activities and tasks to foster student engagement. Preference for practical direct application was voiced throughout the cohorts, and while broader theoretically oriented approaches such as communicative and content-based language teaching, student-centered instruction, learner autonomy, and alternative modes of language assessment were viewed as inspirational and important, participants questioned the appropriateness and practicality. Participants also expressed substantial gains in English language proficiency (as confirmed in their post-program tests); however, they also hoped for more opportunities to practice the target language outside of the institutional setting with local residents in real-life encounters. Teachers overwhelming reported feeling more confident in their ability to teach English and noted a shift in their beliefs about the teacher's

Table 7.2 Cohorts and Data Collection Methods

Cohort	Pre-Arrival	During Program	After Program	Follow-up in China (2018)
2015	Need analysis	Focus group	Focus group	Focus groups, Interviews, Classroom teaching observations
2016	Need analysis, Language proficiency test	Survey, Exit slips	Focus groups, Observations of lesson plan, Interviews, Survey	Focus groups, Interviews, Classroom teaching observations
2017	Need analysis, Language proficiency test, Technology proficiency survey	Survey, Interviews, Exit slips	Focus groups, Observations of lesson plan, Interviews, Survey,	Focus groups, Interviews, Classroom teaching observations
2018	Need analysis, Language proficiency test, Technology proficiency survey	Survey, Exit slips, Interviews	Focus groups, Observations of lesson plan, Interviews, Survey	Focus groups, Interviews, Classroom teaching observations

responsibility in fostering the student motivation and enhancing the conditions for language learning. Almost all participants expressed feeling grateful for the opportunity to travel abroad, to experience Canadian culture and planned to share their experience with the students and colleague and to encourage others to continue learning English for the opportunities it may bring. Knowledge dissemination through state-sponsored initiatives was also reported by select teachers. On top of their daily teaching obligations, all teachers were expected to prepare formal presentations and teaching demonstrations for their colleagues. Other participants were tasked with organizing and delivering regional PD seminars and contributing to provincial ELT curriculum reforms.

In October 2018, author 2 and the program director visited China for the first round of follow-up data collection that included visits to local schools, classroom observations, interviews, and focus groups. Participants recounted the positive outcomes the SA-PD had on their teaching: teachers incorporated activities and strategies learned in the program to engage students in class; students were more engaged in class and enjoyed English more; some teachers expressed how language test scores also improved. Participants reported modest incorporation of teaching strategies, mostly those which fit within existing structure of their curriculum such as using an energizing activity before leading into more text book structured instruction or using a collaborative communicative game to check comprehension after a reading task. Gains in teaching and learning were mainly affective, that is increased motivation among both teachers and students, and increased confidence and curiosity to experiment with student-centered learning. Colleagues and school administrators took notice of the change in the returning teachers and their students' enthusiasm for English class; however, novel approaches were not immediately accepted by all. In our post-program follow up interviews, participants voiced the need for patience and perseverance as it took time for students to engage in the new approaches. One participant explained the resistance to communicative activities and the continuous encouragement students required in order to practice speaking English in pair and group work without the teacher directly present to monitor for accuracy. Breaking the normative routine of drill-based repetition and teacher lead question and answer also required institutional support from colleagues and administrators who were skeptical of free-practice language use without immediate corrective feedback and concerned that unstructured lessons would lead to subsequent problems of classroom discipline. In some cases, introducing communicative activities to encourage student participation was disruptive to the cohesion of the English language program as colleagues questioned the pedagogical benefits that nontextbook individual written work or grammar and accuracy focused learning could bring to the students' language development.

We conclude with one striking example of the transformational potential of ELT-SA-PD informed through post-methods, PPP and KARDS. David (pseudonyms selected by the participant) taught at a remote boarding school in Gansu province. Because of the high regional drop-out rate and the disinterest in English language learning, David found it important to involve parents in their children's learning and began assigning simple homework tasks that engaged parents in English conversation. Students were to ask their parents questions and then report their parents' answers to the classroom Wechat (a popular social media platform) discussion group. The students would use this discussion forum over the weekend to practice writing and reading in English. To verify the authenticity of the students' postings, on Monday morning in front of the entire classroom, David would call the parents to confirm their answers. Hearing their parents' voices echoed through the audio speakers in the English class produced great delight among the students.

What is innovative about the activity is David's ingenuity in connecting technology and parents to their students' learning. This strategy of informal digital reading and writing was not directly introduced in the PD-SA program. Instead, as noted above, there was considerable resistance to the implementation of cellphones for in-class learning with controversy over encouraging the use of technology that might not be accessible to all and concern over "edutainment" based activities that detracted from more important textbook based learning. Yet, months after the PD-SA program, David created a small yet meaningful assignment that made students and parents interested in English language learning.

Challenges

Looking back, developing a collaborative, learner-centered teacher professional development curriculum was not free of challenge and tension. For instance, designing a program responsive to participant needs demands a team of instructors that are flexible and willing to revise content and course materials. Instructors had to be open to learning from the participants, a notion that when put in practice, destabilizes what it means to be an "expert." On this point, we found that there were many moments when we were pushed outside of our comfort zones and forced to question how much we should challenge the teachers to transform their practices while at the same time how much we should customize our program to serve the immediate interests of our participants. Indeed, the visiting teachers might reject the theories and pedagogies we introduce deeming them impractical or irrelevant, but how can learning happen if one is not willing to engage with new ideas? Disruption and uncertainty were necessary for both instructors and visiting teachers. Just as we hoped that the participants would experiment with the material that we brought to class each day, we often wondered how our PD-SA program would lead to transformative teaching practices once the visiting teachers returned home.

Conclusion

This chapter outlines the design and implementation of a PD-SA program inspired by Kumaradivelu's (2012a, 2012b) post-method orientation to teacher education that emphasizes teacher autonomy and pragmatism over the direct replication of Western-centric theories of language pedagogy. Over the course of 4 years, our program hosted over 240 English teachers from Western China, many from remote regions where there was little opportunity to use English in everyday communication or for academic or professional advancement. Aware of the cultural, linguistic, socioeconomic and political difference between the context and conditions of the host university and that of the visiting teachers, we drew on Kumaravadivelu's framework of *particularity, practicality,* and *possibility* operationalized through KARDS as the foundation for our curricular design. We adopted this approach with the belief that empowering teachers to appropriate, transform, and create new techniques, and activities to meet the unique needs of their language learning-communities back home would be more effective than imposing Western-derived theories of language acquisition and associated pedagogies.

Connecting the end of program evaluation to the guiding principles of PPP and KARDS that informed the program design, we noticed that modest changes in teacher beliefs and proposed instructional practices to redress what they viewed as excessively teacher-led, textbook-bound, grammar and memory-based instruction. Arguably, this is consistent with PPP and KARDS that eschews the uncritical adoption of prescribed methods in lieu of locally constructed knowledge and context-appropriate application. While the teachers did not aspire to revolutionize their teaching nor rewrite the local curriculum, the program outcome can still be viewed as transformational in that it equipped participants with the skills and knowledge base to be active and agentic in enhancing their students' English language learning experience. If the teacher's concluded the program with the sense that on the microlevel, they could transform and improve how their students experienced their class, then this humble development was enough to satisfy us as program designers.

In global ELT, government sponsored SA has become a popular mode for in-service EFL teacher PD. SA programs hosted in the target language community offer participants the opportunity to experience linguistic and cultural immersion and to learn *with* (as opposed to *from*) scholars in the field of language education. Countries such as China have established multiple collaborative international programs to ensure that local English language teachers receive quality training and while the overseas experience itself is undoubtably valuable in developing linguistic proficiency and real-life cross-cultural experience, theoretically informed curricular design of SA programs is vital to fostering meaningful PD learning opportunities that can lead to transformative practice. By privileging the rich knowledge and experience that visiting teachers bring and assisting them in creating pedagogic tools, resources, and approaches that best meet the needs of their students, PD-SA programs in ELT can result in personal and professional growth not only for the trainee, but also for the trainers.

References

Brown, Henry D. (2002). *Principles of Language Learning and Teaching*. New York: Longman.

Glasgow, G. & Hale, C. (2018). Policy, pedagogy and transformation. In K. Hashimoto & V. Nguyen (Eds.), *Professional development of English language teachers in Asia* (pp. 61–75). New York: Routledge.

He, Y., Lundgren, K., & Pynes, P. (2017). Impact of short-term study abroad program: Inservice teachers' development of intercultural competence and pedagogical beliefs. *Teaching and Teacher Education, 66*, 147–157.

Hong, P. & Pawan, F. (2014). *The pedagogy of practice of Western-trained Chinese English language teachers*. New York: Routledge.

Kachru, B. B. 1992. World Englishes: Approaches, Issues and Resources. *Language Teaching, 25* (1), 1–14.

Kumaravadivelu, B. (2016). The decolonial option in English teaching: Can the subaltern act? *TESOL Quarterly, 50*(1), 66–85.

Kumaravadivelu, B. (2012a). Individual identity, cultural globalization, and teaching of English as an international language: The case for an epistemic break. In L. Alsagoff, S. Mackay, G. Hu, and W. Renandya (Eds.), *The Principles and Practices for Teaching English as an International Language* (pp. 9–27). New York: Routledge.

Kumaravadivelu, B. (2012b). *Language teacher education for a global society*. New York: Routledge.

Kumaravadivelu, B. (2006). Dangerous liaison: Globalization, empire and TESOL. In J. Edge (Ed.), *(Re)Locating TESOL in an Age of Empire* (pp. 1–26). London: Palgrave/Macmillan.

Li, D. & Edwards, V. (2013). The impact of overseas training on curriculum innovation and change in English language education in Western China. *Language Teaching Research, 17*(4), 390–408.

Li, D. & Edwards, V. (2017). Overseas training of Chinese secondary teachers of English. In N. Van Deusen-Scholl & S. May (Eds.), *Second and foreign language education* (pp. 373–383). Springer International Publishing. DOI 10.1007/978-3-319-02246-8_21

Phillipson, R. (1992). *Linguistic Imperialism*. Oxford: Oxford University Press.

Vargas, D. (2017). Bilingual Panama: EFL Teacher Perceptions, Study Abroad in an Immersion Environment. *Journal of Language Teaching and Research, 8*(4), 669–678.

Wang, F., Clarke, A., & Webb, A. S. (2019) Tailored for China: did it work? Reflections on an intensive study abroad programme for Chinese student teachers. *Teachers and Teaching, 25*:7, 800–820.

Wang, D. (2014). Effects of study abroad on teachers' self-perceptions: A study of Chinese EFL teachers. *Journal of Language Teaching and Research, 5*(1), 70–79.

Zhang, X. (2014). *Impact of residential courses in the UK on the continuing professional development of Chinese teachers of English and educational change in Western provinces in China.* Unpublished PhD thesis, University of Reading, Reading.

Zhao, Y. & Mantero, M. (2018). The Influence of Study-Abroad Experiences on Chinese College EFL Teacher's Identity. *IJELTAL (Indonesian Journal of English Language Teaching and Applied Linguistics), 3*(1), 53–77.

Section 2

Implementation and Introspection in Teacher Study Abroad

8   Experiential Education as a Precursor to Culturally Responsive Teaching

Elizabeth Laura Yomantas

Introduction

In order for preservice teachers to emerge as culturally responsive educators, they should be afforded opportunities for rich field experiences to develop the critical consciousness and awareness of their own positionality required for culturally responsive teaching. In the teacher education classroom, it is easy to lecture about culturally responsive teaching practices, implicit and explicit biases, and strategies to engage all learners. However, the transformation of the teacher does not come from hearing these words in a lecture during a teacher education course—rather, this awareness becomes realized through new field experiences and critical reflections on these experiences (Gay, 2002; Villegas & Lucas, 2002). Study abroad through experiential education (EE) can provide preservice teachers with meaningful learning opportunities (Smith et al., 2011) as a precursor to culturally responsive teaching. Because the learning to teach journey is a complex, nonlinear, and multidimensional process (Cochran-Smith et al., 2014), EE programs can facilitate dynamic spaces for transformative learning (Breunig, 2011).

This chapter details an EE program that took place in rural Fiji. This course was contextualized in a postcolonial framework that acknowledges the western world's history of domination and colonization (Bhabha, 1984; Said, 1978; Smith, 2012; Spivak, 1988), and sought to deconstruct colonial power structures (Delgado & Stefancic, 2017; Lynn & Dixon, 2013) through enacting critical pedagogy. The instructional design of the course aimed to provide participants with opportunities to develop critical consciousness (Freire, 1972) as a beginning point to becoming culturally responsive teachers who practice allyship as a form of activism in the classroom. The Merriam-Webster Dictionary defines an ally as "one that is associated with another as a helper: a person or group that provides assistance and support in an ongoing effort, activity, or struggle." However, the definition I choose to employ extends beyond the notion of being a "helper;" becoming an ally involves joining the collective struggle for justice, accomplishing goals in the concrete reality while continuing to dream of a better tomorrow, and engaging in cyclical praxis to work alongside communities (Anthony-Stevens, 2017;

Freire, 1972). Furthermore, allies maintain the posture of a humble learner and act in accordance with the wishes, desires, and preferences of those they join in this effort for liberation (Berryman et al., 2013; Yomantas, 2020). Allies share power and abide by the ideas Lilia Watson expressed: "If you have come to help me, you are wasting your time. If you have come because your liberation is bound up with mine, then let us work together." Allies stand shoulder to shoulder with the communities and individuals they work alongside in a rich spirit of togetherness.

While there is much available literature about culturally responsive teaching (Gay, 2018; Ladson-Billings 1994, 2006, 2014; Paris & Alim, 2017), I argue that study abroad experiences, particularly through EE programs, can serve as rich opportunities to develop the critical consciousness required for culturally responsive teaching. Darder (2017) noted that teachers cannot liberate anyone, but they are in an exciting and strategic position to invite others to liberate themselves. This chapter reviews the activities and opportunities for reflection before the EE program, during the EE program, and after the EE program that contribute to the development of critical consciousness as a precursor to culturally responsive teaching.

Course Context and Program Overview

Pepperdine University has been sending students to Fiji through study abroad programs since the year 2009. The university gained a connection to Fiji through two different undergraduate students whose families had humanitarian projects that aimed to support the medical and educational needs of a rural community in Fiji. The families connected with the university's volunteer center and international programs office to design study abroad opportunities for students to travel to Fiji for primarily service learning. Students would be able to stay at one of the family's large humanitarian facilities that encompassed a medical clinic, a large farm, spaces for community engagement, and modest dorm-like accommodations. As an undergraduate student, I was able to attend this program abroad in Fiji in 2010 and 2011. My early times in Fiji fostered a great love for this island nation and fueled my graduate studies. In 2017, I returned to Fiji with Ann Cooper, founder of the Fiji Kinde Project, to conduct my dissertation research. I had the privilege of conducting my dissertation study to examine how teachers navigate the complex terrains of modernization and traditionalism in their curriculum. Through these experiences, I have built relationships with local teachers in Fiji.

I now teach at my alma mater. So, when the international programs office staff learned of my continued connection and research in Fiji, they invited me to lead the month-long summer abroad program. While this program formerly had a science emphasis, they invited me to explore my passion and design a course for teacher education (and other) participants based on my dissertation research.

There were 20 undergraduate participants in the program. Half of the participants were enrolled in our undergraduate teacher credentialing program or had plans to pursue education or related fields in their graduate studies or opportunities abroad. The other half of the participants came from other majors or were undeclared. Because this was an elective course that was not contingent upon graduation requirements, it was surprising that so many noneducation participants enrolled in the program. Before the program, I anticipated that more teacher education participants would enroll because it was an EDUC course. Initially, I was somewhat disappointed by the academic diversity of the group as I had planned on having mostly preservice teachers. However, after leading the program, I realized this was actually quite a rich opportunity. By welcoming participants of other majors, this propelled some participants to consider the field of education and also added rich and expansive viewpoints to course discussions. Furthermore, participants made unique links between education and other fields and also realized how there are components of teaching in most professions. They connected the concepts as they considered how culturally responsive teaching may manifest in their future contexts. The information in this chapter applied to all participants who enrolled in the program, but the program was designed specifically with teacher education participants in mind. Therefore, the ideas and examples discussed in this chapter are centered around the participants in the program who plan to pursue careers in the field of education.

As a core component of the program, I designed and taught the course titled EDUC 592: Culturally Responsive Service Learning. The EE program was constructed around the book *Knowing and Learning: An Indigenous Fijian Approach* (Nabobo-Baba, 2006) to center an indigenous voice at the heart of the experience (for more information on the theoretical foundations of the course, see Yomantas (2020). The course explored implicit and explicit bias as a vehicle to develop critical consciousness, engaged with indigenous knowledge through maintaining the posture of a humble learner, and theorized the rights, roles, and responsibilities of becoming an ally. The purpose of these learning activities was to propel participants to think about culturally responsive teaching in new ways for their work in their future classrooms in the United States or to apply the concepts of culturally responsive engagement into their future careers.

Activities Before the EE Program

Before the sojourn to rural Fiji, it was important to provide the participants with an opportunity to be introduced to both the Fijian culture and the new ideas and perspectives that would become the cornerstone of the EE program. The university requires a full day orientation a few months before a study abroad program begins. The orientation is a combination of whole group sessions for all participants studying abroad and smaller breakout sessions for each specific program. In designing the breakout sessions, I asked the international programs office if I could use a small portion of my budget to build the aesthetic and experiential aspects of the orientation that would yield greater cognitive and relational engagement with the ideas introduced. This was a full day orientation, and we had about 5 hours together to engage in these activities.

It is common for the breakout sessions to consist of faculty creating an icebreaker activity followed by a review of the rules and expectations for the program. Rather than follow the traditional format, I decided to renovate the designated classroom to embody the spirit of Fiji. I removed all of the desks and placed a large Fijian mat that I had bought in Fiji during my previous trip there. I placed palm leaves around the room, played traditional Fijian music, and dressed in a Fijian "sulu jaba" (formal Fijian attire). I placed a covered parcel in the center of the mat. I thought through these items carefully and resisted cultural appropriation because of my ties and experiences in Fiji. When in Fiji on my previous trip, I asked permission to share Fijian culture with my dissertation committee and students. I was granted permission and given suggestions and strategies for implementation from research participants, friends, and teacher colleagues. I realize that I must cyclically reflect on this practice through praxis (Freire, 1972), maintain a posture of cultural humility (SooHoo, 2013), and continue to ask permission for the honor and privilege to share Fijian culture with others (Berryman et al., 2013).

When the participants entered, I asked them to sit on the floor in a circle as we would do many times in Fiji. I asked them to introduce themselves by their mountain, river/sea/lake, tribal group, and name. This introduction, respectfully borrowed from Maori curriculum (TKI: Te Kete Ipurangi) and introduced to me through Dr. Suzanne SooHoo, allowed participants the first challenge of thinking about themselves in different ways. Rather than simply stating their major and hometown, they were challenged to introduce themselves and connect with each other in new ways.

Following the mutual introductions, participants then engaged in an activity involving a covered parcel placed in the center of the circle. This activity was based on the work of Wilson (2008) and was furthered when I participated in a workshop that he conducted at the American Indigenous Research Association Conference in 2018. The symbolism of the parcel was to represent indigenous knowledge and ceremony. The questions I designed were to have participants critically consider their assumptions, positionality, and rights for visiting indigenous spaces as western outsiders. We used a talking piece, which is a small object that indicates the person who is holding it has permission to speak. When they are finished speaking, they may pass the object to the next person. If a person wishes to not speak, they may pass the talking piece without verbal contributions. We passed it around the circle answering the following questions:

- What cultural assumptions do you bring into trying to guess what's in the parcel? (Wilson, 2008)
- What right do you have to look in the parcel? (Wilson, 2008)

- What do we need to know in order to find out what's in the parcel? (Wilson, 2008)
- Who benefits from opening the parcel? (Bishop, 1996)
- What should we do to open the parcel? Who should initiate opening the parcel? (Bishop, 1996)
- Who are we accountable to when we open the parcel? (Bishop, 1996)

As participants grappled with the questions, we then transitioned to talking about the meaning of the parcel as indigenous knowledge. We repositioned ourselves from having a right to open the parcel to understanding the parcel as something sacred and reverent; the parcel represents knowledge that we do not have a right to as outsiders. If iTaukei (indigenous) Fijians grant us permission to aspects of their knowledge, it should be treated like a treasured gift.

The participants and I then debriefed the activity with the following questions:

- How are we treating the parcel differently than we would in a US context?
- What elements set the tone for this space to be sacred?
- What elements from this activity will you bring with you into your work in Fiji?
- How is this learning activity different than other ways of learning/ knowing that you have experienced before?

While the concept of the parcel is far greater than its actual contents, the parcel contained a bowl of cassava and taro chips—common foods in Fiji. The chips were placed in a large bowl that was then passed around the circle multiple times and shared with the entire group. This was also modeled after Dr. Wilson's workshop as a tool to begin sharing in community. The purpose of the exercise is to examine the ideas of the parcel rather than simply to explore the actual contents.

The orientation also included a simulation of a traditional Fijian ceremony called a "Sevu Sevu" (Nabobo-Baba, 2006). We discussed the importance of participating in a Sevu Sevu as outsiders before we begin our work in Fiji. A Sevu Sevu includes going to the village chief and asking permission to enter the village and community before we start our work there. We must bring a gift, and we must sit, dress, and speak in a certain way. We discussed this as a first step to honoring cultural practices and honoring iTaukei customs and ways of showing respect. Following the Sevu Sevu, participants then had an opportunity to be introduced to the Fijian concept of *talanoa*, meaning storytelling. As a way of beginning to build relationships, participants were able to tell a story that reflects something about who they are. The participants and I took turns sharing stories as a means of mutual introductions to begin building community. We concluded the orientation with the question "What is something that touched your heart today?"

Pre-Trip Preparation

Following the orientation, the participants and I had three class sessions in which we prepared for the trip. These sessions included three key elements: Fijian history, current events, and an overview of Fijian education. Questions that guided our sessions included:

- In the Fijian history texts, who is telling the story? Whose story is it to tell?
- Do we have a right to view traditional rituals?
- What threatens traditional practices and values?
- How do Christianity and traditional values interact?
- How do education and indigenous values interact?
- How do we honor traditional values while moving into the future?
- What problems did colonization create for Fiji? What impacts does this have on the present?
- Who is a Fijian? What does it mean to be a Fijian?
- What are the differences between tourism and culturally responsive experiential education?
- What does it mean to be a culturally responsive teacher?

In learning about Fijian education, the participants also studied the national curriculum, as it is published online (Ministry of Education, Heritage & Arts, 2020). Participants examined the curriculum pacing guide and created a lesson to teach while in Fiji. Participants were required to plan a lesson with the learning objectives in alignment with the national curriculum. They were then required to bring supplies and resources needed for the lesson. The participants were informed that they were not guaranteed the opportunity to teach this lesson as we needed to ask permission from each teacher upon arrival. The participants would then bring the lesson plan to the guest teacher who was hosting them in their classroom. They would show the lesson plan to the teacher and ask permission to teach the lesson if it was deemed appropriate, in alignment with curriculum standards, and if there was time available. The process of developing the lesson required participants to begin thinking about Fijian curriculum. This served as resistance against the notion that we, as outsiders, have a right to go into a new place and teach without permission, without beginning to understand the cultural context, and without familiarizing to the learners' current curricula. Using the Fijian curriculum as a planning guide, study abroad participants also learned that all students in all contexts deserve lessons that are well planned and intentionally designed.

Activities During the EE Program

This section details the participant activities that took place in Fiji. Each day consisted of fieldwork, class time, and other learning activities. The class met 2–3 days a week for approximately a two-and-a-half to a three-hour block depending on the other scheduled activities of the day. It is difficult to separate the class time and fieldwork time because the learning happened vibrantly in both places and was intertwined. Emergent critical consciousness developed from cyclical action and reflection. Throughout the EE program, participants gained new understandings about culturally responsive service work and teaching as well as the rights, responsibilities, and roles of allies. This section discusses the learning and reflection opportunities and activities through the connections between the course text and class time, field trips, and community service opportunities in Fiji.

This course was taught from a cultural wealth perspective (Yosso, 2005) in which the participants were asked to explore their homegrown epistemologies (Bloomfield, 2013) and critically consider the cultural wealth observed in the communities where we worked. For example, we regularly noted the strengths of the indigenous communities and discussed the ways they preserved culture through their everyday lives. Furthermore, our classroom and living accommodations were at the same site. This was a particularly unique teaching experience as our classroom did not have desks or chairs. The participants and I sat on a straw mat on the floor, and we did not use any technology in the course. Because of limited internet access and electricity, the participants and I relied on the printed text, composition notebooks, and a small whiteboard. As an educator who has used technology seamlessly throughout my teaching career, this was a unique challenge and opportunity. The lack of technology challenged me in my teaching practices and helped to develop rich discussions, class dialogues, and conversations as the allure and distractions of cell phone and computer screens were nowhere to be found.

During class time, the text was used to connect to the local context in order to understand and theorize schooling in Fiji and in the United States. For each class session, participants were required to read a chapter of the text and critically consider a specific aspect of their fieldwork in connection to the text. For example, homework assignments would include questions such as the following: Read *Knowing and Learning* (Nabobo-Baba, 2006) chapter 1 and respond to the following prompt: Create a list of things you notice that seem similar to Western/American schools based on your schooling experiences and/or student teaching experiences (if applicable). Create a list of things that seem different from Western schools. Aspects to consider may include: physical construction of classrooms and schools, curriculum, purposes of school; learning objectives; dress code; procedures, protocols, structures; role of the teacher; and teacher/student relationships.

Then, during class time, we together would consider the following questions in connection to the text:

- What were the purposes of education under colonization?
- How are the purposes tied to cultural erosion?
- What are the connections between curriculum and funding?

To answer these questions, participants worked in groups to create a comprehensive list of things observed in the local schools that they believed reflected Western schooling practices. Then, they decided—does this erode or preserve culture and why? If it eroded culture, participants were asked to suggest an alternative. The class then regrouped for a grand conversation to discuss their ideas. Next we discussed the teacher's role to recognize and preserve culture, particularly in spaces where we are outsiders.

The cultural wealth perspective is a precursor to culturally responsive teaching. Through reflexive self-work, students can simultaneously explore the wealth of the Fijian culture as well as examine their own lived experiences, homegrown epistemologies, and ways of knowing. This important self-work aids individuals in understanding who they are, what gifts and strengths they bring into the work, and how their lived experiences shape their worldview. Furthermore, the cultural wealth perspective allows the preservice teachers to begin understanding their future students from a perspective of strength instead of a perspective of deficit.

To further connect with the course text, guest speakers were also included as a part of the course. Participants had the opportunity to visit a local school and learn from a local eighth grade history teacher about the United States' role in the colonization of Fiji from a historical perspective. Participants also had the opportunity to learn from one of the local program coordinators about the complexities of Fijian mysticism and Christianity. Participants engaged in a program presented by the host staff about the cultural value of the coconut and the many ways that the coconut is used as a life source in Fiji. Following each of these guest speaker opportunities, participants responded to various prompts that asked them to reflect and analyze their new understandings.

Fieldtrips were also an important component of the EE program. Fieldtrips were not scheduled before arrival; rather, they were facilitated based on invitations from local partners and friends. I adjusted class time around invitations for field trips and modeled this flexibility as a culturally responsive practice to honor people above schedules for the participants. While collegiate classes taught in the academy seem to value careful planning and a detailed syllabus, this rigid structure simply cannot work in the Fijian context and contradicts the purposes of this experience. The syllabus listed class times but also included a note that class times may be adjusted based on partnership needs and daily schedules. While the actual activity time was often adjusted, we fulfilled the appropriate number of class hours in order to preserve the integrity of the course. Relationships are of the utmost importance, and so the schedule must be built upon our partners' wishes, availability, and schedules. The schedule falls in line with relationships rather than relationships falling in line with the schedule. In this spirit, field trips were planned as we further built relationships and were granted invitations. Each week, we took a field trip to a local village. We dressed in culturally appropriate ways and had the opportunity to participate in a Sevu Sevu at each site. On each field trip, a local headman (the chief's assistant) took us on a tour and shared with us important aspects of village life. Participants felt welcomed into the community because the headman invited them. The tour did not simply include the buildings and layout of the village; it also included the botany, stories of the complexities between modernization and traditionalism in the village, and daily practices that reflect village life as English is commonly spoken throughout the nation.

Following each village visit, participants were asked to reflect on their observations and new understandings. For example, one of the prompts stated: After visiting Vinikura, discuss which two *I tovo vakavanua* (customs) and aspects of *vanua* (community) you observed. Then, compare/contrast with customs and community values in the United States. What will "remain in your heart" (Nabobo-Baba, 2006, p. 1)? In response to this prompt, one student wrote, "I learned a lot of things about Fijians' culture that I wouldn't have learned if I just went on a random village tour without the knowledge of the headman. For example, when the headman was talking about technology, I learned something new. He explained the questions they are asking—does technology erode the culture? Does it help the culture? That was just really something new for me to grasp. Because I thought that everyone wanted to modernize. On that day, I learned that modernization and westernization can take away from all of the things that the Fijians value. I think that's so hard to balance these two ideas."

In addition to class time, participants also engaged in daily fieldwork. The fieldwork was the heartbeat of the program as this allowed the participants to work alongside local partners and build relationships. Fieldwork projects included participating in manual labor on a farm, assisting in the local schools, volunteering in the on-site medical clinic, and participating in co-constructed village projects to benefit the community. All participants contributed to the different projects and were encouraged to try new experiences. Additionally, we were invited to put on a few programs in the local villages. Even without much preparation time due to short notice, the participants and I worked together to plan interactive, meaningful experiences for Fijian children. Additionally, after asking permission, we participated in a beach clean-up both at the local school and on the property of our local partnership. Participants wrote weekly fieldwork reflections that invited them to consider the activities they participated in, the relationships they built, and the new understandings they gained during the week. The fieldwork reflections were embedded into class discussions and *talanoa* (storytelling) to further unpack the experience.

Activities after the EE Program

Based on principles established in culturally responsive methodologies (Berryman et al., 2013), it is important to sustain and further the relationship between the EE program, the participants, and the university (Grain et al., 2019). In addition to the support needed to unpack the abroad experience

(Dean & Jendzurski, 2013), I wanted participants to have opportunities to share their new understandings with the larger university community. This would bring Fiji to the forefront of the university in order to promote the cultural wealth we experienced, highlight the partnership and connection between the university and the local organization, and to open possibilities to expand the partnership beyond what currently exists. In addition to informal gatherings in which we debriefed the experience, we made the most of opportunities to share about the program. For example, a group of the participants and I presented a "Fijian Word of Welcome" at the Humanities and Teacher Education Division inauguration event to expose our new university president to Fijian culture. The participants and I dressed in sulu jabas, explained and modeled a Sevu Sevu, and each shared a mini story about a value we learned about in Fiji that we wish to bring to the university main campus. We spoke about the Fijian culture in ways that resisted a cultural deficit mindset and instead reported on the cultural wealth (Yosso, 2005) that we experienced. The values the participants shared included connection, prayer, and love.

In addition to this event, the participants self-organized a club convo to further debrief the experience. At the university where I work, participants are required to earn convocation credit each semester. One way to earn this credit is to participate in a club convo, which is commonly student led. I served as the advisor, but the program was student led and student attended. Approximately two-thirds of the participants from the EE program participated in this six-week club convo in order to further discuss ways that the experiences learned in Fiji can be translated into their daily lives. The group continued to grapple with the dominance of fast-paced western ways, the lack of human connection on the collegiate campus, and the desire to connect beyond country borders and cultural differences.

Furthermore, post sojourn, several participants from the group decided to take additional opportunities to study abroad with the university in future semesters. As a result of the EE program, participants made decisions to study in Buenos Aires, Uganda, and Jordan. These study abroad sites are particularly interesting because our university has many study abroad programs in developed countries and popular cities in Europe. The EE program gave the participants confidence to study in developing nations and provided them with a theoretical framework to navigate and co-construct the abroad experience alongside local partners.

Additionally, because the context of the EE program allowed the participants and I to be vulnerable together through our learning, service, and continual critical reflection of ourselves and the world around us, the participants now invite one another and me into dialogue about vocation and purpose. As a result of the program, one student decided to change her major and pursue occupational therapy as a vehicle to connect with others and serve the community. Another student is considering graduate studies regarding culture and cultural interaction with the hope of becoming a sociology professor. Another student now aspires to play basketball abroad before returning to finish teaching credential requirements. Additionally, another student applied for a Fulbright teaching scholarship to further explore different epistemologies, knowledge structures, and cultures. Much of this vocational dialogue continues to happen and is in progress. When the participants come to talk to me about the possibilities that they now consider, they reference personal pivotal moments in Fiji that sparked the transformation and new, expansive ways of thinking about teaching, learning, and human connection.

Lastly, as their instructor, I must continue to model my own emergent critical consciousness and allyship practices. Following this EE program, I noted to the participants my own lack of connection to the indigenous people of the land where our university is built. Since then, I reached out to the tribe's education director, and we began collaborating on projects together. We co-authored a land acknowledgement that I now use to open every syllabus and begin every course with each semester. Furthermore, I am working with our local education partners to consider publishing the land acknowledgement on their campuses as we all are built upon Chumash land. I shared my ideas of connecting the tribe and the university with our new university president, who is open and excited about the possibilities. I share these in-process projects with the participants often. It is important that the participants see my own unfinishedness (Freire, 1972) as a lifelong learner, so I make sure to update them on not just the final outcome, but the in-progress, hopeful, and bumpy transitions. I want to model for them the "patiently-impatient" (Freire, 1972) unfinished work of being an ally. Developing critical consciousness can yield further levels of new consciousness, in which new actions are required. The pursuit of a more just world is powerfully made possible through an examination of teaching and learning abroad and the lessons we have to learn from others. I invite participants to share their in-progress thoughts, hopes, dreams, and actions that they are daring to take in order to concretize some of the concepts and ideas they explored in Fiji.

Conclusion

The activities that took place as a part of this program before, during, and after the trip aimed to provide opportunities for participants to develop critical consciousness as emergent culturally responsive educators. In order to become a culturally responsive teacher who leverages privileged positionality to serve as an ally (Anthony-Stevens, 2017; Brophey & Raptis, 2016), it is critical for preservice teachers to have rich EE experiences that include cyclical action and reflection.

The EE program provided the hands-on opportunity to grapple with the dynamic concepts of culturally responsive teaching in new ways that laid a foundation for career-wide impact. One student noted how she is taking the first steps in considering what it means to be a teacher-ally to her future students. She commented, "As a future teacher, this experience taught me that I need to continue learning about how I can be an ally. I learned that I need to be able ask a lot of hard questions of myself. I learned that when I enter a new community, I have to ask the community if it's okay for me to be there. I am just beginning to think about what this means for me as a teacher. There's a lot to think about, which I think is beautiful and good." The EE program, filled with cyclical action and reflection, opened new spaces for possibility, hope, and transformative teaching and learning.

References

Ally [Def. 2]. (n.d.). In Merriam Webster Online, Retrieved April 15, 2020 from https://www.merriam-webster.com/dictionary/ally.

Anthony-Stevens, V. (2017). Cultivating alliances: Reflections on the role of non-indigenous collaborators in indigenous educational sovereignty. *Journal of American Indian Education, 56*(1), 81–104.

Berryman, M., SooHoo, S., & Nevin, A. (2013). Culturally responsive methodologies from the margins. In M. Berryman, S. SooHoo, & A. Nevin (Eds.). *Culturally responsive methodologies* (pp. 1–31). Emerald.

Bhabha, H. K. (1984). Of mimicry and man: The ambivalence of colonial discourse. *Discipleship: A Special Issue on Psychoanalysis, 28*(1), 125–133. https://doi.org/10.2307/778467

Bishop, R. (1996). *Collaborative research stories: Whakawhanaungtanga*. Dunmore Press.

Bloomfield, V. (2013). A "homegrown" methodology: Cultural intuition, self-trust, and connected knowing at work. In M. Berryman, S. SooHoo, & A. Nevin, *Culturally Responsive Methodologies* (pp. 176–197). Emerald.

Breunig, M. (2011). Paulo Freire: Critical praxis and experiential education. In T. Smith and C. Knapp (Eds). *Sourcebook of experiential education: Key thinkers and their contributions* (pp. 56–63). Routledge.

Brophey, A. & Raptis, H. (2016). Preparing to be allies: Narratives of non-indigenous researchers working in indigenous contexts. *Alberta Journal of Educational Research, 62*(3), 237–252.

Cochran-Smith, M., Ell, F., Ludlow, L., Grudnoff, L. & Aitken, G. (2014). The challenge and promise of complexity theory for teacher education research. *Teachers College Record, 116*, 1–38.

Darder, A. (2017). *Reinventing Paulo Freire: A pedagogy of love*. Routledge.

Dean, K. W. & Jendzurski, M. B. (2013). Using post-study-abroad experiences to enhance international study. *Honors in Practice – Online Archive*. 172.

Delgado, R. & Stefancic, J. (2017). *Critical race theory: An introduction*. New York University Press.

Freire, P. (1972). *Pedagogy of the oppressed* (2nd ed.). Herder and Herder.

Gay, G. (2002). Preparing for culturally responsive teaching. *Journal of Teacher Education, 53*(106), 106–116.

Gay, G. (2018). *Culturally responsive teaching: Theory, research, and practice* (Third ed., Multicultural education series). Teachers College Press.

Grain et al. (2019). Co-constructing knowledge in Uganda: Host community conceptions of relationships in international service learning. *Journal of Experiential Education, 42*(1), 22–36.

Ladson-Billings, G. (1994). But that's just good teaching! The case for culturally relevant pedagogy. *Theory into practice, 34*(3), 159–164.

Ladson-Billings, G. (2006). Once upon a time when patriotism was what you did. *Phi Delta Kappan, 87*(8), 585–588.

Ladson-Billings, G. (2014). Culturally relevant pedagogy 2.0: a.k.a. the Remix. *Harvard Educational Review, 84*(1), 74–84.

Lilia: International Women's Network: About. (2010, January 28). Retrieved from https://lillanetwork.wordpress.com/about/

Lynn, M., & Dixson, A. D. (Eds.). (2013). *Handbook of critical race theory in education.* Routledge.

Ministry of Education, Heritage & Arts. (2020). *Textbooks.* http://www.education.gov.fj/textbooks/

Nabobo-Baba, U. (2006). *Knowing and learning: An indigenous Fijian approach.* University of the South Pacific.

Paris, D. & Alim, H. (2017). *Culturally sustaining pedagogies: Teaching and learning for justice in a changing world.* Teachers College Press.

Said, E. W. (1978). *Orientalism.* Penguin Books.

Smith, L. (2012). *Decolonizing methodologies: Research and Indigenous peoples* (2nd ed.). Zed Books.

Smith T., Knapp, C., Seaman., J. & Pace, S. (2011). Experiential education and learning by experience. In T. Smith and C. Knapp (Eds.) *Sourcebook of experiential education: Key thinkers and their contributions* (pp. 1–11). Routledge.

SooHoo, S. (2013). Humility within culturally responsive methodologies. In M. Berryman, S. SooHoo, & A. Nevin (Eds.), *Culturally responsive methodologies* (pp. 199-220). Emerald Group.

Spivak, G. C. (1988). *Can the subaltern speak?* Macmillan.

TKI: Te Kete Ipurangi. (n.d.) Unit 14: Tō tātou maunga – Our mountain. Retrieved from https://tereomaori.tki.org.nz/Reo-Maori-resources/Ka-Mau-te-Wehi/Introduction-to-the-units/Unit-14-Our-mountain

Villegas, A. M., & Lucas, T. (2002). Preparing culturally responsive teachers: Rethinking the curriculum. *Journal of Teacher Education, 53*(1), 20–32.

Wilson, S. (2008). *Research is ceremony: Indigenous research methods.* Fernwood.

Wilson, S. (2018). *Preconference workshop.* Workshop presented at the 6th annual American Indigenous Research Association Conference: "Research within our paradigm," Polson, MT.

Yomantas, E. (2020). Decolonizing knowledge and fostering critical allyship. In L. Parson and C. Ozaki (Eds)., *Teaching and learning for social justice and equity in higher education* (pp. 303-328). Springer.

Yosso, T. (2005). Whose culture has capital? A critical race theory discussion of community cultural wealth. *Race Ethnicity and Education, 8*(1), 69–91.

9 An International Student Teaching Program in Germany

Partnering with the United States Department of Defense

Rachel Louise Geesa, Thalia M. Mulvihill, Nicholas P. Elam, and Abigail D. Teeters

Introduction

This chapter discusses an international student teaching program in which Ball State University (Muncie, Indiana, United States) student teachers complete their student teaching semester in Germany, while serving United States military children in Department of Defense Dependent Schools through the Department of Defense Education Activity (DoDEA). Student teachers develop with the support of DoDEA mentor teachers, and with university supervisors who reside in Germany during the entire student teaching experience.

Three of the four authors of this chapter have firsthand experience with this program, having served as university supervisors, including one author who also currently serves as the Teachers College Director of International Programs. As we will discuss in the chapter, past university supervisors consistently cite a fostering of independence, self-confidence, and an understanding of culture among the primary benefits to student teachers. These perspectives align with previous studies regarding the benefits of student teaching abroad (Helen & Moss, 2015; Marx & Moss, 2011; Nero, 2018).

This chapter also explores many aspects related to this international program, including its origins and evolution, various program requirements, additional perspectives and reflections of university supervisors revealed through a scholarly study, the program's broader impact, and challenges and areas for improvement unique to the program. We believe this chapter will provide important information to any teacher educator, program coordinator, or prospective student teacher associated with a study abroad program in any nation. The information in this chapter will be especially useful to those who partner, or who are considering a partnership, with schools that primarily enroll children of military service members.

International Student Teaching Program in Germany

Ball State University is a Carnegie classified Public Research University institution comprises seven colleges serving over 22,000 students and offering 205 study abroad programs of various sizes and durations. The university also earned the Community Engagement Classification from the Carnegie Foundation for the Advancement of Teaching recognizing an institution-wide commitment to public service, civic involvement, and community partnerships. Additionally, the university has been named a Military Friendly School for 10 years by veteran-owned Viqtory.

Ball State University's Teachers College awards approximately 300 baccalaureate degrees per calendar year to those who have completed Council for the Accreditation of Educator Preparation (CAEP) accredited teacher education programs. Since 2003, more than 26 university faculty have served as university supervisors and 240 student teachers have completed their student teaching semester in DoDEA schools in Germany, serving United States military children. Typically, these student teachers complete this study abroad student teaching experience during the last semester of their academic degree program which provides them exposure to serving the educational needs of the United States military community while living overseas. When compared to other student teaching assignments, where student teachers are placed in local schools, this program allows student teachers to complete their 16-week student teaching assignment in United States schools while living in Germany.

Origins and Evolution of the International Student Teaching Program in Germany

During the 2002–2003 academic year, deans from colleges of education at Auburn University, Ball State University, and Florida State University received invitations from the National Education Association to explore opportunities to establish student teaching programs with DoDEA on United States military bases in Europe. Upon visits to bases in Belgium and Germany, Ball State Teachers College began a student teaching program in the fall of 2003 in Baumholder, Germany. The student teaching program then moved to United States military bases in Kaiserslautern and Ramstein, Germany, in the spring of 2013, where the program continues to take place each semester. Ball State's program is the only program that continues from the original three universities invited to participate in this partnership.

Typically, 8–16 student teachers participate in the program in the fall semester, and 14–22 student teachers participate in the program in the spring semester. Student teachers tend to participate during their final semester in their teacher education program. Student teachers gain opportunities to demonstrate independence, adaptability, creativity, and knowledge of global issues in their international schools on military bases. Student teachers in early childhood, elementary education, special education, and secondary education teaching programs may participate in this program and serve in PreK-12 grade DoDEA schools on bases in Ramstein and Kaiserslautern, Germany.

Stakeholders throughout the institution are involved in the student teaching program in Germany each semester. One university faculty member serves as the college's international programs director and works directly with each faculty member who supervises student teachers overseas. Opportunities to serve as university supervisors for this program are open to faculty who have experience teaching, supervising, and working in schools in all departments, and the supervisors typically rotate each semester.

Department chairs must support faculty selected for this role, as the responsibilities of university supervisors shift from their typical responsibilities in the department during the semester they are overseas. The international programs director and university supervisors work closely with: (a) the director of clinical practices who oversees all student teacher placements within the college and works with DoDEA to process student teacher applications; (b) the college dean and dean's leadership team; (c) the college director of finance and budgets who assists in setting the program budget semester; (d) the director of study abroad for international programs; (e) a local travel agent to arrange transportation to and from Germany; and (f) German landlords and lodging officials to arrange housing for student teachers and supervisors.

Collaboration Toward Unique Student Teaching Experiences

For more than 17 years, this international student teaching program is open to undergraduate and graduate candidates in all disciplines who are eligible to student teach. Student teachers from other universities are welcome to join Ball State student teachers, as well. While overseas, student teachers have access to resources and materials in the school that promote learning opportunities for international collaboration, twenty-first century school initiatives, and workforce development within the school setting while serving military children. For example, DoDEA schools offer host nation classes and programs that are taught by certified teachers familiar with German language, culture, customs, and geographic areas. Student teachers may collaborate with these teachers to plan lessons, create activities, or go on study trips that support their students' learning of DoDEA standards-based content while also understanding the communities in which they live. This guidance from the host nation teacher is in addition to the support and advice student teachers receive from their mentor teachers.

Additionally, student teachers collaborate with military personnel, German nationals, mentor teachers, fellow student teachers, university personnel, and administrators to enhance school and community partnerships between the university and DoDEA. During their student teaching experience, student teachers live on a military base or close to the base in a nearby German community. Student teachers collaborate with others and support the military and German community as they partake in festivals, attend local events, join common-interest groups, and participate in school activities which take place outside of the regular school hours.

As an interdepartmental and interdisciplinary program, this international student teaching program contributes to the internationalization of the campus by providing elementary and secondary student teachers the opportunity to complete their student teaching experience while living, working, and traveling in Europe. University supervisors meet with prospective student teachers regularly during the semester before student teaching to build relationships, answer questions, and better prepare the student teachers for their overseas experiences. These meetings are especially important for the majority of student teachers who have never traveled outside of the United States or worked within a military community before participating in this program.

Each semester, those university supervisors accompany student teachers to Germany and work with them throughout their student teaching experience. This type of "hands-on" support is distinct to this student teaching program and provides a model for other institutions interested in providing a study abroad experience combined with a student teaching experience. The long-standing relationship between the university and DoDEA is based upon mutual efforts from both entities to provide student teachers with meaningful and high-quality experiences in Department of Defense Dependent Schools. While overseas, university supervisors provide support to student teachers, while they also mentor full-time teachers and offer counsel to school and district administrators, and other community partners that contribute to this partnership.

To assess the impact, strengths, and areas for improvement related to the program, we conducted a qualitative study exploring the perspectives of university supervisors. In 2019, 18 current and past university supervisors each participated in an hour-long one-on-one interview, addressing a wide range of topics. For this chapter, the most relevant topics include: university supervisors' definition of success and keys to success for student teachers and for themselves; university supervisor responsibilities; advantages and challenges unique to the program; and opportunities to improve the program. After transcribing the interviews, we analyzed the interviews through one round of open-coding, then narrowed the list into a manageable number of defined axial codes, then analyzed the interviews again to identify exemplary excerpts for each code. Relevant findings are shared later in the chapter.

Department of Defense Education Activity (DoDEA) Schools

Through the university's established partnership with the DoDEA schools, student teachers have exposure to new opportunities for international careers, professional organizations, travel, and education while working closely with DoDEA teachers, administrators, leaders, and staff. DoDEA schools are on military bases throughout the world, including Bahrain, Belgium, Cuba, England, Germany, Guam, Italy, Japan, Netherlands, Okinawa, Spain, South Korea, and Turkey. The schools have high academic standings throughout the nation, and fourth- and eighth-grade students take the National Assessment of Educational Progress (NAEP) Reading and Mathematics Assessments. In 2019, fourth- and eighth-grade students ranked first in the nation in reading, fourth-grade students ranked first in the nation in mathematics, and eighth-grade students ranked second in the nation in mathematics.

DoDEA teachers and administrators share educational best practices to support and develop progressive and competent student teachers. DoDEA administrators often hire teachers with an international mindset and twenty-first century teaching, leading, and learning skill set, who understand the unique needs of military children and families. In this program, student teachers are able to teach in an international setting at the secondary and elementary school level, work with military communities, and live overseas during experience.

Children or dependents of United States military service members and civilians are a unique population of students to serve in schools, and DoDEA teachers and student teachers need to understand, guide, and address their needs. These students may encounter family member deployments, transfers, injuries, deaths, and separations. Additionally, teachers need exposure and experiences in different cultures to support positive international relationships.

United States military bases and DoDEA schools are placed in host countries and United States civilians and military personnel are guests in those nations. Through teaching and living overseas experiences, teachers and student teachers may develop more acceptance and understanding of others' cultures and opinions. DoDEA students, teachers, and administrators may benefit from student teachers in schools as they learn about new instructional practices, share resources, and exchange backgrounds from different areas of the United States and world. Additionally, these experiences provide student teachers opportunities for future teaching and education-related positions within DoDEA and international schools upon degree completion and licensure.

University Supervisors' Perspectives

The international student teaching program in Germany provides some unique advantages and some student teachers apply to and enroll at this institution for the primary purpose of participating in the study abroad program as seniors. As part of a qualitative study, university supervisors cited in interviews some of the important advantages for student teachers, including gaining a broader view of education as a whole, and developing a frame of reference that will serve them well, even if they teach professionally in the United States exclusively. Student teachers develop connections, a network, and valuable experience in DoDEA schools: "(The Germany student teaching program) opens up the door to work for DoDEA. If that's an interest for the student teachers, which is a wonderful opportunity and experience. So, it kind of sets the stage for them" (Interviewee 12).

Professional teaching positions are among the most coveted and competitive in the DoDEA system. Consequently, participating student teachers enjoy the opportunity to work with high-quality mentor teachers in high-quality schools. These schools serve a unique student population. Students in DoDEA schools have a high level of transience, and often battle distress and anxiety associated with the military deployment of a parent or parent separation. Because of this, student teachers develop firsthand experience and face heightened importance in building relationships quickly with students and tending to their socioemotional needs.

Nearly every former university supervisor cited character-building opportunities as a key advantage of the program—fostering independence, self-confidence, and an understanding and appreciation of culture gained through travel. One supervisor stated:

> Because they don't have their family there, they find out how independent they really are and can be. It gives them additional cultural experiences that you're not going to see in Indiana, that military background that you're not going to see in Indiana.
>
> (Interviewee 17)

Another university supervisor echoed a similar sentiment: "The personal growth during this (program) is astounding. In Indiana, they have their normal support system. (In Germany) suddenly they have to learn coping skills" (Interviewee 3). Interviewee 5 noted that student teachers in this program learn with and from their peers so much more in this program, because of the close, ongoing interactions with peers. Multiple interviewees described the entire experience as "immersive." By living together and traveling together, student teachers are part of a learning community and support network that fosters daily development. Interviewee 2 stated matter-of-factly that this program is a "life-changing event" for student teachers.

While other universities have study abroad programs for student teachers in Germany, the Ball State University program includes a few unique dimensions such as a commitment to on-site university supervisors throughout the entire semester enabling a multidimensional role serving the student teachers, the classroom mentor teachers, and community partners. DoDEA mentor teachers have taken notice and believe the university supervisor presence and insight is invaluable. University supervisors felt that in a traditional student teaching program, student teachers might develop a close relationship with their mentor teacher but maintain a somewhat distant relationship with their university supervisor.

However, the unique nature of this international student teaching program in Germany often fosters strong relationships for student teachers with their mentor teacher *and* their university supervisor. University supervisors felt that ultimately, the greatest success stories for student teachers often materialize *after* completion of the program, after experiencing significant growth as a developing educator, and after gaining employment and starting their professional career, whether in a DoDEA school, traditional public school, charter school, private school, etc. Experience in the international student teaching program distinguishes participants from many of their peers who student taught in the United States in the job market.

Ms. Emmalie Lee (personal communication, June 18, 2020), Principal of Ramstein Elementary School, echoed university supervisors' perspectives about the benefits of travel and immersion in this diverse setting for student teachers. She also expressed her belief that this international student teaching program is especially conducive to preparing student teachers to develop relationships with English language learners and students from diverse cultural backgrounds. "Being unable to understand the local language and cultural norms is a powerful learning experience for the student teachers."

Ms. Lee has developed an intimate familiarity with this international student teaching program by repeatedly welcoming its student teachers into her school, and this approach reflects her belief that the program positively affects the teachers and students in the school. She believes the student teachers "raise the bar for veteran teachers," compel veteran teachers to reflect on their pedagogy by "explaining why they do what they do," and improve the quality of instruction in the school by bringing in "fresh ideas" learned in undergraduate coursework. She believes student teachers' "enthusiasm improves morale for (veteran teachers). The excitement…is infectious."

Program Details: Teaching Timeline

As part of the pre-departure orientation meetings conducted on campus in the United States, student teachers are encouraged to reach out to their mentor teacher, located in Germany, weeks in advance of the semester. Student teachers arrive a week prior to student teaching to begin developing a relationship and to engage in advanced planning, so that they may feel comfortable and prepared at the start of the semester. Over the course of 16 weeks, the international student teaching program directly fosters development and growth in the classroom in a number of ways. The program's structure calls for a gradual transition, first as an engaged observer and contributing on a smaller scale by facilitating small-group and one-on-one instruction. As student teachers are ready, they begin taking ownership of individual class periods and progress until they are ready to plan all lessons and lead their classes from start to finish each school day.

After continuing in this role for a period of weeks, the student teacher transitions to the final stage of the semester, serving in a co-teacher role along with their mentor teacher. In many ways, the co-teaching stage is the most challenging, as it requires the highest level of collaboration, preparation, and finesse. With this in mind, the program's progression is incremental and beneficial in multiple ways for all involved parties. Unlike many student teaching programs, this program saves the most challenging phase of the semester (co-teaching) for the end, when the student teacher is most prepared for the undertaking, and doing so helps to smooth the lasting transition back to the care of the mentor teacher for the children in the classroom.

Program Details: Course Requirements
and Benefits to DoDEA Schools

This program also includes a number of elements more familiar to other successful student teaching programs, and places a strong emphasis on developing rigorous writing skills and fostering self-reflection. Student teachers are required to submit weekly lesson plans, goals, and reflections related to those goals and other knowledge gained, develop their philosophy of education, and assess and reflect on the demographics of their classroom. The most rigorous development opportunity throughout the semester challenges student teachers to not only develop a full instructional unit, but also create, administer, interpret, and act on pre- and post-assessments to measure student growth and the effectiveness of their own teaching in a meaningful way. For years, the university facilitated this process with a proprietary Learning Assessment Model Project (LAMP) but has since done so with the Teacher Performance Assessment (edTPA) program implemented in many teacher preparation programs.

Student teachers' practices are primarily assessed through informal walk-throughs, formal observations, and post-conferences by university supervisors. Informal walkthroughs are typically brief (5–10 minutes) and unannounced. Formal observations last 30 minutes or more are conducted at least four times throughout the semester, and carry with them a post-conference where the student teacher and university supervisor work together to identify areas of strength and areas for improvement, and also result in an evaluation rating (i.e., Distinguished, Proficient, Basic, or Unsatisfactory) based on a rubric rooted in key InTASC standards and sub standards.

Student teachers further develop self-awareness through a course requirement where they record one of their own lessons and analyze it. Student teachers are exposed to different vantage points, different teaching styles, and practices that help shape their own. They are required to observe their peers' teaching and to provide meaningful and constructive feedback, grounding their observation and feedback in a specific InTASC standard, and documenting at least one observed practice that they will implement in their own classroom. Outside of the school day, student teachers are encouraged to grow and embrace the challenge of serving in an extracurricular role, and continue to be immersed in a true learning community, by participating in seminars addressing a variety of topics, from special education practices, co-teaching strategies and inclusion setting strategies, the inner workings of DoDEA schools, navigating the application and interview process, and thriving in a twenty-first century school setting—a uniquely collaborative, open, flexible, and engaging learning environment.

Additional information, grounded in InTASC standards, is included in Table 9.1 below about student teacher roles and benefits to DoDEA schools.

Table 9.1 Student Teacher Roles and DoDEA Partnership Benefits Related to INTASC Standards

INTASC Standard	Student Teacher Roles	DoDEA Partnership Benefits
1 Learner Development	Student teachers work with a variety of students in cognitive, linguistic, cultural, social, emotional, and physical development.	Mentor teachers guide student teachers to support students from military and international backgrounds, in addition to addressing other developmental needs. Student teachers share new resources with mentor teachers.
2 Learning Differences	Student teachers address individual student differences and unique cultures and communities to develop inclusive learning environments.	Mentor teachers facilitate opportunities for student teachers to ensure all students, regardless of educational or cultural backgrounds, are a part of an inclusive classroom. Student teachers provide mentor teachers different ways to promote inclusion for military and international students.
3 Learning Environments	Student teachers collaborate with fellow student teachers and mentor teachers to create collaborative and individual learning environments.	Mentor teachers assist student teachers with identifying ways to encourage students from diverse backgrounds to positively interact with one another. Student teachers demonstrate new ways to actively engage students in their learning.
4 Content Knowledge	Student teachers work together with fellow student teachers and mentor teachers to share expertise in disciplines to guide students.	Mentor teachers work with student teachers to ensure all aspects of learning and subject matter are accessible and meaningful to all learners, regardless of cultural and military backgrounds. Student teachers share new ways to promote equity and inclusion in the classroom.
5 Application of Content	Student teachers provide students unique learning experiences related to twenty-first century skills, competencies, and knowledge for their futures.	Mentor teachers collaborate with student teachers to plan and implement powerful lessons with students from military and international backgrounds may relate to. Student teachers engage mentor teachers in new technologies and resources to support their lessons.
6 Assessment	Student teachers utilize authentic formative and summative assessments to understand students' learning and growth.	Mentor teachers guide student teachers in the development and use of pre- and post-assessments to monitor students' progress, as a transient student population. Student teachers work with mentor teachers to make decisions based on data.

(Continued)

Table 9.1 Student Teacher Roles and DoDEA Partnership Benefits Related to INTASC Standards (*Continued*)

INTASC Standard	Student Teacher Roles	DoDEA Partnership Benefits
7 Planning for Instruction	Student teachers develop and implement rigorous, integrative, and engaging lessons to meet the needs of each student.	Mentor teachers facilitate planning for cross-disciplinary collaboration with student teachers and fellow mentor teachers and opportunities to engage military and international community partners. Student teachers share ways to further develop school-community partnerships.
8 Instructional Strategies	Student teachers implement and share instructional strategies which promote critical and creative thinking in solving real-world problems.	Mentor teachers collaborate with student teachers and fellow mentor teachers to share a variety of teaching and learning strategies to meet the need of diverse learners. Student teachers provide new instructional resources and ways to collaboratively teach.
9 Professional Learning and Ethical Practice	Student teachers participate in continuous professional learning within the school, communities, and university to better support students.	Mentor teachers facilitate and participate in professional learning with student teachers to improve their ability to meet the needs of all students. Student teachers work with mentor teachers to be reflective practitioners in the classroom.
10 Leadership and Collaboration	Student teachers address individual student differences and unique cultures and communities to develop inclusive learning environments.	Mentor teachers engage student teachers building and sustaining collaborative partnerships with families, fellow teachers, military members, and international community members. Student teachers provide new ideas to lead and guide stakeholders.

Program Details: University Supervisor Responsibilities

Along the way, university supervisors are serving in vital roles, striking the right balance between ongoing support and guidance for student teachers, and helping student teachers develop their independence. University supervisors are directly involved with facilitating many of the program elements above, including arranging and facilitating seminar sessions, evaluating and providing feedback for all of the written requirements, and conducting walkthroughs, observations, and post-conferences. During this time, university supervisors strike another delicate balance between positive encouragement and constructive criticism. University supervisors also encourage student teachers to develop their own sense of accountability as they learn to engage in continuous reflection and self-analysis. These skills often are noticeably improved during the post-conferences. University supervisors also maintain clear communication and understanding before and during the semester among student teachers, mentor teachers, school administrators, and university personnel. After the completion of the semester, university supervisors often serve as a reference for many student teachers throughout their job search.

Many of the above responsibilities are common to traditional domestic student teaching programs, too. Beyond this, university supervisors serve in ways emphasized by the study abroad setting. They contribute to the recruitment and selection process, and conduct informational meetings not only with student teachers, but with parents and family members, leading up to the start of the semester. Supervisors also navigate a daunting paperwork process to obtain the necessary clearances and credentials (including Status of Forces Agreement cards—a rough equivalent to a work visa—and base access and base privileges cards).

Additionally, university supervisors take responsibility for the safety and well-being of student teachers, occasionally transporting student teachers as needed to a medical center and helping them to obtain necessary medication and treatment. They provide emotional support when necessary, often caused by homesickness or occasional conflicts that arise between student teachers and mentor teachers, or among student teachers themselves. After completing the program and returning to the United States, university supervisors lead outgoing student teachers through the process of sharing insight, in the form an hour-long presentation, with the next group of student teachers and with select university faculty and leaders. The presentation addresses program requirements, keys to success, the unique elements of DoDEA schools, the wide range of emotions experienced over the course of the semester, and specific living and travel tips. Additional information about university supervisor responsibilities prior to the student teaching semester is included in Table 9.2 later.

Impact of Study Abroad on Teacher Education

The university ensures one or two university supervisors (depending on the number of student teachers) are placed overseas each semester, alongside their student teachers, contributing guidance with a variety of professional and personal matters. Offering field placement on a United States military base coupled with the ability to reach over 50 European countries provides student teachers both a challenging and supportive environment to grow in, ultimately allowing them to become culturally rich individuals inside and outside of the classroom. The travel opportunities connected with this study abroad are thought to develop not only the student teachers' classroom training and connection with students, peers, and mentors, but their personal growth and maturity as well.

Student teachers and university faculty who participate in this international student teaching program in Germany find the experience is often life

Table 9.2 A Stepped Approach for University Supervisors Prior to the Student Teaching Semester

Step		Description
1	Express interest	Ideally, potential university supervisors should share their interest two semesters prior to going sponsoring a program. Potential supervisors should discuss the benefits, challenges, and logistics of being in a different country for a semester with their department chair, international programs director, student teaching director, dean, and study abroad director.
2	Gain approval	Potential supervisors need written approval from the department, college, and university to serve as a university supervisor of an international program. Course schedules, research projects, teaching load, and the feasibility doing other university business while serving as a supervisor should be discussed.
3	Learn processes	Once approved, university supervisors should meet with several people to gain knowledge and understanding about the paperwork processes, logistics, and supervisor responsibilities. Meetings should focus on topics, such as budget, transportation, housing, study abroad and student teaching requirements, school partnerships, supervisor roles, international visas or permits, and personal items.
4	Meet key stakeholders	University supervisors who have not served in this role before should complete a planning trip to the specific program area at least one semester before their supervisor role begins. The purpose of the trip is to meet key school stakeholders, become familiar with the area and cultural norms, and meet with personnel at foreign work permit and residence application offices.
5	Recruit students	After gaining familiarity with the processes and timeline, university supervisors need to work with student teaching and international programs directors to recruit prospective student teachers for the program. Recruitment should begin one to two semesters prior to student teaching, and may include hosting informational meetings, posting information in classrooms and online, and having former student teachers share their experiences.
6	Hold pre-departure meetings	Once university supervisors have recruited prospective student teachers who are committed to student teaching the following semester, supervisors should schedule monthly meetings with the students to complete paperwork, ask questions, build connections with one another, and start planning their international experience. At least one informational meeting should be held with families, parents, and caregivers, as well.
7	Set and adhere to deadlines	University supervisors need to work with student teaching, international programs, financial, and study abroad directors to ensure all paperwork and budgets are authorized and completed. Prospective student teachers should meet all deadlines, and university supervisors are responsible for following up with students who are not in compliance with due dates and planning.
8	Communicate with mentor teachers and school leaders	Once prospective student teachers receive their student teaching school placements, university supervisors should communicate with school leaders and mentor teachers to share contact information and open lines of communication. Additionally, supervisors should have all student teachers contact their mentor teachers.

changing. The cultural engagement with the military community, living in Germany, and having the chance to travel around Europe are notable examples. For some involved with the program, the semester overseas provides a first glimpse of life outside of the United States. University supervisors found that the opportunity to travel throughout Germany and internationally brought forth a greater sense of independence for the student teachers. More importantly, the student teachers' ability to find a balance between travel and tending to student teaching responsibilities also attributed to their personal development.

While university supervisors begin the semester abroad repeatedly stressing the priority that student teaching comes first, it is natural that program participants are excited about the travel opportunities afforded by being part of the program. One former university supervisor (Interviewee 18) stated "One of the biggest transitions is for them to realize when to travel and when not to travel. When to understand the importance of their first task, their first responsibility, and then, how do they mitigate that." Consequently, these opportunities are beneficial in yet another way; helping student teachers successfully learn how to prioritize life tasks and best organize their time as they enter their first years of teaching and come across work, life, and family stressors.

Internationalizing Perspectives and Teacher Identity Development

This international student teaching program in Germany shows how student teachers find ways to translate their international experiences into pedagogical growth in the classroom. The student teachers will often integrate what they are learning about being introduced to different food, art, historical sites, and other more general cultural observations through their immersion within a new community. With these firsthand experiences of cultural engagement, our participants build upon and heighten their content knowledge which can later be shared with their own students.

These experiences contribute to student teachers' development into well-rounded educators with an enhanced understanding of developing international perspectives. For example, one supervisor (Interviewee 18) expressed that "a well-rounded educator is someone who understands not only the local but the global view too." Another supervisor (Interviewee 13) mentioned that their student teachers "see diversity as they travel in the various cultures within Europe. They see customs and ways of doing things," a view shared by multiple other supervisors. In turn, equipped with a more nuanced understanding of global perspectives, student teachers in this program are able to better prepare themselves to appreciate and employ culturally responsive pedagogies within their own classroom, whether teaching in a United States school or in other areas of the world. Ultimately, these experiences within the context of student teaching, shapes the dispositions of these educators in ways that make them open to exploring non-United States based teaching assignments. For example, student teachers, after the completion of their student teaching, find teaching positions abroad through the professional networks maintained by DoDEA. While additional research is needed, there are strong, early indicators that student teachers who opt for a study abroad experience emerge with a newly shaped teacher identity that is more globally encompassing.

Challenges and Future Improvements

University program directors and supervisors are focused on ways to keep this international student teaching program in Germany in a state of continuous improvement. The structure of the program allows multiple faculty to have the opportunity to experience the student teaching program, consider new ways to enhance it and offer various solutions to further improve the program while ensuring its future growth and continued success. These proposed improvements focus on university supervisory preparedness, student teacher selection, and maintaining affordability with the overall program cost.

University supervisors continue to report they enjoy the experience, and it is noteworthy that a number of them request returning to the role again. In fact, more than five supervisors have served more than once, a few as many as three times. Past university supervisors have suggested ways in which they could be better prepared for their supervisory role. University supervisors are on-call day and night, every day, handling both the teaching and non-teaching needs of their student teachers. Based on the circumstances of when supervisors have been selected for this program, different types of training have been provided. Therefore, implementing a university supervisor training, prior to their departure abroad, can better prime supervisors for different scenarios one might face during the semester overseas. An additional suggestion is the creation of a pool of past university supervisors to provide guidance about best practices. This resource would help current supervisors maintain accuracy and consistency within the program.

DoDEA recently built and opened new twenty-first century schools in the Kaiserslautern Military Community, where university student teachers are placed as part of this student teaching program. Shaw noted many key differences between twenty-first century schools and traditional schools. Among them, in a twenty-first century school, the teacher acts as a facilitator or coach (rather than the "center of attention and/or provider of information," as in a traditional school), and the learning process is driven by "exploration, creativity, and twenty-first century skills" (rather than by standardized testing, as in a traditional school) (as cited in Oliva & Gordon, 2013, p. 251). According to Germaine et al. (2016), various organizations have agreed upon the need for these twenty-first century skills (which include critical thinking and problem-solving skills, communication skills, collaboration skills, creativity and innovation skills) in order to help learners be successful in the future. These learning environments further enhance the ability for staff to work more closely together. Teachers willingly assist other students in need and may cross grades and subjects in order to do so.

Many student teachers have completed the program with documented accomplishments, such as leading professional development workshops for school staff, participating in their school's extra-curricular activities like coaching and club advisory, and connecting with more than just their assigned mentor teacher by assisting in additional classrooms. There are, however, rare cases where student teachers do not find such success. This can be for a variety of reasons. While rare, a student teacher may struggle to balance their need to focus on lesson plans and assignments versus their desire to travel and experience new cultures; ultimately putting them behind in their workload and leading to failure within the program. In other situations, some student teachers discover a change of heart with their participation in the field of education, finding it is not the right fit. Therefore, new predeparture training needs are increasing in order to reduce the burden of on-site training in this area. With this in mind, university supervisors have also recommended improving the university's student teaching program through a heightened focus on student teacher preparedness and selection. Providing additional training for the student teachers allows for further preparedness to effectively learn, lead, and work in this state-of-the-art setting.

University supervisors have also suggested a desire to have a more stringent process for accepting student teachers into the program. Albeit, the application process is already quite complex to begin with, as student teachers are required to go through a series of steps in order to reach acceptance. This current process first asks student teachers to indicate their interest and desire to participate in the program. Their applications are then reviewed by the university's Office of Teacher Education Services (OTES). Because this paperwork must be completed meticulously, as the simplest mistakes can result in being turned away, additional stressors surrounding immovable deadlines can materialize. Applications are further worked on between OTES, university supervisors, and those hopeful student teachers, before being sent to DoDEA Headquarters. Prior to submitting paperwork to DoDEA, student teachers truly need to acknowledge their commitment to the program, if accepted. After DoDEA receives and processes the applications, they are sent to the district office in Germany, where student teacher placements are determined. While many applicants are accepted into the program, some are denied due to lack of availability per particular content areas. Considering the distance the student teachers are from home, the length of time they are abroad, and the overall rigor of the program's content, the need to be more selective at the university level helps to ensure a higher likelihood of success for the student teachers. It should also be noted, given the significant need for a more diverse teaching population, the university is also intentionally focusing on expanding the number of applicants of color in the program.

University supervisors have also shared the need to refine the financial structure and overall affordability of the program. As studying abroad demands more financial backing from student teachers, fundraising ventures have become an essential part of the program. These expenses include the cost of housing, transportation between bases, and flights to and from Germany. Student teachers generally pay these expenses out of pocket alongside the tuition they already pay for coursework. The individual costs vary due to (a) the number of student teachers; (b) the number of university supervisors; and (c) the university supervisor's current status (e.g., active, retired). As these expenses continue to increase over time, the number of student teachers able to fund the experience could potentially decrease. This represents an ongoing set of considerations as planning for the future continues.

Conclusion

In this international student teaching program in Germany, student teachers enjoy many of the benefits common to student teaching study abroad programs. These benefits include becoming more student-centered and having better communication skills in the classroom (Çelik, 2017); greater understanding and ability to adapt to new working cultures and different approaches to teaching and learning (Kabilan, 2013); and development of multicultural competencies (Sharma et al., 2011).

Furthermore, student teachers in this program enjoy benefits that are not guaranteed by other programs, including a rigorous focus on reflection and development, outstanding mentor teachers, the fulfillment of serving the children of military service personnel, and a school setting that shares many similarities with what they are likely to be immersed in when they begin their professional teaching career in a traditional public school in the United States. All of these factors help guide student teachers toward successful careers.

References

Çelik, B. (2017). The effects of working abroad on the development of teaching skills. *International Journal of Social Sciences & Educational Studies*, *4*(3), 212–215. Retrieved from https://ijsses.tiu.edu.iq/wp-content/uploads/2018/02/The-Effects-of-Working-Abroad-on-the-Development-of-Teaching-Skills.pdf

Germaine, R., Richards, J., Koeller, M., Schubert-Irastorza, C. (2016). Purposeful use of 21st century skills in higher education. *Journal of Research in Innovative Teaching*, *9*(1), 19–29. Retrieved from https://www.nu.edu/assets/resources/pageResources/journal-of-research-in-innovative-teaching-volume-9.pdf

Helen, M. & Moss, D. (2015). Continuing intercultural learning during the re-entry semester following a study abroad experience. *Journal of International Social Studies*, *5*(2), 38–52.

Kabilan, M. K. (2013). A phenomenological study of an international teaching practicum: Pre-service teachers' experiences of professional development. *Teaching and Teacher Education*, *36*, 198–209. https://doi.org/10.1016/j.tate.2013.07.013

Marx, H., Moss, D. (2011). Please mind the culture gap: Intercultural development during a teacher education study abroad program. *Journal of Teacher Education, 62*(1), 35–47. doi: 10.1177/0022487110381998

Nero, S. (2018). Studying abroad in the Dominican Republic: Preparing culturally and linguistically responsive teachers for 21st-century classrooms. *Annual Review of Applied Linguistics, 38*, 194–200. doi: 10.1017/S0267190518000090

Oliva, P. F., & Gordon, W. R. (2013). *Developing the Curriculum* (8th edition). Pearson Publishing.

Sharma, S., Phillion, J., & Malewski, E. (2011). Examining the practice of critical reflection for developing pre-service teachers' multicultural competencies: Findings from a study-abroad program in Honduras. *Issues in Teacher Education, 20*(2), 9–22. Retrieved from https://pdfs.semanticscholar.org/4656/fbb4ce08dedddc43226ed78e1ccdc62e114a.pdf

10 A Qualitative Analysis of Teacher Candidates' Study Abroad Experiences in Malawi

L. Octavia Tripp, Angela Love, Nancy Barry, Chippewa M. Thomas, and Jared Russell

Introduction

Higher education institutions have allocated considerable resources to advance globalization and internationalization initiatives. Faculty-led academic experiences in international and intercultural settings are increasingly researched. These programs are a means of impacting the cultural awareness, sensitivity, adaptability, competence, and diversity of academic experiences (Cho & Morris, 2015; Leung, Maddix, Galinsky, & Chiu, 2008; Levine & Garland, 2015; Perry, Stoner, Stoner, Wadsworth, Page, & Tarrant, 2013). This increases the variety of academic or service-learning foci and diversifies immersive settings available to students and faculty (Tarrant, Rubin, & Stoner, 2014).

What is more, there has been a paucity of scholarly inquiry into the impact of study abroad experiences on student academic development and global/international awareness (Holmes & O'Neill, 2012; Kulkarni & Hanley-Maxwell, 2015; Lokkesmoe, Kuchinke, & Ardichvili, 2016). However, there are even fewer studies on best models to integrate study abroad experiences into teacher education in terms of teacher best-practices that also include ways to develop professional dispositions that rely on understanding and empathy for diverse cultures (Tripp, Love, Thomas, & Russell, 2017).

The investigators of this study (also the faculty team that led the study abroad program), share an interdisciplinary collaboration led study abroad model where the lived experiences of teacher candidates included (a) designing lessons and teaching in classrooms alongside local teachers; (b) participation in community outreach opportunities; (c) tutoring and mentoring local children in an orphanage; (d) leading professional development for local teachers; and (e) volunteering with a nonprofit organization. The community, school, and village in which the teacher candidates' work supported the development of cross-cultural knowledge, inclusive and culturally responsive skills for best practice, and awareness of attitudes held about teaching and education in the Malawian context. Our study abroad program goals included (a) to contribute to students' awareness of cultural influences on education and learning; (b) to increase students' emerging practitioner self-confidence, and (c) to stimulate

interest in cross-cultural and international learning. This study both intentionally and unintentionally fostered teacher candidates' learning. It did so in
the way that Baptise, Ryan, Araujo, and Duhon-Sells's (2015) research findings reiterated that learning in a real world context is a socially responsible
and an imperative for education in order for it to be transformative, relevant,
and reciprocal. Observing, interacting and then teaching *in vivo* exposed the
teacher candidates to opportunities for change in agency development and
transformation in a different cultural context (Giroux, 1997). Hence, the study
abroad program elements that we incorporated aided the teacher candidates'
learning experientially in active and engaged ways.

This chapter includes an analysis of student reflections from daily journal
entries and field notes on their experiences abroad and pre and post study
abroad discussions. The investigators collaborated across program areas (early
childhood, elementary, clinical mental health counseling, and kinesiology
education), and with a nonprofit organization to create global experiences
in teacher preparation. In this chapter, we share the results of the qualitative analysis of the teacher candidate experiences. Whereas, the study abroad
program faculty (the investigators), the Malawian (cooperating) educators,
school and village personnel, and others engaged with the students; for the
purpose of this study their reflections were not included in the analysis. In
the limitations section of the chapter, the authors briefly describe how some
lessons learned informed the development of future study abroad programs.

Background

Faculty (the investigators) created the Destination Malawi Outreach
Education study abroad program as a result of the institution's memorandum
of understanding (MOU) with a nonprofit foundation that has an established
partnership with the village chieftain to aid and address hunger, malnutrition, and the impact of disease on children in the Lilongwe community in
Malawi. The study abroad program was developed because of the Mtendere
Village and local school's collective desires to advance educative best-
practices and exchange with others. The conception of the study abroad
program was intentionally community-based so that the students, as they
learned, would have an immersion experience that was authentic to the place
where they were. Because of this, the investigators researched best-practices
for insight into how best to achieve the intended program goals. For example, Sipes' (2012) phenomenological study of an undergraduate study abroad
program in Africa revealed seven main themes: "embracing the host culture,
experience of mixed emotions after returning home, critical comparison of
U.S and Africa, challenges in communicating experience, reconstructing
identity, remaining connected to African experience and positive changes in
personal lives" (p. 93). Results of Sipes (2012) study revealed an overall positive connection to the students' experience in Africa, with several students
continuing to include African values into their daily lives, and for all students

"studying abroad in Africa increased the self-confidence....as well as gave them opportunities to be introduced to social practices and worldviews they did not know existed" (p. 139).

Initially the investigators explored interest and feasibility in short-term (one-week) study abroad programs as an option; this allows students an opportunity to participate in international experiences without a long-term time commitment (Payne, Chapman, Daly, Darby & Heft, 2019). An additional program element the investigators considered for the study abroad model was a culture immersion in an educational, service-learning context. This idea propones fostering a sense of importance and social commitment, while developing empathy among participants (Jones & Collier, 2019).

As the investigators synthesized the literature and developed and aligned goals, we explored the notion of delivering a culturally responsive and inclusive study abroad program. However, investigators discovered research is inconclusive about how best to prepare teachers to teach in a culturally inclusive and culturally responsive manner (Daniel & Friedman, 2005; Ray & Bowman 2003). Beyond this, investigators explored the significance of how participants would encounter and respond to the immersion experience. Trilokekar and Kukar (2011) found teacher candidates' frustration stemming from encountering racism at various international locations, as "disorienting experiences", provided rich opportunities for reflection, but also "revealed a limited ability to relate some of their study abroad experiences in ways that would revise or develop new frames of reference" (Trilokekar & Kukar, 2011, p. 1149).

Furthermore, investigators explored other recent studies (Cooper, 2017; Levine & Garland, 2015; Tripp et al., 2017) indicating that the study abroad experience adds value in terms of cultural and language experiences, thus resulting in greater awareness of the diverse needs of students and their backgrounds. This heightened awareness could also inspire teacher candidates' daily learning on return from study abroad as they continue their on-campus programs (Devillar & Jiang, 2012; Kulkarni & Hanley-Maxwell, 2015).

After the study abroad program concluded and data analysis concluded of the teacher candidates' journal entries, the authors reviewed other studies. We identified studies describing the meaning of the themes that emerged from our analysis (i.e., othering, self-realization, sense of belonging, and linguistic and language differences as experiential aspects of this study abroad program). A sense of separation and "othering" can create barriers to successful communication and understanding of the social climate in international settings (Von Wendorff, 2013). Othering, as defined by Powell and Mendian (2018), is "a set of dynamics, processes and structures that engender marginality and persistent inequality across any of the full range of human differences based on group dynamics" (Powell & Mendian, 2018, p. 17). Cooper's (2017) study examining teacher candidates in a study abroad program revealed that self-realization occurred through experiences of daily exploration, intellectual pursuit, and in the context of community. Cooper (2017) also indicated that students felt a sense of belonging and wanted to share what they learned from their lived experiences when returning home. More than that, Mikel's (2019) study abroad research of athletes (training to be teachers) in London, while able to speak English, indicated that the athletes often struggled with differences in linguistic understanding and social norms. Phillion, Malewski, Sharma, and Wang's (2009) qualitative study used teacher candidates' daily journals and interviews to examine the impact of a study abroad program in Honduras.

From literature reviewed, the investigators concluded that successful lived experiences, both locally and internationally (including fieldwork), provide opportunities for teacher candidates to develop greater awareness of and sensitivity to those whose backgrounds differ from their own. While these studies contribute to the knowledge of study abroad program development, there remains a critical need for data to inform international program developers about specific academic and cultural benefits and potential challenges associated with study abroad experiences. These studies helped develop a contextual view, inform the approach and design of the study, and helped to clarify the results presented in this chapter.

Purpose and Significance

Teacher education programs need specific venues and organizational structures that support professional development within learning communities in the context of a study abroad program. The purpose of this study was to examine teacher candidates' reflections on their experiences in a study abroad program in Malawi during a three and one-half-week summer session (of a summer semester). Investigators accessed local schools and opportunities for interaction with administrators, teachers, and students, and included structured time for addressing professional development needs in the community. The qualitative study explores graduate and undergraduate teacher education participants' personal and professional growth associated with a study abroad experience in Malawi. While the experiences of the investigators as participants in a qualitative research process are integral, see Tripp et al. (2017) for further discussion of these reflections. With the goal in mind of building a program in Malawi a second year, the following research questions provided an initial framework for analysis: what cultural and educational benefits do participants believe they gained from the study abroad program; and what changes in participants' intercultural attitudes occurred during the study abroad experience? The Institutional Review Board at the university that employs the investigators approved the research procedures involving human subjects in the study described in this chapter.

Methods and Procedures

The faculty team intended that the summer outreach education study abroad program prepare teacher candidates to understand multiple cultural perspectives, which could lead them toward becoming culturally responsive teachers and leaders. As remarked by Zull (2012), immersion study abroad experiences, in particular, foster powerful learning due in part to a variety of sensory experiences (e.g., smell, taste, sight, emotions) that engage students. This study examined participants' open-ended daily journals that included field-notes and faculty-assigned daily reflections in response to their experiences while in-country. At the conclusion of the program, participants submitted their journals, and they were then copied for review and assessment. After the faculty review of the journals, faculty returned the journals to teacher candidates.

Participants

One graduate student, eleven undergraduate students, and four university faculty traveled together to Malawi during the summer of 2012. Some of the students had previously traveled abroad, but for some this event was their first international travel experience. The program was open to all matriculating advanced undergraduate (juniors and seniors) and graduate majors in the College of Education at a large, predominantly white public university (PWI) in the southeastern United States. The graduate student and ten undergraduate teacher candidates were European American; one undergraduate teacher candidate was African American; all were women. Students represented several different areas of study in K-12 teacher preparation programs, including elementary, early childhood, and physical education. The faculty team consisted of three African Americans and one European American, one male and three females, from four disciplines, namely, counseling, kinesiology, elementary, and early childhood education. The faculty team intended the study abroad model to provide a support network from different perspectives and diverse areas of study, as well, for the teacher candidates who participated. The elementary and early childhood education faculty facilitated the teacher candidates' learning, using observations and note-taking from their field experiences, writing lesson plans, personal and group reflections, participating in tutoring sessions, and discussing daily observed and learned educational strategies. The counseling faculty facilitated the support for those who had difficulty dealing with issues of diversity, interpersonal/intrapersonal concerns, and other adjustment issues while being miles away from their home and familiar environment. The kinesiology faculty addressed physical and mental health, including personal choice times as well as organized sports, and discussions of healthy choices.

Settings

The collaborative partnership between the university and 100X Development Foundation, a nonprofit organization located in the same state, collaborated and assisted with the study abroad program. The nonprofit organization set up meetings with local Malawian stakeholders, arranging lodging, meals, and in-country transportation while the College of Education faculty planned the program itinerary and recruited the student participants. Once in Malawi, the faculty team and student participants lived in housing provided by the nonprofit organization and the local children's village. There, we stayed for three weeks in a supervised children's community with 80 orphaned children, 12 House Mothers, additional educational and healthcare staff, and a few additional staff from the United States employed by the nonprofit organization.

The establishment and opening of the Mtendere Children's Village by 100X Development Foundation in 2004, was for children orphaned from the impact of disease and malnutrition on local families. Mtendere Children's Village, located in Lumbadzi, Malawi, is 22.53 kilometers from the capital city of Lilongwe. It includes room and board for the orphaned children, medical care at a center, and preschool, all sponsored and managed by 100X Development Foundation in partnership with a local chieftain. This particular children's village and community was a good fit for the teacher candidates' cultural immersion experience, due to the availability of onsite accommodations and opportunities to interact with residents at the orphanage, the village, and community school. Every morning, the teacher candidates walked to school with the village children, and taught in their classrooms alongside their teachers.

Centrally located in Africa, Malawi is affectionately known as "The Warm Heart of Africa". The official languages are Chichewa and English. Education in Malawi is free, except that students pay for their own uniforms, books, pencils. Education is not compulsory, and many children drop out, often repeatedly, depending on their family's work status and configuration. There is also a tremendous teacher shortage, averaging 96:1 ratio, when the recommended ratio by the government is 60:1 (Ripple Africa, 2020).

Accommodations at the children's village were comfortable and safe, but quite modest and, perhaps to some, inconvenient in comparison to accommodations at local hotels (e.g., cold showers, limited water, regular power outages, and limited Internet connectivity). However, staying at the guest cottages at the orphanage provided a more authentic, shared, community-based experience. The teacher candidates also enjoyed two in-country cultural excursions, an overnight stay and safari at MVUU-Liwonde Game Park in northern Malawi, and an overnight stay at Lake Malawi, the third largest, and most ecologically diverse lake in Africa.

Research Methodology

The investigators employed a qualitative methodology for this study based upon phenomenological and grounded theory approaches (Age, 2011; Moustakas, 1994). Owning our interest in an indepth, richly detailed profile of participants' perspectives of the lived experiences studying abroad, the theoretical framework worked well for grouping participants' reflections into themes (as evidenced by the process-orientated analysis type selected). The investigators examined the ways that participants engaged in this experience, seeking insight into their developing global attitudes from both emerging professional and more general perspectives. Students' daily journals were the primary data source that depicted emerging understandings reflexive of their daily experiences in Malawi (Moustakas, 1994; Matua & Van Der Wal, 2015).

Data Analysis

The investigators engaged in a cyclical, ongoing process of collaboration and deliberation as outlined by Age (2011). Investigators began the cyclical process of data analysis with an "attitude of openness" (p. 1600), as we explored and discussed emerging concepts. Investigators then explored and discussed emerging concepts in cyclical rounds as well. The coding process occurred through five overlapping cycles. In the first cycle, each of three coders identified themes that appeared repeatedly through reading and rereading student participant journals. Emerging themes were documented, including code families of themes or constructs, plausible code names, code descriptions, illustrative quotations, related literature, and theoretical memos from each coder. Finally, the coders categorized, then refined, sub-themes through collaborative discussions until data analysis reached saturation. The investigators then began the theoretic writing process in which "all the details of the substantive theory are brought together in an overall conceptual description that is then integrated with [...] the extant literature on the subject" (Age, 2011, p. 1600). Because of multiple investigators and constant comparison, an audit trail was employed to ensure the trustworthiness of the outcomes (Guba & Lincoln, 1981).

Results and Discussion

Analyses revealed that working and being in Malawi helped teacher candidates understand the values and benefits of this international, educational experience. The data analysis addressed both research questions stated earlier in the background (purpose and significance) section of the chapter. Five overarching themes emerged in the saturation process: (a) othering, (b) communication and language, (c) disorienting/eye-opening experience, (d) similar/different cultural experiences, and (e) two-way learning experience. Investigators discuss each of these themes and include participant statements below. Pseudonyms used in this chapter ensure the confidentiality of study participants.

Othering

Students expressed an idealized impression of the country and people of Malawi, particularly during the first week of the study abroad experience. Comments such as "it's like a dream" and references to movies, such as "The Lion King", illustrated this theme. Woolf (2006) observed that study abroad participants sometimes view people from non-US cultures as exotic or romanticized; others support these findings. Participants themselves felt like "the other", because of a lack of knowledge of social norms, as well as linguistic miscommunication.

> Natalie, "I remember looking outside at the Malawi airport and thinking that I had just landed in paradise. The people smelled like warm corn, and they smiled and helped me haul our luggage into the van".
>
> Beverly, "When we went to visit and tour the school it was like I had stepped into a story or movie".
>
> Melanie, "I don't feel like I am in Africa. It's like a picture. It is not what I expected... It was amazing".

As they wrote about initial feelings and reactions to the immersion experience (e.g., grateful, compassion-filled, dissonant, and disoriented), teacher candidates described themselves as "outside" of the culture/people of Malawi; revealing perceptions of being the "other" (Woolf, 2006). A common reaction of study abroad students visiting cultures vastly different in terms of disparities that vary from their own, is a desire to do something; they want to help or save those they have met and encountered. Some scholars refer to his attitude as the "White Savior Complex" (Cole, 2012; Machado, 2016). This way of thinking does not always cause one to stop and reflect on whether this desire to "help" would meet the needs of the people or community. Consequently, study abroad encounters can reinforce romanticizing, presuppositions, and prejudices rooted in privilege that lead to dispositions of othering (e.g., engaging as a spectator). While the teacher candidates started their stay in Malawi with this perception, the characterizations of their lived experiences and reflective discussion content with faculty, as well as with their peers, later begin to shift.

Communication and Language

Communicating meaning across language barriers and cultural norms can be both challenging and exciting for study abroad participants (Phillion, Malewski, Sharma, & Wang, 2009). This occurrence seems to be most evident in statements made by students who attended a church worship service with several of the House Mothers.

> Beverly, "I can tell a difference in myself even just between being at that church a week ago and being there today...I felt much more comfortable being out of my accustomed environment".
>
> Jamie, "... The language barrier ... and being the only white people in the group of people made this feel different".

When the teacher candidates faced the challenge of using the Chichewa language to communicate, they experienced the village youth as caring and warm, and fond of their efforts to acquire their home language. At the same time, the village youth were studying English to become proficient (Mancini-Cross, Backman, & Baldwin, 2009). Teacher candidates did not expect that their lack of understanding the primary language would also be the key to so many positive experiences. A participant remarked that they ventured out one evening to buy groceries at the village market, and said that the locals were at first not very helpful, but once the teacher candidates attempted hand gestures and words in the native language the local people warmed up.

> Beverly, "I've been hesitant to use the [Chichewa] language here, but I really want to break out of my comfort zone and try it out".

The teacher candidates were hesitant in the beginning of the experience and felt they were different in physical appearance; their thoughts also reflect the disequilibrium that normally precedes a shift in perception or disposition (Kim, 2001).

Disorienting/Eye-Opening Experience

Participants felt challenged by the experience of being an outsider, as contrasted with the experience of privilege and taking one's identity, and fitting in for granted in the United States. The disequilibrium of these challenges also enabled a sense of newness, slightly disorienting, but leading participants to a more open perspective of trying something different. Even more than this, witnessing the unexpected, such as extreme poverty, caused teacher candidates to reflect on many interrelated issues, such as feelings of helplessness, immobilization, disorientation, and cross-cultural stress (Phillion et al., 2009).

> Lisa, "It's a weird feeling being stared and waved at wherever you go".
> Jamie, "These moments, driving by, make me feel so helpless to these people who need so much... I knew poverty existed, but I had never witnessed it".
> June, "Very eye opening experience. I saw what poverty was all about for the first time. We had to travel down a dirt road. Children running and asking for food or money. None of the houses had anything more than a thatch roof protection. My heart aches for these people".
> Barbara, "These poor, sweet children were so excited just to get an empty bottle [for] water. The difference between what I saw today and cities in Alabama was shocking. How can things be the same and so different at the same time?"

Reflecting on the unexpected, several teacher candidates described perceptions they held about African (Malawian) culture and people, as well as observing that the village youth were eager, capable, smart, and savvy-thinkers. They noticed also that beauty and poverty could exist at once. They commented on tasty and familiar foods as well.

Jamie, "It's amazing to me to see such beautiful scenery in such a poor country".

Further, students expressed surprise in simple things, such as.

Jill, "We had chicken, rice and coleslaw. This was not what I was expecting",

Lisa, "I am so surprised at how much the children know".

Barbara, "A first grader in the village could recite her multiplication tables 2 [through] 8. This just shows that any student in a situation can learn whatever they set their minds to".

The teacher candidates' pondered the contexts in which the youth who lived at the children's village learned, and perceived the eagerness and respect with which the village youth approached authority and education; particularly toward the end of the stay.

Melanie, "These kids are so smart and it amazes me how determined they are".

Lisa, "I was very surprised how well the boys paid attention to our lesson. They never asked to go to the bathroom and didn't show signs of being mentally tired until an hour into the lesson".

Barbara, "I am surprised at how much the children know".

June, "I was expecting the people to have nothing and while they have very little, they are able to make their resources [go] so far".

Lisa, "They may lack stuff in my eyes, but in their [eyes] they have everything they need and are very joyful people".

Beverly, "It is amazing to me how little the people here complain. Even when we were at the afternoon tutoring time and the desks were all 'smooched up' next to each other and they were having to crowd over each other to find a seat".

Journal entries reflected shifts in comfort-level and dispositions as the students neared the end of the abroad experience; thus addressing the second research question related to changes in attitudes.

Jill, "I realized I needed this trip for personal growth. I really needed to step out of my normal box...I am enjoying my experience; it's already changing me as a person, making me continue to step out of my box".

Together, these findings suggest shifts in dispositions that facilitate participants' multicultural competence development for personal and professional growth (Phillion et al., 2009). Their reactions relate to their experiences around race/ethnic group membership and identity, outsider status, risk-taking, differences, and poverty. These responses appear to have influenced participant's ability to develop empathy for and authentic interest in ethnically diverse people (Desai & Kukar, 2011). The teacher candidates' attitudes shifted from surprise, shock, and disequilibrium toward more acceptance of the perceived unexpected differences. As well, participants believed at first that their teacher training was so different that they would not be able to collaborate with the cooperating teachers. But overtime teacher candidates reflected in their journals that they were learning, and how they were grateful for the experience to work with the cooperating teachers.

Similar/Different Cultural Experiences

Cross-cultural and intercultural interactions presented unique sets of challenges and benefits. When study abroad participants lack awareness, knowledge of the culture, or the interpersonal skills to manage responses to their lived experiences, these circumstances further compound the situation (Robson, 2002). The present study allowed participant exposure through immersion and exploration opportunities they might not have otherwise experienced. Some of the study participants observed that the teachers of the host country were open and kind, genuine, and compassionate, which were similar to their experiences with teachers in the United States. The study participants reported of themselves as warming up to and developing fondness of the local people and culture as time unfolded.

> Lisa, "I see the love for the children by the teachers. The teachers here are as teachers in the states, embracing the students with praise and kindness in the classroom".
>
> Jamie, "[The teacher] was pretty strict with the kids, but I noticed many practices similar to those in the US".
>
> June, "We met teachers that we would be working with, as well as went on a tour. I am surprised at how [many] decorations and posters were in English".
>
> Missy, "The way teachers teach here is so different from how we are taught to teach in America. I can already tell this is going to be an experience that I will never forget!"

These similarities and differences observed and about which study participants journaled, became more and more palpable as they began to cross-culturally adjust and adapt. Participants said at times they were homesick, felt melancholy, and yet, examined their own bias; others felt a sense of awe and wonderment. The faculty processed these reactions with the teacher candidates as part of group discussions about psycho-emotional, cognitive, and sociocultural adjustment and adaptation. Cross-cultural adjustment occurs in stages and happens because the values, traditions, customs and beliefs may be different and unfamiliar (Lokkesmoe et al., 2016; Ward & Kennedy, 1993; Zhou, Jindal-Snape, Topping, & Todman, 2008). As participant narratives in the next section reveal, cultural adaptations included the participant's ability to listen, observe, ask questions, and use the Chichewa language.

Two-Way Learning Experience

Teacher candidates' journal entries written early in the program reflected a "one-way" attitude of coming to help the "poor, African people", rather than being open to learning from the Malawian hosts. As such, the teacher candidates did not acknowledge or express specific interest in what they could learn from the native Malawians they encountered or how our native hosts could contribute to a learning exchange. As participants gained more onsite field experience in the schools and while getting to know the staff at the Mtendere Children's Village, participants shifted in perspective toward two-way learning. Phillion, Malewski, Sharma, and Wong's (2009) study revealed two-way, interactive learning, "We thought we were coming here for ourselves; [instead,] they were teaching us how to be good teachers" (p. 333).

> Jamie, "There was a moment that we were staring at each other, but not in an unfriendly way...Dinner was delicious and it was great to sit around and get to know the group in a light-hearted fashion".
>
> June, "After I changed my ways of teaching, things went smoothly. I finally understand the teaching strategies of Malawi teachers".
>
> Melanie, "Co-teaching made things better because we worked together to understand".
>
> Beverly, "Working and planning [together] to see how we can best help these students is a great practice in learning how to take others' views that are different from my own and build on them to create a better experience overall".

After three and a half weeks, participants reflected on their experiences with warm feelings, even as they expressed their excitement about returning home to share what they learned.

> Beverly, "The people in Malawi have opened my heart and my mind in a way that will last forever".
>
> Melanie, "The experience I have gained in the classroom is one like no other. It is one that I will cherish but also ... bring so much back to my future classrooms like games and songs from these three weeks".
>
> Jill, "I will be excited to teach the songs that I have learned to my future classroom".
>
> Maribeth, "The nation as a whole has an ambitious reforestation agenda, which I am interested in following over the next few years. In some ways Malawi is way ahead of the US when it comes to discussion of climate change and taking action. If the country had the resources to implement their plans it would be revolutionary".

Participants indicated that this study abroad experience had a profound impact upon their thinking, particularly about how they relate to and perceive others (Cooper, 2017).

Melanie, "This journey has changed the way I look at life down to even the way I look at a situation or a person".

Lisa, "Even though I'll be going home, Malawi will always have a place in my heart. I will never forget the things I've learned and seen [and] all the wonderful, precious people I've met. This truly was a life-changing experience".

Limitations

There are several limitations to this study. The investigators learned that teacher candidates need to have targeted preparation before departure. In discussion among faculty, it was thought a two-week introduction of professional development to culture, language, and simulations of the Malawi living environment would support teacher candidates in a better understanding of what to expect when they arrive in-country. Faculty discussions informed what should be specific, international coaching to journal reflexively before departure, while in-country, and upon re-entry to the home country. These would aid students in more productive processing of disorienting experiences (Mikuleu, 2019) and aid in processing lived experiences abroad, both personally and professionally. Investigators are interested in the impact the program has on participants now teaching, or in some capacity working in servicing careers. More interviews or focus groups with the teacher candidates may inform researchers more comprehensively about the experiences of each teacher candidate's new ways of thinking, teaching, and working in service careers. This would have helped to support investigators in more ways to integrate pre-and post-departure discussions and reflections in a way that could further aid in processing teacher candidates' lived experiences abroad, again both personally and professionally.

Conclusion

The goals of the study abroad program were to (a) provide information about teacher candidates' awareness of cultural influences on education and learning, (b) increase students' emerging practitioner self-confidence, and (c) stimulate interest in cross-cultural and international education. The research questions of the study presented in this chapter confirmed what cultural and educational benefits participants believe they gained from the study abroad program experience and revealed what changes in their intercultural attitudes occurred during the study abroad experience. The Destination Malawi Outreach Education study abroad program provided experiences that would aid participants' perceptions of educational and cultural benefits while building their confidence and teacher knowledge. Consequently, these findings further support the notion that study abroad programs do promote intercultural, social, and language skills that help develop cultural awareness and sensitivity (Doyle et al., 2010). This study abroad program sought to help teacher candidates cultivate awareness and cultural sensitivity. Results of the study demonstrated how the teacher candidates adapted to situations, became resourceful, and persisted in the challenges they faced on a daily basis.

The investigators realized after the completion of the project, they would plan a second Destination Malawi program to better model cultural frameworks for experiences in self-efficacy, increased adaptability, and global awareness in teaching. The results of this study added further insight for program development. In future studies, the investigators will explore developing working relationships with other universities in the regions where a study abroad program is implemented. This would provide teacher candidates an opportunity to work with teacher candidates from in-country educational institutions to exchange and share teaching strategies. Finally, the investigators sought to refine the study abroad model to support teacher self-confidence, improve cross cultural experiences and contribute to professional development through "funds of knowledge", (González, Moll, Amanti, 2005) including cultural and family influence on education and learning. Results of this study have influenced the development of other teacher candidate study abroad programs carried out (in Malawi; Monteverde, Costa Rica; Seoul, Korea; and Oslo, Norway). Further research needed includes longitudinal study of teacher candidates' classroom beliefs and practices as informed by their study abroad experiences. As the investigators have pondered and rethought the study abroad programs, ensuring specific guidelines are in place to assist the teacher candidate goal-set is paramount. In so doing, the teacher candidates may be more likely to better understand their personal goals in relationship with cross-cultural experiences, and how this can lead to improved teaching and equity behaviors in the classroom (Walters, Garil, & Walters, 2009).

The 21st century schooling in the United States requires an alternative perspective to address the needs of culturally and linguistically diverse students in today's classrooms (Asia Society, 2008). Studying abroad can give teacher candidates the necessary experiences to do just that; it allows for developing and growing in ways that are near impossible when only studying in a relatively homogeneous environment in their home country. The participants learned a variety of skills, including being resourceful, utilizing materials more effectively, and motivating the village community students, teachers, and house mothers in a way that sharpens understanding and appreciation for preparing to teach in the United States. The results of this study on teacher candidates' study abroad experiences can be professionally informative for a larger learning community. This information is equally salient for teacher education programs and anyone involved in planning international field experiences for teachers and teacher candidates. Melanie, a teacher candidate [study participant], said it best, "This journey has changed the way I look at life, even the way I look at a situation or a person".

References

Age, L. (2011). Grounded theory methodology: Positivism, hermeneutics and pragmatism. *The Qualitative Report*, 16, 1599–1615.

Asia Society. (2008). *Going global: Preparing our students for an interconnected world*. New York, NY: Author.

Baptiste, H. P., Ryan, A., Araujo, B., & Duhon-Sells, R. (Eds.). (2015). Multicultural education: A renewed paradigm of transformation and call to action. San Francisco: Caddo Gap.

Cho, J., & Morris, M. W. (2015). Cultural study and problem-solving gains: Effects of study-abroad, openness, and choice. *Journal of Organization. Behavior*, 36, 944–966. doi. org/10.1002/job.2028

Cole, A. (March 21, 2012). The white-savior industrial complex. The Atlantic, https://www.theatlantic.com/international/archive/2012/03/the-white-savior-industrial-complex/254843/

Cooper, C. M. (2017). Transformation through disorientation: A narrative approach to perspective change in study-abroad contexts (Doctoral dissertation). Retrieved from ProQuest LLC. ED578447

Daniel, J., & Friedman, S. (November, 2005). Taking the next step: Preparing teachers to work with culturally and linguistically diverse children. *Young Children*. Retrieved from www.naecy.org/yc/pastissues/2005/november

DeVillar, R., & Jiang, B. (2012). From student teaching broad to teaching in the U.S. classroom: Effects of global experiences on local instructional practice. *Global Experience, Local Practice*, 39, 7–24.

Doyle, S., Gendall, P., Meyer, L., Hoek, J., McKenzie, L. & Loorparg, A. (2010). An investigation of factors associated with student participation study-abroad. *Journal of Studies International Education*, 14, 471–490. doi: 10.1177/1028315309336032

Giroux, H. A. (2010). Rethinking education as the practice of freedom: Paulo Freire and the promise of critical pedagogy. Policy Futures in Education, 8(6). https://www.wwwords.co.uk/PFIE

González, N., Moll, L. C., & Amanti, C. (Eds.) (2005). Funds of knowledge: Theorizing practices in households, communities, and classrooms. New York: Routledge.

Payne, E., Chapman, H., Daly, A. Darby, S., & Heft, M. (2019). Short-term study-abroad: The students' perspective on London 2019. *Athletic Training Education Journal*, 14, 269–274.

Guba, E., & Lincoln, Y. (1981). *Effective evaluation*. San Francisco, CA: Jossey-Bass.

Hendershot, K., & Sperandio, J. (2009). Study-abroad and development of global citizen identity and cosmopolitan ideals in undergraduates. *Current Issues in Comparative Education*, 12, 45–55.

Holmes, P., & O'Neill, G. (2012). Developing and evaluating intercultural competence: Ethnographies of intercultural encounters. *International Journal of Intercultural Relations*, 36, 707–718.

Jones, A. & Collier, R. (2019). Implementing and evaluating culturally responsive teaching for historical black colleges and universities through study-abroad programs. In L.O. Tripp & R. Collier (Eds.), *Culturally Responsive Teaching and Learning in Higher Education* (pp. 53–82). Hershey, PA: IGI Global.

Kim, Y. Y. (2001). *Becoming intercultural: An integrative theory of communication and cross-cultural adaptation*. Thousand Oaks, CA: Sage.

Kulkarni, S., & Hanley-Maxwell, C. (2015). Preservice teachers' student teaching experiences in East Africa. *Teacher Education Quarterly*, 42, 59–81.

Levine, K., & Garland, M. (2015). Summer study-abroad program as experiential learning: Examining similarities and differences in international communication. *Journal of International Students, 5*, 175–187.

Leung, A., Maddix, W., Galinsky, A., & Chiu, C. (2008). Multicultural experiences enhances creativity: The when and how. *American Psychologist. 63*, 169–181. https://doi.org/10.1037/0003-066X.63.3.169

Lokkesmoe, K., Kuchinke, K., & Ardichvili. A. (2016). Developing cross-cultural awareness through foreign immersion programs: Implications of university study-abroad research for global competency development. *European Journal of Training and Development, 40*, 155–170.

Machado, A. (2016). 4 ways Americans are taught the 'white savior complex' (and what we can do about it). Retrieved from https://matadornetwork.com/change/4-ways-americans-taught-white-savior-complex-can/

Mancini-Cross, C. Backman, K., & Baldwin, E. (2009). The Effect of the language barrier on intercultural communication: A case study of educational travel in Italy. *Journal of Teaching in Travel & Tourism. 9*, 104–123. doi.org/10.1080/15313220903042004

Matua, G. A., & Van Der Wal, D. M. (2015). Differentiating between descriptive and interpretive phenomenological research approaches. *Nurse Researcher. 22*, 22–27.

Mikuleu, E. (2019). Short term study-abroad for preservice teachers: Personal and Professional growth in Brighton, England. *International Journal for the Scholarship of Teaching*: 13(1), Article 1. doi.org/10.20429/ijsotl.2019.130111

Moustakas, C. (1994). *Phenomenological research methods.* Thousand Oaks, CA: Sage.

NAFSA, (2018). *Trends in U.S. study-abroad.* Retrieved from http://www.nafsa.org/Policy_and_Advocacy/Policy_Resources/Policy_Trends_and_Data/Trends_in_U_S_Study_Abroad/

Perry, L., Stoner, K., Stoner, L., Wadsworth, D., Page, R., & Tarrant, M. (2013). The importance of global citizenship to higher education: The role of short-term study-abroad. *British Journal of Education, Society & Behavioral Science, 3*, 184-194.

Phillion, J., Malewski, E.L., Sharma, S., & Wang, Y. (2009). Reimagining the curriculum: Future teachers and study-abroad. *Frontiers: The Interdisciplinary Journal of Study abroad, 18*, 323–339.

Powell, J. & Mendian, S. (2018). The problem of othering: Towards inclusiveness and belonging. In A. Grant-Thomas, R. Galloway-Popotas, S. Mendian, M. Omi (Eds.), *Othering and Belonging Expanding the Circle of Human Concern* (pp. 14–39). Berkley, CA: Haas Institute for a Fair and Incisive Society.

Ray, A., & Bowman, B. (2003). *Learning multicultural competence: Developing early childhood practitioners' effectiveness in working with children from culturally diverse communities.* Final report to the A.L. Mailman Family Foundation. Initiative on Race, Class, and Culture in Early Childhood. Chicago, IL: Erikson Institute.

Ripple Africa. (2020). General information about education in Malawi. Retrieved from: https://www.rippleafrica.org/ra_projects/more-info-education/

Robson, E. (2002). 'An Unbelievable Academic and Personal Experience': Issues around teaching undergraduate field courses in Africa. *Journal of Geography in Higher Education, 26*, 327–344.

Sipes, A. (2012). Reconstructing identity: Sociocultural and psychological factors affecting U.S. college students' re-entry adjustment after studying abroad in Africa. (Electronic Master's Thesis). Bowling Green, Ohio: Bowling Green State University. Retrieved from https://etd.ohiolink.edu/

Tarrant, M., Rubin, D., & Stoner, L. (2014). The effects of studying abroad and studying sustainability on students' global perspectives. *Frontiers: The Interdisciplinary Journal of Study-abroad. XXVI*, 68–82.

Trilokekar, R., & Kukar, P. (2011). Disorienting experiences during study-abroad: Reflections of pre-service teacher candidates. *Teaching and Teacher Education: An International Journal of Research and Studies, 27*(7), 1141–1150.

Tripp, L. O., Love, A. Thomas, C. M., & Russell, J. (2017). Teacher education advocacy for multiple perspectives & culturally sensitive teaching. In Thomas, U., (Ed.), *Advocacy in academia and the role of teacher preparation programs.* IGI Global Publisher: http://www.igiglobal.com/

Von Wendorff, F. (2013). *Top 5 Challenges of Studying Abroad.* Retrieved from: https://www.topuniversities.com/blog/top-5-challenges-studying-abroad

Ward, C., & Kennedy, A. (1993). Psychological and socio-cultural adjustment during cross-cultural transitions: A comparison of secondary students overseas and at home. *International Journal of Psychology, 28*, 129, 147, doi.org/10.1080/00207599308247181

Walters, S., Garil, B., & Walters, T. (2009). Learning globally, teaching locally incorporating International exchange and intercultural learning into pre-service teacher training. *Intercultural Education*, 20. Suppl S1-2 p. S151-S 158 2009.

Woolf, M. (2006). Come and see the poor people: The pursuit of exotica. *Frontiers: The Interdisciplinary Journal of Study-abroad, 13*, 135–146.

Zhou, Y., Jindal-Snape, D., Topping, D., & Todman, J. (2008). Theoretical models of culture shock and adaptation in international students in higher education. *Studies in Higher Education, 33*, 63-75. doi: 10.1080/03075070701794833

Zull, J. E. (2012). The brain, learning and study-abroad. In M. Vande Berg, R. M. Paige, & K. H. Lou (Eds.), *What our students are learning abroad, what they're not, and what we can do about it* (pp.162–187). Sterling, VA: Stylus.

11 Implementation of an Interprofessional Study Abroad Experience in Botswana for Special Educators and Speech-Language Pathologists

Amy J. Rose & Karena Cooper-Duffy

Introduction

Although some teacher education programs have begun to incorporate study abroad experiences and activities (Byker & Putnam, 2018; Gay, 2010; Olmedo & Harbon, 2010) into their pedagogy, there remains limited research on the impact of educator study abroad programs for current and future special educators and speech-language pathologists (SLPs). Educator study abroad programs typically provide opportunities for future professionals to spend just a few weeks in the summer exploring a country of interest, a semester abroad attending a college program, or an entire year in a discipline-specific experience.

It is recommended that short-term study abroad programs take place for three to four weeks to achieve the most commonly stated programmatic aim of fostering intercultural competence and/or skills to work with diverse students (Morley et al. 2019; Nguyen, 2017; Schenker, 2019). For students working on degrees that place them in the public or private school sector after graduation, a well-designed study abroad experience may have a substantial impact on future student/classroom success in an increasingly interconnected world. Three phases in a study abroad program are recommended and should include a pre-departure phase, an in-country phase, and a post-overseas phase (He et al., 2017; Paras et al., 2019). According to Morley et al. (2019), a thoroughly planned study abroad experience for future professionals should contain the following: (a) language/culture immersion or training activities, which align with the goal of fostering intercultural competence, (b) internship or student instruction opportunities to work with diverse populations, (c) hands on practice activities, (d) reflection on global knowledge and practical application of the experience in the life of the professional, and (e) cost effective ways to enable all students an opportunity to participate in a study abroad course. Students are encouraged to complete reflections about the experience throughout the three phases of the experience. In addition, study abroad courses need to be planned collaboratively with partners in the country where the study abroad course will take place.

Despite the significant literature on how to prepare for a quality study abroad experience, there is scarce research on experiences designed for professional graduate programs (Baecher, 2019). Even more limited is scholarly research on the study abroad experiences of current and future special educators and SLPs learning and working together. Preparing professionals from two disciplines to demonstrate interprofessional collaborative practices during a study abroad course can expand the literature on study abroad experiences. Additionally, teaching interprofessional collaboration practices within the study abroad course can facilitate the importance and application of cross-cultural collaboration with professionals across countries.

Special education teachers and SLPs regularly work together in educational settings with the common goal of increasing communication skills in children with language-learning disabilities (Archibald, 2017; Flynn & Power-deFur, 2013), however there are few to no interprofessional educational experiences to prepare them to work collaboratively with diverse populations upon graduation. There is a considerable need for these future professionals to appreciate the diversity of the children they will serve through experiences that focus on increasing intercultural awareness, knowledge, and sensitivity (Baecher, 2019; Gay, 2018; He et al., 2017). Baecher (2019) also notes that by engaging in these experiences, the future professional's ability to "understand, respect, engage with, and ultimately teach diverse cultural groups" will intensify. Study abroad programs can help provide interprofessional collaborative opportunities and effective experiences for both special educators and SLPs to learn to work with diverse populations.

Ethical standards in SLP and special education national associations and programs of study further support the need for increased cultural competence and linguistic competence. For example, the American Speech-Language-Hearing Association (2017) includes the following statement in their Issues in Ethics document:

> As the 21st century has moved forward, the ethnic, cultural, and linguistic makeup of the United States has been changing steadily. The different traditions, beliefs, and values present in the United States have created one of the most diverse societies in history. Audiologists, speech-language pathologists, and speech, language, and hearing scientists practicing in the 21st century must recognize the similarities among culturally diverse populations while respecting and acknowledging the important differences that make people distinct and that can affect service delivery, research, and professional/supervisory relationships. (p. 1)

Similarly, the National Education Association (NEA, 2019) answers the question "Why Cultural Competence?" by noting that American classrooms are becoming increasingly diverse and cultural competence is a key factor in enabling educators to be effective with students from cultures other than their own. This project focuses on current and future special education teachers and SLPs incorporating strategies and activities designed to increase cultural competence in the context of Interprofessional Education (IPE). The following three elements of cultural competence are addressed: (a) understanding of one's own cultural background and the ways that cultural background influences personal attitudes, values, and, beliefs; (b) understanding and knowledge of the worldviews of individuals from diverse cultural backgrounds; and (c) the use of culturally appropriate interventions (Hook et al., 2013).

An additional component of this project was a strong foundational and reciprocal relationship that has been established between the programs of Special Education and Communication Sciences and Disorders (CSD) at the university and the Department of Special Support Services (DSSS) in Botswana leading to a successful grant award for a four-week Fulbright-Hays Group Project Abroad (GPA).

Reciprocal Relationship between the University and Botswana

Botswana, officially the Republic of Botswana, is a land-locked country located in Southern Africa. Since gaining independence from Britain in 1966, Botswana has been striving to meet the educational needs of the nation and prepare students for the job market with over 800 primary schools. Their National Policy on Education states that the government is committed to the education of all children, including those with disabilities (Denbow et al., 2006; Government of Botswana, 1994). In 2013, the DSSS in Botswana completed a Project on Diagnostic Assessment of Learners with Special Needs (Department of Special Support Services, 2013). Several critical issues were identified impacting the quality of special education provision in Botswana, including 1) a wide gap between policy and practice; 2) persistently negative attitudes in schools and parents towards learners with special education needs; 3) school managers generally not informed about special education issues; 4) a belief that special needs learners should be taught separately; 5) limited continued professional development; 6) regional disparities in parental involvement, and, 7) the need for collaborative practices to be strengthened (Department of Special Support Services, 2013).

A partnership effort to address special education along with other areas of need in Botswana has been established between North Carolina (NC) and the Ministry of Basic Education in Botswana through the National Guard State Partnership Program (and more recently through the State's Department of Military and Veterans Affairs). In September of 2015, a Memorandum of Understanding (MoU) was signed between North Carolina and the Republic of Botswana with efforts to increase cultural awareness, understanding of shared values, and promotion of common interests through cooperation between various agencies along with sharing of human resources and expertise and providing the opportunity for professional, scholarly, and governmental staff exchanges.

The partnership between NC and the Republic of Botswana is further supported by the State Board of Education. Included in this partnership is a collaboration between the university and the DSSS under the Ministry of Basic Education in Botswana. This collaboration has included reciprocal visits by participants from each country. Specifically, activities have included an initial visit by one of the authors to Botswana in June of 2015, a visit from a Training Attaché with the Botswana Embassy to the university in September of 2015, a two-week international service-learning course for university students to Botswana in May of 2016, a presentation and meeting in the State's capitol regarding the State/Botswana bilateral partnership in January of 2017, and a two-week educational experience from a 14 member Botswana delegation which included teachers and administrators to NC in July of 2017. This partnership has a bi-directional relationship where educators from both countries have participated in study abroad experiences to learn about teaching students with disabilities.

Interprofessional Education

Interprofessional Education (IPE) is a priority of the project. IPE is a critical focus for current and future professionals in education as delivery of educational strategies for children with special needs requires a team-based and collaborative approach. While special education teachers and SLPs commonly work together as members of interprofessional teams in school settings, there is limited interaction and collaboration in pre-professional educational programs (Coufal & Scherz, 2016). Successful preparation and achievement of optimal performance outcomes requires programs to change from being solely "discipline-centered" to students and professionals demonstrating discipline-specific knowledge in interprofessional contexts (Coufal & Scherz, 2016). Flynn & Power-deFur (2013) stress that single-discipline perspectives cannot drive service delivery decisions; rather professionals must view students with disabilities in the context of the entire education system. This project provided an interprofessional and global context for practice and implementation of these collaborative models.

Fulbright-Hays GPA

The large individual costs of study abroad in general has historically meant that study abroad is more accessible to affluent students (Norton, 2008). To provide access to a quality study abroad course for four weeks for current and future professionals in special education and speech-language pathology, a Fulbright-Hays GPA grant was acquired. The Fulbright-Hays GPA program provides grants to support overseas projects in training, research, and curriculum development in modern foreign languages and area studies for teachers, students, and faculty engaged in a common endeavor. Projects may include short-term seminars, curriculum development, group research or study, or advanced intensive language programs (Fulbright-Hays Group Projects Abroad Program, 2019). Objectives for the Fulbright-Hays GPA included: (1) enhancing participants' knowledge of Botswana history, culture, and language; (2) developing participants' intercultural competence and cross-cultural communication skills; (3) strengthening the collaboration between Botswana and US teacher educators and teacher candidates; and (4) developing accessible curricular activities to enrich the integration of African culture and language instruction in K-12 area studies.

The project outlined in this chapter covers three phases: pre-departure phase, the in-country phase, and the post-overseas phase. Description of activities, assessment measures and results, discussion, and implications for practice are provided. The research questions included:

1 What is the effect of an educator study abroad program on enhancing participants' intercultural sensitivity?
2 What is the effect of an educator study abroad program on developing participants' intercultural knowledge and competence?
3 What is the effect of an educator study abroad program on developing Setswana language and communication skills?

Methods

Design

A mixed methods design was used for this research, including both quantitative and qualitative analysis. For quantitative analysis, a one-group pretest-posttest quasi-experimental design was used (Shadish et al., 2002). Quasi-experiments are most likely to be conducted in field settings in which random assignment is difficult or impossible. They are often conducted to evaluate the effectiveness of a treatment. In a pretest-posttest design, the dependent variable is measured once before the treatment is implemented and once after it is implemented. This design lacks a comparison or control group, and thus threats to internal validity are possible. Qualitative measures included weekly debriefing meetings with small group discussion, reflections expressed in individual participant daily blogs, and daily observations by project instructors during school visits, language and content seminars, and cultural site visits.

Participants

Current and Future Professionals

A total of 12 current and future professionals who support students with disabilities participated in all three phases of the project. There were two males and ten females. The average age of the participants was 38 with a range of 24 to 56. Seven of the participants were 31 years of age or over and five participants were 30 years of age or younger. Seven of the participants were first time international travelers. Six of the participants were professionals working in the public-school system, three were SLPs, and three were special education teachers. The remaining six participants were graduate students, three of the graduate students were pursuing a Master's degree in Communication and Science Disorders and three graduate students were pursuing a Master's degree in Special Education.

Instructors

There were three instructors who participated in the educator study abroad project, including the two authors. One instructor was a professor in the Communication Sciences and Disorders program and took the lead on collaborating with the Botswana partners and providing cultural content; the second instructor was a professor in the Special Education program and was responsible for data collection and supporting the teams; and the third instructor was a clinical supervisor and a speech-language pathologist who took care of day to day items such as financial management, problem solving, and travel arrangements.

Botswana Partners

The Director of the DSSS in Botswana provided oversight of the collaboration and assigned four professionals to accompany participants and facilitate the educator study abroad project in Botswana. The four professionals included a lecturer from Tonota College, the former director of the DSSS, a governmental SLP, and a behavior analyst who was also the President of Autism Botswana. The lecturer from Tonota College and the former director of DSSS engaged participants in both Setswana language classes and cultural content seminars. The governmental SLP facilitated all school visits and cultural activities. The behavior analyst coordinated workshops and worked alongside current and future professionals in classrooms.

Three Phases of the Project

Phase 1 - Eight Week Pre-Departure Instruction

The pre-departure phase provided students with information about the trip, culture, language and travel tips. There were eight pre-departure sessions (see Table 11.1), held once a week online using Blackboard®, a learning management system with a web conference tool known as Collaborate®. This online tool was used to allow the instructors and participants to see and talk with each other while showing their computer screens in real-time (http://www. blackboard.com/about-us/index.html). In this format, participants attended synchronous sessions with the course instructors.

Table 11.1 Pre-Departure Weekly Sessions

Weekly Session	Topic(s)	Activities
1	Introductions, syllabus review	Ice-breaker; syllabus and assignment review; group selection of cultural activities; travel reminders (e.g., travel insurance, vaccinations).
2	Fulbright-Hays GPA program; roles and responsibilities	Video-conferencing with President of Autism Botswana; overview and expectations of Fulbright-Hays GPA; Review of Roles and Responsibilities Agreement.
3	Botswana Partnership History	Reviewed the history of the Botswana/University partnership, laws and safety, and travel tips; LinguaFolio introduced with homework assigned; downloaded WhatsApp on phones for communication while in Botswana.
4	Linguafolio	Explored the LinguaFolio fact sheet, website and join codes; provided a LinguaFolio overview and participants registered; practiced uploading evidence in LinguaFolio, and downloaded LinguaFolio To Go on phones.
5	Intercultural sensitivity and 21st Century Skills	Participants registered for Smart Traveler Enrollment Program (https://step.state.gov/step/); cultural activities sign-up; review of cultural sensitivity standards; completion of intercultural survey and 21st Century Standards self-evaluation.
6	Botswana language, culture, history, and traditions	Continued discussion on 21st Century Skills and intercultural sensitivity; reviewed article on Botswana cultural considerations; reviewed James Denbow et al., 2006 book about the culture and customs of Botswana; practiced basic Setswana (tips on pronunciation, watched videos on Setswana Language).
7	Universal Design for Learning (UDL)	Overview of Universal Design for Learning principles; application strategies for final curriculum project for the course and techniques for working with students with disabilities.
8	Curriculum activities/ projects; team building	Overview of team building skills using a team effectiveness model with five stages of team development; read article on effective team practices; teams planned their goals, roles, process, communication strategies and evaluation. Continued to lay a foundation and structure for curriculum projects with each team responsible for developing accessible curricular activities integrating Botswana culture and language instruction in K-12 studies.

During each weekly session, the instructors provided participants with an agenda, written directions, reading materials, assignments, and video and web links. Meetings were video-recorded for later or repeat viewing.

Following the eight weekly online videoconferencing sessions, participants came to the university for a full day of predeparture workshops. Activities included continued team building, itinerary review, goal setting, and small group work on curriculum activity planning. Additionally, the Director of the university's International Programs and Services led a session addressing travel "nuts and bolts" and safety. A representative from Botswana joined by videoconferencing to share information about Botswana's language, culture, and educational system, and answered participant questions.

Participants were divided into four work teams with representation by current and future special education teachers and SLPs. Current and future SLPs served as language coaches to assist the group in highlighting similarities and differences in the English and Setswana language systems. Participants with special education experience assisted other participants in their group in integrating UDL principles in curriculum activity design to ensure that the activities would be accessible for all learners in K-12 school settings. Each working group set common goals, established group norms and peer support approaches, and made decisions about project timelines and implementation strategies consistent with the overall project design.

Phase 2 - Four Weeks' Study Abroad in Botswana

The in-country phase provided instruction to participants in four different Botswana cities; the capital city of Gaborone located in the southeast corner of Botswana, Francistown (a four-and-a-half-hour drive north from Gaborone), Kasane (a 6-hour drive northwest from Francistown), and Maun (a six-and-a-half-hour drive south and west from Kasane). Bus transportation was provided by the DSSS for travel to each city and for attendees at all activities. Participants, instructors, and Botswana partners stayed together in local hotels in each city.

There were four different structured activities implemented during the in-country phase: (a) work in eight different schools with students who have severe disabilities, and their teachers, (b) instruction in Setswana language and culture of Botswana, (c) daily experiences and exploration of cultural activities, and (d) culminating curriculum projects and presentation.

Work in Schools. School visits were the most significant part of this project as participants directly interacted with Botswana teachers and students to learn about the K-12 curriculum being implemented in Botswana schools. Participants visited eight schools across different geographic regions of Botswana: (a) Solomon Dihitsu Primary School, Gaborone; (b) Batlokwa National School, Tlokweng; (c) Ramotswa Centre for Deaf Education, Ramotswa; (d) Ledumang Primary School, Gaborone; (e) Camphill Community Trust, Otse; (f) Francistown Centre for Deaf Education, Francistown; (g) Maun Senior Secondary School, Maun; and (h) Moremi Primary School, Maun.

There were two schools for children who were deaf or hearing impaired and had intellectual disabilities, four schools with self-contained classes for students who had severe disabilities, one school with all students included in general education classes, and one private school for students with autism. While at each school, the participants were greeted by the administrators of the school with a traditional welcome ceremony that included formal introductions, tea, demonstration of the children's talents (e.g., dancing, selecting names for the guests, presentation of art created by the children), and a description of their school. Each team went to an assigned classroom where they observed a lesson, worked with a student with severe disabilities, and exchanged information with the classroom teacher. The participants had opportunities to ask the classroom teachers questions about the lesson they observed and the participants answered questions from the classroom teacher about strategies for working with students who have severe disabilities. The participants collected information about teaching materials, instruction strategies, and curriculum to use in creating their curriculum projects.

Content and Language Seminars. Participants engaged in six sessions (18 hours) of instruction. Setswana language classes included instruction in conversational Setswana, verbal and non-verbal communication strategies, and Setswana cultural norms. Participants learned functional phrases, correct pronunciation of sounds and words, and common grammatical patterns. They also learned when and how to use both formal and informal language.

Content specific seminars provided in-depth discussion on Botswana history, culture, traditions, and their connections with Botswana, including the development of the education system. Seminars on specialized education services provided a forum for cultural comparisons and ways to differentiate instruction for learners with various needs. Participants learned about the instructional practices and curriculum activities in K-12 settings that embrace Botswana's language system and culture.

The Setswana language classes and content seminars provided participants with more knowledge and ideas to integrate Botswana culture and language elements into the K-12 curriculum activity design for their curriculum development projects.

Daily Experiences and Exploration of Cultural Activities. Each day the participants had the opportunity to interact with the people of Botswana and to experience the information they learned about in the seminars and in the schools. Participants ate traditional meals, shopped in grocery stores, explored open markets, and navigated through everyday activities. Participants were encouraged to use the language they learned from the seminars and experience a day in the life in Botswana. Cultural site visits were selected for this program with the purpose of broadening participants' scope of knowledge of Botswana culture and traditions. Participants had the opportunity to learn about village life, including the Kgotla which is a public meeting, community council or traditional law court of a Botswana village. They also learned about ancient traditions, observed and engaged in traditional dance, and visited national parks and game reserves to learn about African wildlife.

During the first week of the in-country phase, participants remained in and around the capital city of Gaborone with a game drive and dinner at Mokolodi Nature Reserve, a day trip to Baharutse Cultural Village, a tour of the Three Chiefs statues, shopping and dinner at Main Mall in the city center, shopping and lunch at Botswanacraft, and several traditional meals at the Central Resource Center and local schools.

Visits to other regions were incorporated into the program in subsequent weeks. Participants visited Maun, the tourism capital of Botswana with a rural atmosphere along the banks of the Thamalakane River. Activities in Maun included game and boat drives in the Okavango Delta, Chief's Island, and Moremi Game Reserve. Participants also visited Francistown which is the second largest city in Botswana. A visit was made to Kasane which is close to Africa's "four corners" where the four countries of Botswana, Namibia, Zambia, and Zimbabwe meet. Activities in Kasane included a daytrip to Victoria Falls along with boat and game drives in Chobe National Park. These significant concepts were later used by the participants and teachers of Botswana to create lessons plans to be used in classrooms in the US and in Botswana.

Curriculum Projects. Each team completed a culminating K-12 curriculum project integrating Botswana culture and language elements at the end of the four weeks in Botswana (see Table 11.2). The participants worked on their projects with Botswana partners and classroom teachers from the eight different schools visited during the in-country phase. Project ideas and design arose from working in schools, attending content and language seminars, and engaging in daily experiences and exploration of cultural activities.

All finalized curriculum activities included a unit outline, activity descriptions, lesson plans, instructional materials, assessment measures, and supplementary materials and resources. Finalized curricular projects were presented by the four work teams at the Central Resource Center in Tlokweng with invitations sent to administrators, teacher educators, and teacher candidates in Botswana. Approximately 30 individuals attended the presentations, including the Ambassador and other representatives from the United States Embassy. After the presentations, participants had the opportunity to dialogue with the audience and receive further feedback to improve their curriculum activity design.

Phase 3 - Post-Overseas Phase (After Return to the United States)

The post-overseas phase provided students the opportunity to apply the study abroad experience to their profession. Upon return from Botswana, participants engaged in (a) continued curriculum activity development;

Table 11.2 Curriculum Projects

Components	Description of Activities with Links to Interprofessional Work and Team Building
Curriculum/classroom observations	Description of observations in the eight different Botswana schools that impacted the team's curriculum project ideas.
The curricular project	Project includes a plan of instruction of Setswana language, history, culture and/or traditions to be taught in K-12 class. The plan includes the use of differentiated instruction, 21st Century Standards, instructional practices, and curriculum used in Botswana. Specific cultural activities are included in the plan.
Elements of the curricular activities	Unit outline, lesson objectives, lesson plans, activity descriptions, assessment measures, materials, and instruction strategies.
Adaptations or strategies for culture, language, individual school and student needs	Emphasis is on literacy, language, and behavioral skills.
Collaboration with your team, teachers, assistants, and other Botswana professionals	Illustrate specific examples of collaborative experiences that informed the team's curricular project. Describe the team's interprofessional skills working within the team and with Botswana partners.
Other considerations identified presentation styles	Additional needs, ideas for future interaction/collaboration, etc.
	Provide a team presentation of the curriculum assignment at the end of the study abroad course. Present the content listed in the six items above.

(b) curriculum implementation; and (c) professional development presentations. These activities were designed to help participants internalize their learning from their experiences in Botswana and allow them to empower more educators to integrate Botswana language and culture into the K-12 curriculum. Additionally, an in-person debriefing session was held to talk with the participants about the impact of their experiences in Botswana. Each participant shared their feelings about the experiences they had that profoundly impacted them. Instructors discussed questions the participants had and explored ways to apply what they learned to their profession. Over the following three months the participants implemented the curriculum projects in the NC schools.

Quantitative Measures

Intercultural Sensitivity Survey

The Intercultural Sensitivity Survey was chosen to address the first research question on the effect of an educator study abroad program on enhancing participants' intercultural sensitivity. This measure has been used previously to assess the development of intercultural sensitivity in short-term study abroad programs and includes measures of global competency (substantive knowledge, perceptual understanding, and intercultural communication) as well as stages of intercultural sensitivity (denial, defense, minimization, acceptance, adaptation, and integration) (Olson & Kroeger, 2001). It consists of 48 questions self-rated using a 5-point Likert scale as well as several objective questions necessary for obtaining demographic information. Students rated themselves on each item as 1= Never Describes Me, 2= Seldom Describes Me, 3= Describes Me Some of the Time, 4=Describes Me Well, or 5=Describes Me Extremely Well. Each participant scanned the QR code from the instructor to access the survey. The survey was compiled and analyzed in Qualtrics. This survey was administered during Phases 1, 2, and 3.

Intercultural Knowledge and Competence Value Rubric

The Intercultural Knowledge and Competence Value rubric (Association of American Colleges and Universities, 2009) was chosen to address the second research question on the effect of an educator study abroad program on developing participants' intercultural knowledge and competence. This measure was developed by teams of faculty experts representing colleges and universities across the United States through a process that examined many existing campus rubrics and related documents for each learning outcome and incorporated additional feedback from faculty (Bennett, 2008). This rubric contains six indicators, **Knowledge**: cultural self-awareness, **Knowledge**: cultural worldview framework, **Skills**: empathy, **Skills**: verbal and nonverbal education, **Attitudes**: curiosity, and **Attitudes**: openness. Each indicator is rated with the following four performance criteria: 1= benchmark, 2 & 3= milestones, and 4= capstone. Faculty rated the participants on a scale of 1–4 as a comprehensive assessment at the end of the project using qualitative measures (e.g., individual daily blogs, weekly debriefing sessions, and direct observations).

Linguafolio

LinguaFolio is an online language learning portfolio that promotes autonomous learning through formative assessment (https://linguafolio.uoregon.edu/). This measure was used to address the third research question, the effect of an educator study abroad program on developing Setswana language and communication skills. This tool enables learners to set goals based on Can-Do Statements, track their progress toward accomplishing the statements, and upload work samples to showcase their abilities. Learners are enabled to truly understand the differing levels of language proficiency through examining and practicing the language functions embodied by the Can-Do Statements. They can create evidence to include in their portfolios on a regular basis to showcase their work, which helps them see how they are building the capacity to use the target language. Learners have a clear voice in tailoring their learning experiences to their own needs, wants, and interests (https://linguafolio.uoregon.edu/). Learners complete activities and set goals using three modules: Biography, Passport, and Dossier. Included in these modules are learning profiles and inventories, and self-assessment checklists to record proficiency levels and ongoing progress with language learning. LinguaFolio Online contains five sections for self-rating on Interpersonal Communication, Interpretive Listening, Interpretive Reading, Presentational Speaking, and Presentational Writing questions. Participants rated themselves on each item as (a) this is a goal, (b) can do with help, (c) can do, or (d) can do well during Phases 1, 2, and 3. The data was compiled and analyzed within LinguaFolio to determine the level of language mastery for each participant.

Qualitative Measures

Debriefing Meetings

Debriefing sessions were held weekly for approximately one hour each session during Phase 2 of the project with both whole and small group discussion. A final debriefing meeting was held upon return to the United States during Phase 3. Topics ranged from reflecting on activities, planning for school visits, airing frustrations and working through team dynamics.

Daily Blogs

All participants reflected on experiences through daily blogs. Participants were creative in designing their own blogs with formats including written journals, online applications, and web pages. Visuals were encouraged by instructors with photos shared daily through a WhatsApp group page.

Observations

Project instructors completed direct observations during school visits, language and content seminars, and daily activities. Instructors worked side-by-side with participants in classrooms and engaged in Setswana language learning. Participant feedback was provided daily during activities.

Results

In Figure 11.1, The Intercultural Sensitivity Survey data show the average scores for all 12 participants for each category, Phase 1 (pre-departure), Phase 2 (in-country), and Phase 3 (post-overseas), calculated for the study abroad course. This measure was selected because the variables relate strongly to interprofessional collaboration. The first six categories on the survey

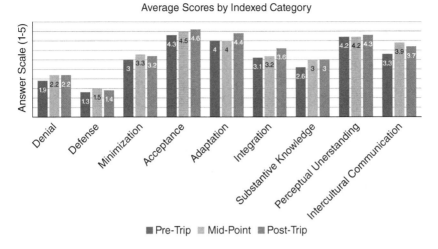

Figure 11.1 Participant average scores on the Intercultural Sensitivity Survey

represent the stages that an individual goes through to become culturally sensitive; from denial to integration. The greatest score increases from Phase 1 to Phase 3 were in the categories of acceptance (4.3 to 4.6), adaptation (4.0 to 4.4), and integration (3.1 to 3.6).

The next three categories on the survey are measures of global competency and include substantive knowledge, perceptual understanding, and intercultural communication. Growth was noted in all three areas with the greatest score increase in intercultural communication from Phase 1 to Phase 2 (3.3 to 3.9) with a slight decrease noted in Phase 3 (3.7). Substantive knowledge was the second area to show a score increase from Phase 1 to Phase 3 (2.6 to 3); and perceptual understanding had a slight increase (4.2 to 4.3).

In Figure 11.2, there were five questions in the survey that showed the greatest increase from Phase 1 to Phase 3. Three of these questions were in the intercultural communication domain:

- Question 41: *I have learned how to produce work with people from other places in the globe.*
- Question 43: *I have lived abroad and experienced intense interaction with a variety of people from this other culture.*
- Question 44: *I have long-term friendships with several people from other cultures.*

Question 18 was in the adaptation domain where participants were asked to rate themselves on *I have added to my own cultural skills new verbal and nonverbal communication skills that are appropriate in another culture.* Question 26 related to substantive knowledge with participants rating themselves on *I have substantive knowledge about at least one other culture outside the United States, and I apply this knowledge with confidence in my professional work.*

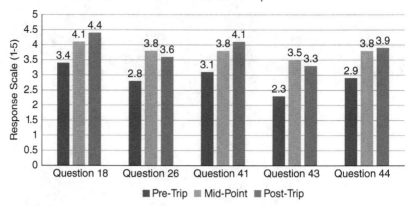

Figure 11.2 Top five questions from the Intercultural Sensitivity Survey with the greatest increase across probes

In Figure 11.3, scores from the Intercultural Knowledge and Competence Value Rubric are represented. This measure was completed by the three instructors in Phase 3 as a culminating assessment of each participant in the course and included review of qualitative measures noted above. Participant scores were variable with some participants scoring at the "benchmark" level and others at the "capstone" level. Previous international experience, chronological age, openness, and flexibility may have contributed to these

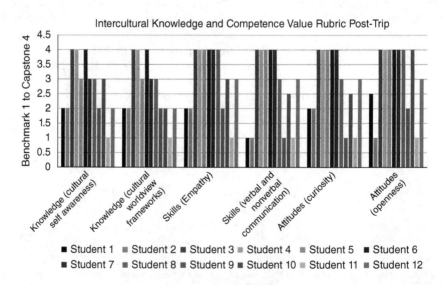

Figure 11.3 Post departure ratings per participant on the Intercultural Knowledge and Competence Value Rubric

results. Six out of the 12 participants demonstrated high scores for openness and empathy, followed by verbal and nonverbal communication, and curiosity. The individual scores for cultural self-awareness and cultural worldview frameworks were more variable.

All 12 participants completed self-evaluations using LinguaFolio. For Phase 1, all participants reported skills in the **Novice Low** for the five sections of Interpersonal Communication, Interpretive Listening, Interpretive Reading, Presentational Speaking, and Presentational Writing. For Phases 2 and 3, (the results were the same for both time points) with skills increasing into the **Novice Mid** and **Novice High levels of performance** on all five sections. In the Interpersonal Communication section, an example of a novice low question was "I can tell someone my name", a novice mid question was "I can talk about places I know", and a novice high question was "I can ask about and identify familiar things in a picture".

Discussion

Results obtained from qualitative and quantitative measures revealed growth across all research questions moving from Phase 1 to Phase 3 of the project, particularly in the adaptation and integration stages of intercultural sensitivity, intercultural communication, and increasing Setswana language and communication skills. Additionally, the collaboration between Botswana and United States teacher educators and teacher candidates during all three phases of the project was strengthened with team development of accessible curricular activities. For example, participants and teachers from Botswana created and maintained professional communications regarding instruction after Phase 3.

For intercultural sensitivity, participants reported the highest scores in the stages of acceptance and adaptation with growth also noted in integration during Phases 2 and 3. Acceptance is the stage where individuals recognize and appreciate patterns of cultural difference and embrace a deeper understanding of cultural differences. Adaptation is the next stage on the continuum where individuals shift cultural perspective and focus on learning adaptive strategies. Participant growth in the stages of acceptance and adaptation was further supported by generally high scores in "openness" and "empathy" on the Intercultural Knowledge and Competence Value Rubric. Integration is the final stage of intercultural sensitivity which is rare and difficult to achieve. This finding is also supported by the variable scores on the cultural self-awareness and worldview framework sections on the Intercultural Knowledge and Competence Value Rubric. Cushner et al. (2012) note that the integration stage requires "deep self-awareness and an individual being able to move in and out of their own worldview" (p. 165).

Unexpectedly, participants reported minimal growth in "perceptual understanding" on the Intercultural Sensitivity Survey. Perceptual understanding has been identified to include open-mindedness, resistance to stereotyping, complexity of thinking, and perspective consciousness (Olson and Kroeger, 2001). This finding may be due to participants already possessing many of these skills prior to departure or may be consistent with the variability in scores found on the Intercultural Knowledge and Competence Value Rubric with results displaying the uniqueness of each participant (i.e., differences in personalities, prior knowledge, learning styles, levels of independence, and background experiences). This was the first out-of-country experience for 7 out of the 12 participants and the first time to Africa for most of the participants. Morley et al. (2019) emphasized that programs can "inadvertently reinforce harmful stereotypes" which often occur when participants travel from the global north to global south (Morley et al., 2019, p. 5). Inequities, privilege, and power dynamics within educator study abroad programs need to be understood and reflected upon through all stages of planning and implementation.

All 12 participants reported growth in learning the Setswana language with "can do" statements changing from "this is a goal for me" to "I can do this" in categories of exchanging information, meeting personal needs, and expressing preferences. The ability to communicate in Setswana with children and teachers in the classroom setting and during activities in local communities helped make the program a success. Exposure to Botswana history and culture was interwoven throughout the experience with score increases on related questions on the Intercultural Sensitivity Survey and review of participant reflections.

Implications for Practice

Throughout the planning and execution of this project, the instructors noted several implications for practice. When providing study abroad experiences, it is important to provide a variety of experiences that include language seminars taught both at home and abroad, cultural content seminars taught both at home and abroad, experiential cultural opportunities, and time to communicate and spend with people from the host country. The richness and purposefulness of activities is significant in facilitating cultural competence and cross-cultural communication skills for future professionals (e.g., creating lessons for children to learn about Botswana).

The instructors found that providing pre-departure information, such as information about the Botswana culture and learning some key Setswana phrases proved helpful to participants. Additionally, creating opportunities for participants to interact directly with people from Botswana through a video platform was positively received. They could ask questions about what to wear, what to expect, how to greet others, and about specific needs experienced by children with autism and developmental disabilities along with their families and teachers. Clearly stating goals prior to leaving the country and revisiting these goals throughout the project activities in Botswana helped to keep participants focused and engaged. The instructors found that sharing the Bennett's Model of Intercultural Sensitivity stages during the pre-departure phase helped participants know what to expect while experiencing a new culture and being far away from the comforts of home.

Team building was a component of the project that was emphasized from the beginning to the end of the project. During Phase 1, teams were formed and participants worked on team building skills using a step by step team building process that included setting goals, assigning roles, outlining steps to reach goals, types of communication, and strategies to evaluate effectiveness. This process was referred to and expanded throughout Phase 2 as participants worked in teams to create curricular projects and activities and Botswana partners worked alongside team members to assist with creating curriculum projects. While this project incorporated interprofessional education with special educators and SLPs, and the assessment variables involved interprofessional collaboration, a specific interprofessional measurement tool was not utilized. Consideration for future interprofessional educator study abroad experiences should include a tool from the Interprofessional Education Collaborative Core Competencies which addresses Values/Ethics for Interprofessional Practice, Roles/Responsibilities, Interprofessional Communication, and Teams and Teamwork (Interprofessional Education Collaborative, 2016).

The instructors cannot overstate the importance of the partnership created with educators and administrators in the host country and the support provided by the grant. Many of the participants would not have had the opportunity for an international experience without grant funding. Partners in the host country took the lead in preparing for school visits, accommodations, transportation, meetings, and cultural activities. Additionally, several of our host country partners accompanied the group throughout the trip and assisted with navigating challenges that arose. This close partnership facilitated participant growth in cultural competence.

Conclusion

Educator study abroad programs are a high impact practice which should be increasingly employed by higher education programs, including programs in special education and speech-language pathology. Educators of children with disabilities have increasingly diverse population in their classrooms where development of cultural competence is critical. Intercultural sensitivity, knowledge, and competence can be strengthened through reciprocal partnerships with countries who share similar professional goals such as improving services for individuals with severe disabilities and autism. While the three phases of the project were a considerable time commitment for instructors, participants, and Botswana partners, results and feedback demonstrate considerable success and carryover into classrooms in both the United States and in Botswana. This experience also led to enduring relationships with ongoing collaboration and communication between the participants and Botswana partners which have a daily impact on learning for children with disabilities.

References

American Speech-Language-Hearing Association. (2017). *Issues in ethics: Cultural and linguistic competence.* Available from www.asha.org/Practice/ethics/Cultural-and-Linguistic-Competence/.

Archibald, L. M. (2017). SLP-educator classroom collaboration: A review to inform reason-based practice. *Autism & Developmental Language Impairments,* (2), 1–17. https://doi.org/10.1177/2396941516680369

Association of American Colleges and Universities (AAC&U). (2009). *The Intercultural Knowledge and Competence Value Rubric.* Retrieved from https://www.aacu.org/value/rubrics/intercultural-knowledge

Baecher, L. (2019). Study abroad in teacher education. *Global Education Review, 6*(3), 1–3.

Bennett, J. M. (2008). Transformative training: Designing programs for culture learning. In M. A. Moodian (Ed.), *Contemporary leadership and intercultural competence: Understanding and utilizing cultural diversity to build successful organizations* (pp. 95–110). Sage. https://doi.org/10.4135/9781452274942.n8

Byker, E. J., & Putnam, S. M. (2018). Catalyzing cultural and global competencies: Engaging preservice teachers in study abroad to expand agency of citizenship. *Journal of Studies in International Education, 23*(1), 1–22.

Coufal, K., & Scherz, J. (2016). *Interprofessional Education: Challenges to Preprofessional Programs in CSD.* Retrieved from American Speech-Language-Hearing Association (ASHA): http://www.asha.org/Academic/questions/Challenges-to-Preprofessional-Programs-in-CSD/

Cushner, K., McClelland, A., & Safford, P. (2012). *Human diversity in education: An intellectual approach.* McGraw Hill.

Denbow, J. R., Thebe, P. C., & Thebe, P. C. (2006). *Culture and customs of Botswana.* Greenwood Publishing Group.

Department of Special Support Services. (2013). *Project on Assessment of Learners with Special Needs.* Gaborone, Botswana

Flynn, P. F. & Power-deFur, L. (2013). Collaboration in the schools: Let the magic begin. *American Speech-Language and Hearing Association Annual Convention,* Chicago.

Government of Botswana. (1994). *The Revised National Policy on Education (Government Paper No. 2).* Gaborone, Botswana: Government Printer.

Fulbright-Hays Group Projects Abroad Program. (2019). Retrieved from https://www2.ed.gov/programs/iegpsgpa/index.html

Gay, G. (2010). *Culturally responsive teaching: Theory, research, and practice, 2nd edition.* Teachers College Press.

He, Y., Lundgren, K., & Pynes, P. (2017). Impact of short-term study abroad program: Inservice teachers' development of intercultural competence and pedagogical beliefs. *Teaching and Teacher Education, 66,* 147–157. https://doi.org/10.1016/j.tate.2017.04.012

Hook, J., Davis, D., Owen, J., Worthington Jr, E., & Utsey, S. (2013). Cultural humility: Measuring openness to culturally diverse clients. *Journal of Counseling Psychology, 60*(3), 353. https://doi.org/10.1037/a0032595

Interprofessional Education Collaborative. (2016). *Core competencies for interprofessional collaborative practice: 2016 update.* Washington, DC: Interprofessional Education Collaborative.

LinguaFolio® Online network. (2008). Retrieved 2018, from http://lfonetwork.uoregon.edu/learner-interculturality/, Site maintained by Center for Applied Second Language Studies (CASLS).

Morley, A, Braun, A., Rohrer, L., & Lamb, D. (2019). Study abroad for preservice teachers: A critical literature review with considerations for research and practice. *Global Education Review, 6*(3). 4–29.

National Education Association. (2019). *Why Cultural Competence?* Retrieved from https://www.nea.org/home/39783.htm

Nguyen, A. (2017). Intercultural competence in short-term study abroad. Frontiers: *The Interdisciplinary Journal of Study Abroad, 29*(2), 109–127. https://doi.org/10.36366/frontiers.v29i2.396

Norton, I. (2008). Changing the face of study abroad. *Chronicle of Higher Education, 55*(5), B12. Retrieved from http://www.chronicle.com/

Olson, C., & Kroeger, K. R. (2001). Global competency and intercultural sensitivity. *Journal of Studies in International Education, 5*(2), 116–137. https://doi.org/10.1177/102831530152003

Olmedo, I., & Harbon, L. (2010). Broadening our sights: Internationalizing teacher education for a global arena. *Teaching Education, 21*, 75–88. doi:10.1080/10476210903466992

Paras, A., Carignan, M., Brenner, A., Hardy, J., Malmgren, J., & Rathburn, M. (2019). Understanding how program factors influence intercultural learning in study abroad: The benefits of mixed-method analysis. *Frontiers: The Interdisciplinary Journal of Study Abroad, 31*(1).

Schenker, T. (2019). Fostering global competence through short-term study abroad. *Frontiers: The Interdisciplinary Journal of Study Abroad, 31*(2), 139–157. https://doi.org/10.36366/frontiers.v31i2.459

Shadish, W. R., Cook, T. D., & Campbell, D. T. (2002). *Experimental and quasi-experimental designs for generalized causal inference.* https://doi.org/10.1086/345281

"The contents of this chapter were developed under a grant from the Fulbright-Hays Group Projects Abroad (GPA), U.S. Department of Education. However, these contents do not necessarily represent the policy of the Department of Education, and you should not assume endorsement by the Federal Government."

12 Internationalizing Teacher Practice through the Arts

Exploring the Impact of a Drama-Infused Study Abroad Program

Carmel O'Sullivan & Linda Krakaur

Introduction

Learning throughout life takes on new meaning in the 21st century. Continuing education is framed as a process for people to return to education to successfully navigate novel situations in their personal and professional lives. As educators, we require intentional and ongoing professional development to support our work which often takes place in "unforgivingly complex" (Cochran-Smith, 2003, p. 4) professional spaces. Rapid societal and political changes have resulted in classrooms that are more racially and ethnically diverse, communities that are more economically stratified (Clark et al., 2020), and learners who are more consumed with technology than ever before (Kumar Saini & Goel, 2019). With the uncertainty of a changing socio-economic landscape and recognition that new paradigms are needed in society and schools, the arts have been framed as educational processes to help teachers and students apply reason, thought, action, creativity, and passion to their learning journeys. Greater access to arts education is presented as a means to help students both survive and thrive (Barton & Baguley, 2017). Dewey's *Art as Experience* (1934) has been re-examined to validate art education as an "incomparable organ of instruction", and to usher in renewed support for arts education (Jones & Risku, 2015, p. 78). Yet, orienting instruction toward such creative and interpretive goals requires a significant shift in how we as teachers conceive of ourselves, our learners and the curriculum. Transformational shifts in practice from educator as transmitter of knowledge to educator as creative and dialogical pedagogical expert requires professional development focused on a unique set of skills, knowledge, and dispositions (Teo, 2019).

In this chapter, we describe how we collaborated to internationalize a graduate program in teacher education with an arts-integration focus. Both institutions shared a common mission of globalizing teacher professional development (TFD), and an interest in implementing drama-based approaches as a transformative learning experience. Examples of arts-infused teacher education study abroad programs are relatively rare, and therefore we begin by presenting the theoretical landscape underpinning the program, positioning it as an area for further development within the wider study abroad literature.

We then explore the distinctive features of the model, discussing the mechanisms through which this innovative area of practice evolved. Finally, we consider its efficacy through feedback provided by participants.

Precedence for Arts Education

The UNESCO General Assembly recommended major shifts in teaching and learning at the precipice of the new millennium. The *International Appeal for the Promotion of Arts Education and Creativity at School* [1999] declared an urgent need to increase creativity and arts in schools to counter the adverse effects of globalization on adolescents and children (UNESCO, 2000). Framed within an agenda of peace, UNESCO (2000) prioritized the teaching of artistic values and subjects as a method to inspire greater creativity in learners, and as a by-product, greater hope in humanity. More recently, UNESCO (2019) highlighted the role of arts education and international cooperation to help build resilience and students' capacity to respond to future challenges. Given the weight of the economic, social and political impact of globalization, exchanging ideas and resources across traditional boundaries (e.g., disciplinary, governmental, transnational) is enthusiastically encouraged. In recognizing the power of arts education and intercultural dialogue to create new opportunities, UNESCO (2019) urges us to move forward in a "spirit of mutual assistance and concern" (p. 3) to improve the lives of diverse and vulnerable student populations.

Reflecting on how classrooms could be transformed during a time of great social and political upheaval at the turn of the 20th century, and armed with a desire to make education meaningful to children, arts education pioneers like Harriet Finlay-Johnson (1912) and Henry Caldwell Cook (1917) brought the playful, imaginative, and creative qualities of drama into their subject teaching to enable their students to experience the curriculum in what is now recognized as a form of embodied learning and cognition (Kemp & McConachie, 2019). This tradition has evolved, and today drama-infused pedagogic practices using the elements of make-believe, story, improvisation, and role-play are used to address complex challenges extant in society. As a kinesthetic mode of knowing, positioning teacher and students as agentic players in a shared learning process, drama in education addresses a common criticism globally: that school curricula may lack opportunities to link knowledge to real world contexts. Drama in education has recently been classified within the transformative end of the teacher professional development model (O'Keeffe, 2019) and as such, orients the study abroad program under discussion here.

Challenges to the Vision

Twenty years have passed since UNESCO first appealed to nations to bring greater creativity through arts education into classrooms. However, while creativity has been extensively studied from multiple perspectives, evidence of its impact on school practices has been slow to emerge (Regier & Savic, 2020). Regarded as central to students' career success, the perception that schools can 'kill' creativity is still widely held (Adobe, 2016; Hennessey, 2015). Confused epistemic beliefs about creativity can stem from teacher education programs (Katz-Buonincontro et al., 2020), and research suggests that over emphasis on standardized testing and highly structured curricula rather than problem solving, critical thinking, and collaboration impact instructional decision making (Rubenstein et al., 2018).

Students who have teachers that model flexible mindsets and risk-taking have long been recognized as more likely to develop these dispositions themselves (Wiggins, 1989). As such, teachers need to perform complex roles in classrooms to promote creativity, intellectual curiosity, and socioemotional well-being. Meaningful, challenging and enjoyable experiences can switch learners "on" to learning, but negative experiences can have detrimental effects, damaging curiosity and motivation, and limiting students' creative, imaginative, and entrepreneurial potential in later life. Arts rich environments create opportunities to develop students' concepts of self-awareness, social justice, deep conceptualization, consciousness, creativity, and imagination; pre-requisite skills for global curricular reform.

Like many nations, schools in the United States are facing an increase in vulnerable populations due to global economic and social forces. Simultaneously, greater competition and higher academic demands place additional pressures on teachers. Developing global learners who are curious about the world, able to communicate cross-culturally, and think creatively about relevant societal matters remains an elusive but critical goal. A narrowed educational agenda and intense oversight of teacher performance leaves little room for teacher ingenuity and instructional innovation. Globalizing the teaching framework is an important aim. Currently, some classrooms are led by teachers who start their careers with only superficial knowledge of the world (Longview Foundation, n.d.). Educators may not have received adequate preparation to create globally significant spaces where cross-cultural communication, problem-solving, creativity, and cultural competence are prioritized (Engel et al., 2020). Traditionally, teacher education has to a large extent been shaped and interwoven by nationally oriented agendas (Bodovski & Apostolescu, 2020; Leutwyler, 2017). Schools of Education are considered among the least internationalized programs on campus, with many pre-service teachers having limited interaction with international students and few opportunities to consider global influences and perspectives during their studies (Engel et al., 2020). Framing curriculum within an internationalist dimension requires major institutional and instructional shifts away from isolated knowledge toward global understandings, thereby facilitating a change in teachers' epistemology from an absolutist understanding of knowledge (as fixed and factual), to what Parkinson and Maggioni (2017) refer to as an evaluativist perspective (seeing knowledge as changing and contextual). Teachers in the former category are more likely to support teacher-centered pedagogical practices, while those who believe knowledge is constructed, interactive, and changeable tend to advocate greater learner autonomy, collaboration, facilitation of individual needs and difference, critical thinking, and experiential learning through the arts (Schraw et al., 2017). Teacher study abroad programs can challenge the negative impact of a standardization agenda in teacher education. The most innovative of such programs tend toward transformative learning experiences, fostering criticality, rational dialogue, inquiry-based learning, and critical reflection (Cranton, 2016). These characteristics underpin the drama-infused partnership study abroad program under discussion here.

Background to the Partnership

This partnership was initiated by Dr. Krakaur, who at the time was a doctoral student at a large public university on the East Coast of the United States. As a project assistant supporting a grant to improve teacher quality, she worked with faculty to design arts integration courses. Integrating the arts across the curriculum was identified as a method to both orient teacher instructional decision making toward the needs of the whole child, and provide enhanced learning opportunities for all students. Due to the positive impact of the grant on teacher performance, Dr. Krakaur and her colleagues proposed a new graduate program, *Teacher Leadership with a focus in Arts Integration*. The team developed a program of studies by using established courses in the College of Education (leadership, policy, research) and arts education (history and aesthetics). They partnered with The School of Theater, Dance and Performance Studies to offer electives in dance and music education. With no drama education courses available in the program, Dr. Krakaur initiated a partnership with the second institution.

Located in a large urban center in Ireland, the second institution offered a well-established M.Ed. program in drama in education designed to serve an international audience. Graduate students in the program, representing six continents, completed a year of study on site, or two (or more) years of summer study followed by research and practice at a home location. As a graduate of the M.Ed., Dr. Krakaur contacted her former master's dissertation supervisor, Prof. O'Sullivan, to determine if a partnership could be negotiated allowing a group of visiting scholars from the United States to attend the summer school component. Our two institutions were keen to collaborate based on shared interests to develop a new generation of skilled drama in education practitioners and to broaden opportunities to integrate critical international perspectives through experiential learning.

Dr. Krakaur worked through the university's Education Abroad Office to establish and promote a new study abroad program titled *International Perspectives in Drama and Learning*. Recruitment targeted graduate students from across the United States, in-service teachers, teaching artists, and other professionals who viewed drama as a potential medium to improve their practice. No more than six visiting scholars would be allowed to participate in the summer school in order to maintain a balanced and culturally rich learning opportunity at the host university. The first cohort included four participants (a professor, a special educator, and two drama education graduate students from other universities). This program ran for five summers, serving 25 participants.

Program Structure and Goals

As a blended learning, modular program designed to support distance learners and international students, the Drama in Education Summer School offered the flexibility and academic rigor necessary to serve the needs of both institutions. The diverse backgrounds of the visiting US participants fitted well within the program of the host institution which served K-12 through tertiary education, theater artists, youth leaders and facilitators, and others with a professional interest in the arts in education. Based on the assets of the host institution (i.e., subject-area expertise, academic resources, location, participant demographics) and the academic needs and characteristics of the visiting scholars, we developed the following goals for our study abroad program:

- develop teachers who can compare the imperatives for arts-based instructional practices within an international, national, and local context;
- foster best practices, so teachers can design and facilitate high quality drama in education experiences for students with diverse abilities and cultural backgrounds; and
- increase awareness and capacity to participate as global citizens in an international community.

Program Costs

The Education Abroad Office at the US institution collected student fees to pay for tuition, housing, insurance, and two performances. These fees were negotiated to make the program cost effective for participants while also accounting for the instructors at both universities. Housing costs were paid to a third university who offered dormitories in the city center close to campus. Dr. Krakaur stayed in the housing with participants, as did some of the international M.Ed. students. The US participants shopped for groceries, walked to campus, frequented local restaurants and shops, and took excursions whenever possible. They were encouraged to take advantage of the thriving city life.

In Preparation

Recognizing that study abroad programs can provide both an exciting but unsettling experience, we discussed ways to constructively explore cultural differences and varied academic traditions with the US participants before departure. These included the level and extent of criticality and analysis associated with the academic tradition in Europe, sociocommunication skills when interacting in an international context, and sensitivity around transnational identities. Dr. Krakaur prepared participants through advance course readings on drama in education and informal discussions regarding cultural norms and expectations in the host country. We also helped participants get their bearings when they arrived in Ireland by providing a preliminary orientation experience to help them acclimatize and settle into life in a different country.

Curriculum

On this program, we conceptualized drama as both an art form and as an effective learning, teaching, and assessment strategy in formal and nonformal educational settings. Participants were introduced to the philosophies underpinning this educational approach, its history, and to a wide range of drama, theater, and arts-infused techniques. Topics covered included the nature of the art form and key components in drama; arts infusion and arts integration; drama strategies and approaches to planning; applied theater; drama and second language learning; drama and special educational needs; drama and early childhood education; dramatic meaning and engagement; philosophy of the arts; theater in education, devising theater and physical theater; musical theater; critical pedagogy and embodied cognition; and the work of pioneers and playwrights such as Dorothy Heathcote, Gavin Bolton, Cecily O'Neill, David Davis, Jonathan Neelands, Augusto Boal, Edward Bond, Bertolt Brecht, Constantin Stanislavski, and key educational theorists such as Dewey, Freire, Giroux, Bourdieu, Bernstein, Bruner, Vygotsky, Bandura, Piaget, Kirkpatrick, Gardner, Erikson, Maslow, Kolb, Apple, among others.

Emphasis was placed on what Shulman (1986) describes as subject content knowledge, pedagogical content knowledge, and curricular knowledge. In this way, participants were introduced to the content of drama and theater in education and to ways of developing, using and adapting learning, teaching and assessment procedures and approaches in their own educational contexts.

Schedule

During the program the US participants became fully immersed in summer school. They participated in both weeks of intensive, hands-on workshops and discussions led by a team of international experts. They worked in collaboration with the host university's international cohort from 9.30 am to 5.30 pm, Monday through Friday, with twilight sessions taking place two evenings each week (6.30 pm–8.30 pm). Participants collaborated in small and large groups to explore and critically examine the course content while also finding opportunities to engage in relevant conversations around topics such as global educational trends, national politics, cultural values, and daily life. Both groups integrated during all aspects of the two weeks including cultural enrichment opportunities organized by the university and by students themselves. These included live theater, music and dance excursions, eating out, visiting cultural and historical sites, and socializing during free time.

Teaching and Learning

Much of the course content was new to the visiting participants. While arts integration is well established in the United States, drama in education presents a slightly new frame for exploration placing greater emphasis on teaching for understanding than teaching for performance. We both facilitated experiential and active learning strategies in the presentation of content at the host university as did other professors from the institution as well as a renowned figure in theater in education from England. The M.Ed. cohort and visiting scholars merged into one entity who experienced evidence-based, practice-focused workshops and seminars, interweaving theory and practice throughout.

Reflection and Assessment

To monitor the intellectual, cultural, and socioemotional growth of the US participants, Dr. Krakaur conducted daily check-ins and weekly discussions. As participants began to connect the pre-readings to the course content, they raised questions about how they might apply the philosophical and methodological imperatives of the program to the institutional realities of teaching and learning in the United States. Dr. Krakaur encouraged the group to problem solve together and with the M.Ed. cohort, provided examples from her own practice, and reminded them that they would have the opportunity to plan a drama integrated lesson as their summative assignment. During these discussions, the participants also noted common and disparate points of professional and personal experience that they identified within the larger collective of summer school students.

Methods to Assess the Impact of the Program

In order to assess the efficacy of this program, we designed a small-scale study. Data from all 25 participants' program evaluation forms, voluntarily and anonymously completed at the end of summer school each year (2013–2108) were included. Many opted to sign their form.

In addition, we invited the 25 participants to respond to a 12-item online survey in 2020 to elicit their retrospective opinions about this experience and its influence, if any, on their professional identities, range of pedagogical and arts-based practices, underlying beliefs and assumptions about teaching and learning in arts enriched settings, and wider global awareness. Ten completed the questionnaire in full, which included former participants from each cohort, excluding the one year Dr. Krakaur did not travel with the program.

Table 12.1 Participants in the Study

Professional status (while participating)	(N)	Characteristics
Graduate students	7	Arts integration
		Elementary education
		Dance education
		2 Drama education from other US universities
Teachers	13	2 to 30 years experience
		Elementary education
		Special education
		Arts education
		High school English
Teaching artists	3	Drama-based
Professor	1	Theatre
College administrator	1	Resident life

Respondents included three teacher education students (two now working as teachers), two experienced elementary and two experienced high school teachers, a well-established teaching artist, an associate professor of theater education, and a successful program management specialist (see Table 12.1). We received ethical approval to conduct the study from Trinity College Dublin.

Data were coded and analyzed thematically (Braun & Clarke, 2006), and the findings are presented below. Survey respondents identified three primary reasons for registering for the program: developing new teaching practices, expanding subject area knowledge, and studying in an international context. More than half also attributed graduate credits as a motivation.

Findings

Feedback from Participant Evaluation Forms

Eighty-eight percent (22) reported being "extremely satisfied" when asked about the quality of program content, relevance to practice, methodologies used in presenting, and quality of tutors' facilitation. One-hundred percent (25) noted that the program met or exceeded their expectations, citing that they would use elements of it in the future in terms of content/knowledge, methodologies/skills, materials/resources, approaches to assessment, and reflection/self-evaluation.

As teacher educators, we were excited to see several themes emerge relating to our program goals. The first was developing greater global awareness, which was encapsulated in one participant's comment of "Being with kindred spirits from all over the world". Participants spoke about the value of working in a creative, interactive, task-based manner, which highlighted the diversity of the group, including unexpected perspectives. While many felt prepared for cultural diversity, the US participants in particular expressed less readiness for more finely tuned differences in relation to education, ideology, belief structures, religion, social standing, modes of verbal and nonverbal communication, including cultural norms relating to eye contact and physical touch. Participants reflected that some lessons were learned the hard way through experiences countering generalized notions of cultural norms such as eating habits, politeness, deferring to others, and proximity of seating habits during group discussions. However, it was the degree of similarities between the two groups that appeared to most surprise US participants. Confirmation around the commonality of humanity emerged, with participants noting the "generosity of the group", "the depth of thought we reached," "the sense of togetherness and group dynamic" so quickly established, where "great friendships and bonds" were formed. As one participant put it, "Encountering more diverse worldviews made it challenging and intense, but we met great minds with new ideas! Really enjoyed the activity-based classes with a mix of music and drama, and the mix of nationalities". The international experience provoked one experienced teacher to reflect on her own identity and personality, challenging cultural homogenization when she remarked, "I am enjoying this course – I find it really empowering. I have been teaching for over 20 years and it gives me hope for the future, but I want to be understood by others as a separate, different American".

A second theme emerged in relation to participants' perceived ability to apply elements of Shulman's (1986) content, pedagogical content, and curricular knowledge in their work contexts. On completion of the program, participants expressed a degree of confidence in their ability to design and facilitate high quality drama in education experiences for students with diverse abilities and cultural backgrounds, noting for example, that "This course has given me enough knowledge to understand more and go deeper. I feel able to give much more to my students now". We return to this below when discussing the follow-up survey to ascertain whether participants had actually used what they learned. Many attributed the success of this arts-infused program to its sensorial nature as a form of embodied cognition: "My senses were involved, not just my mind," "Working through the arts was inspirational, a mind opening experience for me," "Mind blowing practices, opening the possibility of revealing my inner self as a teacher, … being objective about my practices through the drama tasks we did led to deeper understanding about what I do with the kids in my school". Almost a third told us that the "the in-depth theory explorations and the exercises that connected theory with the practice" were challenging and intense but effective in expanding their horizons and knowledge base as creative educators. As one participant said, "This experience activated all my senses. I came here wanting to know how to get administrators on board and I think I now know how. I've learnt more creative and fun ways to hook people into learning and that matters".

Other themes emerged in relation to the facilitation style and quality of tutors, and to the interactive, experiential and creative pedagogy, or what participants called the "living through" experience. However, the intensity of the program was identified as both a strength and a weakness, with several reporting extreme levels of tiredness and both mental and physical fatigue: "It's way too intense and I am really tired, but in a good sorta way," "I am tired and emotionally and physically drained and have to leave a day early but I don't want to miss any of the amazing stuff I have been doing!" Calls to extend the program for an additional week were counterbalanced by others who suggested that they would further digest and reflect on the experience over the months and year ahead. In order to explore whether this had happened, and to what extent, we invited all participants from between 2013–2018 to respond to a recently administered survey, and the results are shared below.

Impact Over Time on Instruction

All survey respondents (n = 10) stated that the program had positively impacted their instruction with a majority (8) indicating that it had a significant impact. Half noted that the reflective aspect shifted their perceptions of their roles as instructional leaders. One participant who was a graduate student at the time stated, "It made me think about instruction in a different way than what I had been taught in other education courses". One early-career elementary teacher stated that "learning new ways to approach not being a didactic teacher turned my perspective of what teaching looks like upside down. This course was the most transformative class I've ever taken as it finally showed me models and philosophies that made sense to how to connect with my 21st century students". Engaging in global conversations around the purpose of drama in education strongly influenced how participants viewed the classroom dynamics during this short study abroad experience. Practical experience of drama in education forms and conventions were also deemed to be of value by a majority of participants (7). "The application of drama for special education students was something I used in my classroom to reach some of my more difficult students". The experienced English teacher stated, "This course gave me the tools I needed to create more meaningful arts integrated lessons through process drama and drama in education strategies and techniques." Participation in the program also informed how non–school-based educators viewed education in general: "Though I don't directly teach in my current role, it changed the way I think about effective instruction and gave me a deeper understanding of just why the dramatic arts are so important". While a majority (7) stated that the summer school provided many new practices, tools, and techniques for them to utilize, three mentioned that they weren't able to use drama in education methods within their professional context. Administrative expectations for traditional teaching methods, an abundance of curriculum standards, and a lack of time were cited as factors that limited the use of drama in education methods.

Despite the differing educational and professional backgrounds of participants, the program appeared to stimulate critical reflection and support long-term growth as individuals who strive to support learners, although in varied capacities. As one graduate student stated, "this course was utterly eye-opening and life-changing. I do not teach an age group at the moment that would benefit most from Drama in Education (PreK), but the influences of the form are extremely significant and I hope to find a way to integrate them into my practice at some point in my career".

Impact Over Time on Professional Identity

Seven respondents stated that the course impacted how they viewed themselves as professionals, with three indicating that it had moderate to no impact on their professional identity. As one teaching artist stated, "I came in knowing that I believed in this work. That was just confirmed". While the program did not change their daily professional roles, all respondents mentioned the value of taking a "deep dive" into drama in education within an internationalist perspective, pointing to the impact of the course on their content knowledge and understanding of the field. Although these particular individuals did not experience a shift in their professional roles after the program, the experience had expanded their knowledge of "what is possible". Per the influence of being in an international context, several pointed to this aspect as the most important. "I had never worked with a group of international teachers before...that had such an impact on my perspective of my profession" stated the special education teacher. Another teacher commented, "going abroad gave me the opportunity to see a different culture than mine...I not only participated as a teacher and learner, but I became a part of a community which strengthened my identity and transferred into finding joy as a teacher and learner". Participants discovered not only what was possible, but what existed beyond the parameters of their own professional and personal experiences.

The study abroad program reinforced some participants' identities while also influencing others to modify their career aspirations. The theater professor, a member of the first group of scholars, explained that the program continues to impact her today: "This program affirmed my teaching philosophy while encouraging me to connect with other drama in education programs on a national and international level. I now have significant international contacts". The high school English teacher noted that the course provided the impetus to take on a greater leadership role:

> After this course, I pursued a graduate degree in Teacher Leadership, Policy, and Learning with a focus in Arts Integration. I became the Arts Integration Lead Teacher at my school (I still serve in this role) and I have led and participated in several professional development opportunities on the school and county levels based on my arts integration practice. I still refer back to resources from this program and the knowledge I gained while studying at TCD on a regular basis and I have recommended the program to several colleagues.

One graduate student decided to leave teaching altogether after her first year. Yet, inspired by the program, she returned to the host country to attend graduate school in museum education. One arts educator noted that "the course helped to alter my perception of education as a construct set forth by our policy writers…it showed me there was another answer worth looking for that will deeply affect students educationally and socially." He recently left public school in search of greater teacher autonomy in a small, private school.

Discussion

When assessed against Dwyer's (2004) claim that while "study abroad changes people's lives, little evidence exists to explain what kinds of tangible changes occur and for how long (p. 161)", the data in this small scale study are significant as respondents were enrolled between 2–7 years prior to the survey. This is long enough to determine if they had internalized the experience and applied it in their practice. While all respondents commented positively on the impact of study abroad in terms of increased cultural awareness and exposure, it is noteworthy that participants still remember the content and skills, more so than the excursion value of a study abroad program, which often emphasizes generic and transversal skills. Less emphasis was placed on marketing the experience as a holistic or cultural opportunity, and more on the integrated learning experience for visiting scholars. The data suggest that a content rich, intensive study abroad program in a stimulating academic environment had both short and longer-term impacts on these participants' professional identities as educators. Although the literature does not generally consider short experiences always rigorous enough (Sanger, 2019), respondents' experiences appear to support what Iqbal (2019) found in his study. His students reported greater gains in their personal, professional, and intercultural growth in a short program than in semester or year-long programs. In addition, while much is written about the impact of short-term faculty led programs (Interis et al., 2018), less attention is given to the impact of intensive programs led by tenured professors from the host institution, as occurred here. Having international peer role models (Brux & Fry, 2010) and international professors and tutors was noted as expanding the visiting scholars' intellectual and professional curiosities, which appears to have sustained and propelled several of them in their careers.

While the data are limited, there is evidence of critical reflection about transmission and skills-based models of education in contrast to multisensory and interactive learning environments. The novel intersection of drama in education with a study abroad opportunity facilitated lively and engaged critical reflection about professional assumptions and prior teaching experiences. Underpinned by Mezirow's (2012) conceptual framework of transformative adult learning, this partnership brought teachers from diverse and varied sociocultural and geographical backgrounds into a collective critical examination of value judgements, normative assumptions and expectations, prompting what Mezirow (1978) calls "a disorienting dilemma" (p. 7). Understood as the beginning phase of the transformative process, Mezirow (1991) refers to this disorientation as a process through which adult learners query and explore old meanings and perspectives which can be perceived as inadequate when faced with heightened awareness or new knowledge. In trying out new roles and experimenting with new perspectives through arts education, it appears that our participants entered the first phase of transformation of beliefs and assumptions during the summer school, with a degree of integration into some of these educators' frames of reference occurring over time. However, in emphasizing the value of the arts-based study abroad experience, located within a critical and creative internationalist perspective, respondents highlighted an unanticipated weakness in the program. It appears that while many of the participants were ready for change, their education system at home may not have been. This phenomenon was reported by many of our US participants and also by our M.Ed. students living and working in diverse global contexts, including Ireland. It highlights a much larger challenge for education systems worldwide.

Conclusion

With universities in the United States pledging to double participation levels in study abroad programs, the experience of our participants, while not generalizable, point toward an innovative and effective model which could be further developed, and adapted for use in other disciplines. Establishing a shared vision about the nature of drama-based TPD among both partners was a prerequisite to success, as was an explicit emphasis on experiential and creative intellectual engagement. We positioned teachers as creative pedagogical experts and reflective practitioners who could master arts-based instructional methods to meet the needs of learners from diverse backgrounds, abilities, cultures, and circumstances. This model of international cooperation framed global perspectives, transformative practices, and arts-based learning as methods to empower and prepare a new generation of life-long learners.

References

Adobe (2016). *State of create: 2016.* Retrieved from: https://www.adobe.com/content/dam/acom/en/max/pdfs/AdobeStateofCreate_2016_Report_Final.pdf [Accessed on June 5 2020]

Barton, G., & Baguley, M. (2017). *The Palgrave Handbook of Global Arts Education.* London: Palgrave Macmillan.

Bodovski, K., & Apostolescu, R. (2020). The pull and push forces in the internationalization of education in Russia. In L. Engel, C. Maxwell, & M. Yemimi (Eds). *The machinery of school internationalization in action: beyond the established boundaries* (pp. 88–102). New York: Routledge.

Braun, V., & Clarke, V. (2006). Using thematic analysis in psychology. *Qualitative Research in Psychology, 3,* 77–101.

Brux, J. M., & Fry, B. (2010). Multicultural students in study abroad: Their interests, their issues, and their constraints. *Journal of Studies in International Education*, *14*, 508–527.

Caldwell Cook, H. (1917). *The play way. An essay in educational method*. New York: Frederick A. Stokes Company.

Clark, H., Coll-Seck, A.M., Banerjee, A., Peterson, S., Dalglish, S., Ameratunga, S., Balabanova, D., Kishan Bhan, M. … de L Costello, A. (2020). A future for the world's children? A WHO–UNICEF–Lancet Commission. *The Lancet*, *395*(10224), 605–658.

Cochran-Smith, M. (2003). The unforgiving complexity of teaching: Avoiding simplicity in the age of accountability. *Journal of Teacher Education*, *54*(1), 3–5.

Cranton, P. (2016). *Understanding and promoting transformative learning: A guide to theory and practice* (3rd ed.). VA: Stylus Publishing.

Dewey, J. (1934). *Art as experience*. New York: Capricorn Books.

Dwyer, M.M. (2004). More Is better: The impact of study abroad program duration. *Frontiers: The Interdisciplinary Journal of Study Abroad*, *10*, 151-163.

Engel, L., Maxwell, C., & Yemimi, M. (2020) (Eds). *The machinery of school internationalisation in action: Beyond the established boundaries*. New York: Routledge.

Finlay-Johnson. H. (1912). *The dramatic method of teaching*. London, UK: Ginn and Company.

Hennessey, B.A. (2015). Reward, task motivation, creativity and teaching: Towards a cross-cultural examination. *Teachers College Record*, *117*(10), 10.

Interis, M.G., Rezek, J., Bloom, K., & Campbell, A. (2018). Assessing the value of short-term study abroad programs to students. *Applied Economics*, *50*(17), 1919-1933.

Iqbal, Z. (2019). Eastern promises fulfilled: The differential impact of marketing-focused short-term study abroad programs in India and Japan. *Frontiers: The Interdisciplinary Journal of Study Abroad*, *31*(2), 158-179.

Jones, A.G., & Risku, M.T. (2015). The butcher, the baker and the candlestick maker: John Dewey's philosophy of art experience saving twenty-first art education from limbo. *Education and Culture*, *31*(1), 77–87.

Katz-Buonincontro, J., Perignat, E., & Hass, R. (2020). Conflicted epistemic beliefs about teaching for creativity. *Thinking Skills and Creativity*, 36, doi.org/10.1016/j.tsc.2020.100651

Kemp, R., & McConachie, B. (2019). *The Routledge companion to theater, performance, and cognitive science*. New York: Routledge.

Kumar Saini, M., & Goel, N. (2019). How Smart Are Smart Classrooms? A Review of Smart Classroom Technologies. *ACM Comput. Surv.* *52*(6), doi.org/10.1145/3365757

Leutwyler, B., Popov, N., & Wolhuter, C. (2017). The internationalization of teacher education: Different contexts, similar challenges. *Bulgarian Comparative Education Society (BCES)*, *15*, 66–78.

Longview Foundation. (n.d.). *Internationalizing teacher preparation*. Retrieved from: https://longviewfdn.org/programs/internationalizing-teacher-prep/ [Accessed on Feb 28 2020.]

Mezirow, J. (1978). Perspective transformation. *Adult Education*, *28*(2), 100–110.

Mezirow, J. (1991). *Transformative dimensions of adult learning*. San Francisco, CA: Jossey-Bass.

Mezirow, J. (2012). Learning to think like an adult: Core concepts of transformation theory. In: E.W. Taylor, P. Cranton, & Associates (Eds.), *The Handbook of transformative learning: Theory, research and practice*. San Francisco, CA: Jossy-Bass.

Parkinson, M., & Maggioni, L. (2017). Changing preservice and in-service teachers' beliefs. The potential of course interventions to change pre-service teachers' epistemological beliefs. In: G. Schraw, J.L. Brownlee, L. Olafson, & M. Vanderveldt Brye, (Eds.), *Teachers' personal epistemologies: Evolving models for informing practice (Current Perspectives on Cognition, Learning and Instruction)*. Charlotte, NC: Information Age Publishing, 215–238.

O'Keeffe, L. (2019). *'Teaching an old dog new tricks!' The impact of a master in education in drama in education on teaching practices and beliefs*. Unpublished master's dissertation, Trinity College Dublin, Ireland.

Regier, P., & Savic, M. (2020). How teaching to foster mathematical creativity may impact student self-efficacy for proving. *The Journal of Mathematical Behavior, 57*, 1–18.

Rubenstein, L. D., Ridgley, L. M., Callan, G. L., Karami, S., & Ehlinger, J. (2018). How teachers perceive factors that influence creativity development: Applying a social cognitive theory perspective. *Teaching and Teacher Education, 70*, 100–110.

Sanger, J. (2019). *The power of international education. Impact analysis of IIE administered programs, 2005-2015*. New York, NY: Institute of International Education.

Schraw, G., Brownlee, J. L., Olafson, L., & Vanderveldt Brye, M. (2017). (Eds.) *Teachers' personal epistemologies: Evolving models for informing practice (Current perspectives on cognition, learning and instruction)*. Charlotte, NC: Information Age Publishing.

Shulman, L. S. (1986). Those who understand: Knowledge growth in teaching. *Educational Researcher, 15*(2), 4–14.

Teo, P. (2019). Teaching for the 21st century: A case for dialogic pedagogy. *Learning. Culture and Social Interaction, 21*, 170–178.

United Nations Educational, Scientific and Cultural Organization (UNESCO, 2000). *Records of the general conference, 30th session*. Paris, Fr. Resolutions, Volume 1.

United Nations Educational, Scientific and Cultural Organization (UNESCO, 2019). *Promoting awareness of arts education and the international arts education week: Draft resolution*. Retrieved from: https://unesdoc.unesco.org/ark:/48223/pf0000371470?-posInSet=6&queryId=1e9b548a-1291-43ec-84b6-eea4554fdd76 [Accessed on April 25th 2020]

Wiggins, G. (1989). The futility of trying to teach everything of importance. *Educational Leadership, 47*(3), 44–59.

13 "We Learned Together"

Amplifying the Impact of International Experience for Pre-Service Teachers through Cross Program Collaboration

Andrew Gilbert and Kathleen Ramos

Introduction

A critical component of teacher education in the United States is to prepare educators who embrace the idea that content learning and language and literacy development go hand-in-hand across grade levels and content areas (de Oliveira, 2016). This notion is especially important given the likelihood that all teachers will need to meet the needs of emergent bilingual children as the number of PK-12 English learners (ELs) continues to grow throughout the nation (Besterman et al., 2018). Since it is our premise that content and language integration is an essential component for preparing 21st century teachers, we designed a unique initiative to link pre-service teachers (PSTs) seeking licensure in the English for speakers of other languages (ESOL) program with those enrolled in a generalist elementary education (ELED) licensure program in an international context. The goal was to enact active, immersive learning experiences that supported content learning and fostered language and literacy development for the PSTs so they could transfer this knowledge to their own practice. We viewed this collaboration as important to teacher development given the professional reality that both ESOL and

We utilized an instrumental case study to investigate this innovative study abroad program. The cross-collaboration required that graduate-level PSTs design and implement a three-day inquiry-based science and language learning experience while abroad. PSTs were assigned to teaching teams that included at least one member from each program and those teams were assigned to a particular grade-level. In total, the PST teams offered the science and language experiences to how many bilingual (Spanish–English) children across grades K-7 in a Costa Rican school. We envisioned this collaborative program as a key innovation that blended the challenge and benefits of international teaching experiences with opportunities to collaborate in ways that will be expected in professional teaching roles. Developing teacher skills related to increasing integration and collaboration among elementary teaching teams can enhance student learning particularly for ELs (York-Barr et al., 2007).

ELED teachers ideally work together in a collaborative approach to meet the needs of emergent bilingual children. Collaboration also supports both content and ESOL pre-service teachers in viewing English learners through a strengths-based lens (Calderón et al., 2011).

This cross-program approach was especially novel in the context of study abroad teacher education programs and we were interested if PSTs from both programs gained insights into developing areas of their teaching practice. As such, the program was woven around the following key idea: collaboration between pre-service science and ESOL teachers in designing hands-on science learning while enhancing language and literacy development through engagement with science content. This chapter describes the approach and addresses the following research question: How did PSTs describe their experiences and insights regarding their engagement with this type of cross-program approach to study abroad in teacher education?

Theoretical Framework

This project brought future teachers into a new cultural context to teach science and language to Costa Rican children, therefore we utilized a theoretical framework steeped in culturally relevant pedagogy (Ladson-Billings, 1995). We envisioned culturally responsive pedagogy as the synergistic relationship between the home and school cultures of both children in Costa Rican classrooms and the PSTs enrolled in the experience. The reason for this theoretical position rested upon the notion that meaning-making must be constructed through dialog between and among social actors (Ladson-Billings, 1995). We were also guided by Gay (2018) who linked the importance of cultural understanding in building relevant community-based experiences where teachers view children according their strengths. This focus on pedagogy provided an essential lens for our team in order to connect the classroom with the surrounding community. These sociocultural positions framed how we intended to build student learning and facilitated future teachers in navigating home and school communities with children in a different culture.

Buxton et al. (2015) identified the connections between sociocultural theory and culturally relevant pedagogy in the context of emergent language learners in science stating,

> science curriculum and instruction must not only make stronger connections to their prior knowledge, but must also pay specific attention to building students' linguistic competence and comfort in using the academic language of science, including home language support (p. 25).

This complexity in regards to science learning with emergent bilingual children guided us in conceptualizing that in order for inquiry-based approaches to reach their potential, PSTs must understand the worldviews and experiences that inform student thinking. This theoretical position framed all aspects of this study as we collaborated across programs and across cultures to deliver a community science program for both PSTs and emergent bilingual children.

Integrating Inquiry-Based Science Learning with Language and Literacy Development

A wide body of literature addresses preparing teacher candidates to view learning content, and language and literacy development as interdependent (de Oliveira, 2016; Buxton et al. 2015; Shaw et al., 2014). Yet, many pre-service teachers receive minimal preparation for teaching content to ELs (Darling-Hammond, 2006). At the same time, when inquiry, language, and science content learning intersect, ELs' achievement in science grows (Lee et al., 2013; Shaw et al., 2014).

Integral to content learning and language and literacy development is student-to-student interaction (de Oliveira, 2016; Wright, 2016). Emergent bilingual children benefit from opportunities to make their thinking visible and use language actively to explore and express understanding with their peers (Heritage et al., 2015). Contextualizing learning around content aligns with the idea of hands-on, minds-on science learning (National Academies of Sciences, Engineering, & Medicine, 2017) and makes space for actively using language to learn content (de Oliveira & Lan, 2014).

Viewing Emergent Bilingual Children from a Strengths-Based Lens

Creating ample opportunities for emergent bilingual children to actively learn content through contextualized experiences while using language to read, write, speak, listen, and use multimodal expressions of understanding is a way for ELs' cultural, linguistic, and knowledge capitals to emerge naturally (Gibbons, 2015; Zwiers, 2014). For example, connecting inquiry-based science learning to ELs' experiential knowledge opens a space for making learning relevant, expanding existing understanding, and leveraging the first language (L1) as a tool for strengthening English language and literacy development (Echevarria et al., 2015; Heritage et al., 2015). Embracing the idea that emergent bilingual children's cultures, languages, and experiences are assets, rather than deficits, is a critical notion in teacher education, and fostering ample opportunities for talk during active learning unveils those strengths (de Oliveira, 2016; Walqui & Heritage, 2018; Wright, 2016).

Preparing Teacher Candidates for Teaching English Learners Through Study Abroad Experiences

It is important to create affordances for future educators to value other cultures and cultural practices during teacher education, and short-term study abroad experiences are one way to meet this goal (Cunningham, 2019). Study abroad provides opportunities for broadening global perspectives through interacting with diverse learners (Linder & McGaha, 2013), an increasingly critical piece of teacher education, especially given ever-growing numbers of culturally and linguistically diverse (CLD) learners in PK-12 US schools (Santoro & Major, 2012). Another benefit is the strengthening of both content and ESOL PSTs' readiness to design effective instruction for PK-12 ELs. Research suggests that content teachers need to enhance their skills in language and literacy instruction given that content learning cannot be only the responsibility of ESOL teachers who may lack content knowledge in academic disciplines (Lee et al., 2013) and conversely, content teachers lack knowledge of language development. Baecher and Jewkes (2014) suggested that teacher education programs under-prepare future teachers to work with ELL students. They found that by bringing together PSTs from early childhood and TESOL programs to engage in collaborative inquiry increased content confidence as well as enhanced the delivery of classroom pedagogy. This provides a lens for the power and benefits of collaboration by bringing together ELED and ESOL pre-service programs and represented the main reasoning for our program cross-collaboration.

Context for the Global Discovery Abroad Program

Vision and Process for the Global Discovery Experience

We were inspired by our university's commitment to global learning experiences and answered a university-wide call for proposals regarding study abroad programs that could be embedded within current course offerings. Upon being awarded a *Global Discovery Abroad* grant for 2018–2019, we designed our program to link the goals of two teacher education graduate courses *ELED 553 – Science Methods for the Elementary Classroom* and *EDCI 516—Bilingualism & Second Language Acquisition Research* through a global discovery experience in Costa Rica. The program included readings, a pre-departure orientation, delivery of an inquiry-based science learning and language enrichment program in Costa Rica, and two excursions to natural environments within Costa Rica after the school-based experience. The program grant included the cost of lodging, in-country transportation, most meals, materials, excursion fees, and faculty travel expenses. Students purchased their own airfare and some meals over the week-long program. The length of the experience was designed to fit George Mason University's embedded program structure that creates one- or two-week programs built into an existing course.

The authors modeled a co-teaching approach through our own activities as co-designers of the program by co-selecting and embedding readings and discussion opportunities linked to integrating science learning with language and literacy goals throughout both courses. We modeled our own collaboration as a science expert and a language specialist in order to encourage the

PSTs to value the way that their varied strengths, experiences, and knowledge would provide a strong teaching foundation in a team-teaching context.

The School Context

The St. Sebastian School (pseudonym) is a private, PK-12 international school in the suburban San José region of Costa Rica that serves approximately 350 Spanish–English bilingual learners. Instruction at St. Sebastian is mainly in Spanish, but there is a strong commitment toward fostering bilingualism and biliteracy in English across grade levels with the children having varied levels of English language and literacy strengths. Per the principal's suggestion, we planned the global discovery experience for the first week of December 2018, which followed the end of the Costa Rican school year and was the first week of their summer vacation, where interested students volunteered for the STEM/English language experience. This timeframe coincided with the final week of our university semester.

The connection between our university and St. Sebastian was forged a year prior, when the first author traveled with a delegation from a local school district to study teaching approaches in Costa Rican elementary schools across the San José region. The principal of St. Sebastian, an American working as an educator in Costa Rica for more than 20 years, reached out about the possibility of bringing PSTs to her school to provide additional English language opportunities for students. She promoted our program with parents as a three-day inquiry-based science and English language development summer enrichment program, arranged lunches for the teachers and children, observed and connected with the PSTs during teaching, and joined the group for a daily debriefing session each afternoon.

Collaborating to Bring Science and Language Learning to Life

We worked with the principal to generate a theme for the program that would be relevant and exciting for the bilingual children, choosing the theme *Caring for Water in Our Homes, Our Communities, and Our World.* This theme afforded opportunities for the PSTs to learn about the children's home and community water uses as well as their thinking and understanding of local concerns about water conservation. Together, we created a set of resources consisting of easy-to-implement, inquiry-based science experiments about properties of water that could be adapted across grade levels, as well as educational websites, videos, and children's literature around the theme of water conservation. Each day, we gathered in the school's science lab to walk through the hands-on science activities related to properties of water. For instance, we demonstrated counting how many drops of water can be placed on a coin before the water spills over the coin's edge and invited the PSTs to consider what could be learned about surface tension, the structure of water molecules and the nature of their bonding from this simple experiment. This initial activity provided a foundation for follow-up experiences such as dissolving candy canes in different temperatures of water as a means to engage children in thinking about solutions, an important notion when considering environmental issues related to protecting watersheds. We guided our PSTs to think about the conceptual science knowledge as well as about the many ways that attention to language could be integrated into the lessons. For example, we generated ideas for opportunities to use language to draw and label observations, create graphic organizers and bilingual dictionaries, use cognates to learn vocabulary (e.g., conservation and conservación), make hypotheses, articulate procedures, and share noticing and wonderings, to name a few. We discussed ways that the PSTs could invite students to make their thinking visible through extended opportunities to talk, including in L1 Spanish, as well as ways that drawing visual representations of their science learning could support talk, which could then support writing. We shared ideas for using word banks and cloze sentences and for being creative in generating ideas for multimodal representations of understanding.

Space does not permit a full description of all of the science and language learning activities that occurred over the three days. However, one of the more powerful happenings occurred when our PSTs came up with the idea to have a culminating project where student groups (across all grade levels) would offer public presentations regarding their ideas for protecting the water in their community. This event took place in the school gymnasium and represented a community celebration for the science and language engagement over the duration of the three-day enrichment experience. In the following sections, we provide a description for how we investigated PSTs' perceptions of this innovative integration of science and language experience as well as the resulting implications for study abroad possibilities with PSTs.

Methods

Participants

There were 15 PSTs who took part in the program with seven teacher candidates (call them this rather than students to avoid confusion) enrolled in EDCI 516 *Bilingualism & Second Language Acquisition Research* and eight students enrolled in the ELED 553 *Science Methods for the Elementary Classroom*. The second author constructed teaching teams based on grade-level preferences of the PSTs, placing them in teams of three across five student groups (two groups of K-1 and one group each of grades 2-3, 4-5, and 6-7). Each of the PST teams was given a curriculum map to provide a skeleton outline of possible approaches to fit the school-requested theme of exploring properties of water, water conservation and how water helps to meet the needs of their community. The students from ELED 553 were familiar with some of the approaches, as they had engaged with them in the methods course, but teams were encouraged to further develop and adjust activities based on the experiences in their Costa Rican classroom context. There was an overarching goal to connect the science content to the lives and experiences of the children's local context as well as to utilize language skills to articulate their ideas for addressing these issues in their own communities. We wanted our teaching teams to be creative about creating opportunities to actively use language as well as to expand or change the science approaches based on the needs and interests of children within their individual class groupings.

Study Design

We envisioned the approach of this qualitative study as an instrumental case study (Stake, 1995), which differs from the traditional approaches to case study research, because the questions of the researcher are at the center of the study as opposed to the primary goal of understanding the case itself. This method was chosen because we found ourselves in a condition where, "we have a research question, a puzzlement, a need for general understanding, and feel that we may get insight into the question by studying a particular case" (Stake, 1995, p. 3). We were primarily interested in understanding PST experiences and insights into the cross-program collaboration, where we treated the entire program as a single case.

Data Collection and Analysis

The data collected included observations of PSTs team teaching, PST journal entries, post-experience focus group and individual interviews. All interviews and focus groups were recorded and transcribed by the first author. In an effort to build credibility, data sets were subjected to multiple complete readings by both authors in which we generated a list of emergent themes, and then coded all data into those categories (Corbin & Strauss, 2015). The emergent themes from this analysis included: *positive experience, challenges, importance of collaboration,* and *international experience as reflective lens.* This chapter will focus solely on the importance of collaboration. The following section highlights the major findings from this process to synthesize the impacts and challenges of bringing collaborative content and language practices to fruition in an international context.

Findings

Facing Fears

The first challenge for us as directors of the program was that each of our PST groups expressed trepidation when it came to spanning the boundary between science and language teaching with bilingual children possessing varied language and literacy skills in English. In an effort to facilitate PST thinking, we provided a series of readings and facilitated discussions to help them consider key ideas related to teaching science and language in an integrated way. However, the PSTs expressed the worries that they carried with them into the experience as evidenced by ESOL PST Laurie (all participant names are pseudonyms):

> I think it was a little bit hard for me with not knowing the science beforehand and having to learn it the day before to really be able to expand on the ESOL part of it. So that part was hard for me.

We assumed that providing the curricular map and demonstrating and discussing science content and language usage opportunities through modeling the hands-on experiments would support the PSTs in integrating content learning and language development in their teaching. However, engaging with the science only the day before using it in the classroom impacted Laurie's ability to bring more substantial ESOL approaches to her team. Interestingly, ELED PSTs had similar fears of science content, despite university classroom engagement with the science activities, which were in addition to their language content concerns as evidenced by Connie:

> Even though I knew I would be challenged and thrown into it, I think the excitement and the passion just, I overcame that fear. There is still that fear of the unknown... So personally, between teaching science and teaching with the language difference, both were so unknown and uncomfortable that it was like accepting all of it as a new experience.

Thus, we learned that even after extensive content experience, ELED PSTs can often still carry content fears into the classroom, which is consistent with research regarding the preparation of elementary teachers (Gilbert & Byers, 2017). These worries linked to one of our hopes around collaboration—for the PSTs to notice that ESOL and science teachers need to work together to maximize learning with emergent bilingual children. Each group of PSTs carried anxieties into the experience but looked to one another for support, which seemed to lessen their worries as they faced the classroom teaching challenge at St. Sebastian. This was often on display each evening, when teaching teams would meet to refine plans for the following day. We would often witness cross-team interaction and collaboration to shore up ideas and content-related questions during these evening planning sessions.

Importance of Collaboration

One unexpected outcome from our program was how quickly relationships were forged across the PST teams. These began prior to arrival as some teaching teams discussed teaching and travel plans before leaving for Costa Rica. These collaborations accelerated on day one in Costa Rica as the PSTs participated in a school tour and shopped for workshop supplies. The first evening, the PST teams took the initiative to meet in the hotel cafe and work through their plans for the following day's activities, a gathering time that would continue throughout the duration of the project. This organic process reflected the heart of the collaborative efforts across the teams. Sierra, an ESOL PST who had yet to gain any classroom-based field experience and who was paired with ELED students who had already completed two semesters of school-based teaching experience, noted:

> So that really helped me because, at times I was like, oh I don't really know what to do because I've never actually been in a classroom, and lesson planning. So when we would come back from the school, we would sit down, and we would all work together. And so that helped me a lot. I mean they knew how to do different approaches, and how to get students' attention. So that helped me as well.

The PSTs seemed to view each other through the reflective lens of a more capable peer in terms of areas where they saw their own possibilities for growth. This was clear in Erin's reflection around working with ESOL PST, Marie, and shows the value she placed on language teaching skills in this context:

> I could have learned more from Marie throughout the experience...I could've maybe taken a step back and let her lead more...because she, for me, I felt like...I felt like those teachers were the most valuable...they had a different skill set than I did.

Marie's understanding of language-based content and pedagogy struck Erin as the "most valuable" skill set and reminded her of the value of what others bring to the table. This realization that science and language teachers can complement and learn from one another to enhance children's learning was a central one that we wanted our students to make.

There were multiple occasions where PSTs articulated the power of collaboration but also saw their individual role in building toward the classroom teaching goals. Olivia, an English–Spanish bilingual ESOL PST, highlighted how she saw her language-based pedagogy knowledge coming through as she described her role within the teaching group:

> But they understood the content much better, so I think for us coming with the language and trying to build that bridge with, for example, we did one of the Spanish-English dictionaries. That part of it, I think we had that to offer to bridge the language gap.

Olivia continued by describing her role as a bridge builder between content and language, supporting the children to make sense of the content through building Spanish to English language guides complete with sketches of the science phenomena. We found this type of insight to be a powerful reminder for us to encourage future teachers to recognize their own strengths while also noticing the critical importance of collaboration in meeting the needs of ELs in classroom instruction.

In the same conversation, Tina (ESOL) adds to Olivia's point, describing the impact on the children of constructing visual bilingual dictionaries, "That, of everything that we did, that experience really stuck with me because I could really see the students taking pride in that. And they were so happy that they could bring their first languages to the classroom". We are reminded of Lee et al.'s (2013) emphasis that language skills are gained when children engage with the language of science in the context of building scientific understandings through meaningful action. Additionally, this experience brought to life the importance of bringing students' first language into the classroom as a means to build both content understanding and language development (Garcia, 2017).

One of the key ideas that emerged from the experience was not just that collaboration reduced stress and anxiety through sharing the responsibilities for designing and implementing integrated content and language instruction. We found that the shared connection toward answering the challenge of teaching in this context was a driver to creating a meaningful experience in the study abroad context. As Connie (ELED) articulated:

> It's not just about the content. We learned together and it was an experience. It's something everyone involved will remember, and I think when you connect over content or curriculum and science, that's a shared experience. That's what brings it to life, I think.

Connie, who previously conveyed having to overcome substantial fears to join this study abroad program, clearly articulated the power of these connections by emphasizing, "We learned together and it was an experience" that "everyone involved will remember". The learning together model provided an organic space for building a respect for the knowledge that other teachers bring into the classroom and reinforcing the key notion that content and language learning truly go hand-in-hand. Most importantly, though, this notion of "shared experience" was what brought this program to "life" for Connie. This, again, points to the positive attributes associated with the innovation we introduced through the integration of our two programs to deliver the inquiry-based science and language enrichment experience with children.

Future Practice

Ultimately, seeing each other as more knowledgeable peers within their respective areas of science and language teaching seemed to quickly build trust across teams and simultaneously support the PSTs' confidence as teachers of content and language. We were also buoyed by the fact that this process was something that the PSTs envisioned would provide helpful skills in future teaching positions. As Tina noted,

> I was very scared of the content, just because in our program they teach us well how to address English language learning. But it was really nice to work with a fellow colleague because, often it is going to happen for us and we're going to be placed in a classroom with another teacher, so we're going to have to learn how to co-teach, how to work together.

Teacher education programs work tirelessly to find placements for students and often they get to work closely with a mentor teacher in the same subject area but do not often get to enact these types of cross-curricular and integrated co-teaching arrangements. Tina sees this as a clear benefit of this innovative team structure. Interestingly, she continued that working through these challenges in delivering the content and language lessons also helped her better understand the challenge her students face in the classroom:

> You get to have a sense of what your students back home must be feeling too, because now you're the visitor. You're the outsider and you have to adjust yourself to that situation, so it's always good to take those experiences back with you into schools here.

Reminding teachers of the discomfort of taking on new challenges helps them better understand the trepidation their future students might experience on a daily basis. Building empathy is essential for future teachers working with children, particularly when those children may be working to not only learn new content but also learning in a new language.

Discussion: Reflecting on Our Collaboration and Ways Forward

We started this project based on our shared intuition as teacher educators that combining language, science, and international teaching experience would provide a unique opportunity for the future teachers in both of our programs to grow professionally. We have articulated the ways that our global discovery abroad collaboration was positive for our students and led to powerful understandings about integrating science learning with language and literacy development with ELs in culturally responsive ways. For us as teacher educators, study abroad proved to be a productive space for modeling collaboration and affording elementary and ESOL educators with a meaningful way to practice real-world collaboration in an authentic and well-supported setting with emergent bilingual children.

At the same time, we recognized ways that we could strengthen the study abroad experience for our graduate students. One enhancement would be to bring the PSTs together more than once before the study abroad experience. Additional meetings would provide a space for the PSTs to generate ways to teach a science concept with emphasis on actively using language for content learning. In our context, making this interaction happen would have been challenging given that the EDCI 516 course was an asynchronous, online course, and that many of our students work during the day. Yet, we could take advantage of the affordances of technology to meet in an online space. Another change would be to create more opportunities for debriefing upon return (Santoro & Major, 2012), which could also take place in an online space.

To connect to emerging research around study abroad in teacher education, we could include more discussion around what our students could learn beyond teaching, and what they might notice about their own cultural selves as important for teaching culturally and linguistically diverse children. Cunningham (2019) noted the importance of promoting PSTs' capacity to be culturally responsive teachers during study abroad programs. She emphasized inviting participants in short-term study abroad experiences to reflect on their own cultural noticing and cultural responding capacities. She defines *cultural noticing* as "the cultural practices, values, and behaviors a group of individuals engage in within a particular social context" and *cultural responding* as "as actions a person takes or adapts as a result of cultural noticing" (p. 1264). We worked to build a sense for the abilities of ELs and the value of the surrounding communities as called for through the lens of culturally relevant pedagogy (Ladson-Billings, 1995) and culturally responsive teaching (Gay, 2018). However, in future programs we need to more sharply focus those efforts on PSTs own reflective journeys in terms of their cultural noticing. Integrating this emphasis into a study abroad experience would not be difficult and could open more spaces for exploring a salient aspect of teaching culturally and linguistically diverse children (Lindahl et al., 2020).

We are also intrigued by the idea of including service learning in the study abroad experience for teacher education students. Although applied to language education, Palpacuer et al. (2017) highlighted community-based service learning as an avenue for building intercultural competence and noticing the benefits of multilingualism and multiculturalism for PSTs. This idea connects with a recent review of the literature on community-based teacher education as a space for fostering culturally responsive teaching in teacher education programs (Yuan, 2018). It makes sense to us that exploring ways to include service learning within global community contexts could contribute to research around the ways that study abroad experiences may strengthen PSTs' preparation for teaching culturally and linguistically diverse children.

Conclusions

As STEM disciplines are an integral part of 21st century education, it is imperative that aspiring STEM educators are ready to be responsive to the needs of emergent bilingual children (Besterman et al., 2018). It was our desire to offer our ELED and ESOL PSTs a unique, collaborative opportunity to gain first-hand experience integrating content teaching with language and literacy development while immersed in another culture that inspired our innovative study abroad program. Often, one of the greatest hurdles to integrated practice are the institutional structures that govern how we deliver student experiences, such as the separation of preparing content teachers from the preparation for language and literacy educators. Working across these boundaries can offer exciting possibilities for strengthening faculty professional learning and provide powerful examples for future teachers to engage across the curriculum. This cross-curricular thinking provided PSTs with a more realistic vision for the classroom content challenges they will face as well as the relationships they will need to build in their future classrooms. We found that this innovative cross-curricular approach provided PSTs with reduced stress and anxiety since they could lean on their partner's expertise, which ultimately led to positive experiences for both PSTs and the children they served. We also recognized there exist areas of growth for future iterations of this global program as we navigated the challenges of running an embedded international program within a semester structure. These would mainly serve to expand pre-departure connections with participants, lengthen the program time in-country, and provide greater opportunities for post-travel debriefs. Despite these challenges and areas for possible growth, we are buoyed by the increased content confidence and connections the PSTs gained from this international experience that can be applied when teaching ELs in their future teaching. For these reasons, we invite others engaged in developing international teacher education experiences to consider the inclusion of cross program collaborations.

References

Baecher, L. & Jewkes, A. (2014). TESOL and Early Childhood collaborative inquiry: Joining forces and crossing boundaries. *Journal of Early Childhood Teacher Education*, *35*(1), 39-53.

Besterman, K.R., Ernst, J., & Williams, T.O. (2018). Developments in STEM educators' preparedness for English language learners in the United States. *Contemporary Issues in Educational Research*,*11*(4), 165-176. https://doi.org/10.19030/cier.v11i4.10211

Buxton, C., Salinas, A., Mahotiere, M., Lee, O., & Secada, W. (2015). Fourth-grade emergent bilingual learners' scientific reasoning complexity, controlled experiment practices, and content knowledge when discussing school, home, and play contexts. *Teachers College Record*, *117*(1), 1–36. https://www.scopus.com/record/display.uri?eid=2-s2.0-84922829929&origin=inward&txGid=250a0dfd9c167be13523114b-89f1cc69

Calderón, M., Slavin, R., & Sánchez, M. (2011). Effective instruction for English learners. *The Future of Children*, *21*(1), 103–127. http//:www.jstor.org/stable/41229013

Corbin, J., & Strauss, A. (2015) *Basics of qualitative research: Techniques and procedures for developing grounded theory* (4th ed.). Sage.

Cunningham, H. (2019). Responding to what we notice: International student teaching as a pathway to cultural responsiveness. *Urban Education*, *54*(9), 1262–1289. https://doi.org/10.1177/0042085919860569

Darling-Hammond, L. (2006). Securing the right to learn: Policy and practice for powerful teaching and learning. *Educational Researcher, 35*(7), 13–24. https://doi.org/10.3102/0013189X035007013

de Oliveira, L. (2016). A language-based approach to content instruction (LACI) for English language learners: Examples from two elementary teachers. *International Multilingual Research Journal, 10*(3), 217–231. https://doi.org/10.1080/19313152.2016.1185911

de Oliveira, L., & Lan, S. (2014). Writing science in an upper elementary classroom: A genre-based approach to teaching English language learners. *Journal of Second Language Writing, 25*, 23–39. https://doi.org/10.1016/j.jslw.2014.05.001

Echevarria, J., Frey, N., & Fisher, D. (2015). What it takes for English learners to succeed. *Educational Leadership.* http://www.ascd.org/publications/educational-leadership/mar15/vol72/num06/What-It-Takes-for-English-Learners-to-Succeed.aspx

Gay, G. (2018). *Culturally responsive teaching: Theory, research, and practice* (3rd ed.).Teachers College Press.

Garcia, O. (2017). Translanguaging in schools: Subiendo y bajando, bajando y subiendo as afterword. *Journal of Language, Identity & Education, 16*(4), 256–263. https://doi.org/10.1080/15348458.2017.1329657

Gibbons, P. (2015). *Scaffolding language scaffolding learning: Teaching English language learners in the mainstream classroom* (2nd ed). Heinemann.

Gilbert, A. & Byers, C. (2017). Wonder as a tool to engage preservice elementary teachers in science learning and teaching. *Science Education, 101*(6), 907–928. https://doi.org/10.1002/sce.21300

Heritage, M., Walqui, A., & Linquanti, R. (2015). *English language learners and the new standards: Developing language, content knowledge, and analytical practices in the classroom.* Harvard Education Press.

Ladson-Billings, G. (1995). Toward a theory of culturally relevant pedagogy. *American Education Research Journal, 32*(3), 465–491. https://doi.org/10.3102/00028312032003465

Lee, O., Quinn, H., & Valdés, G. (2013). Science and language for English language learners: Language demands and opportunities in relation to next generation science standards. *Educational Researcher, 42*(4), 423–433. https://doi.org/10.3102/0013189X13480524

Lindahl, K., Hansen-Thomas, H., Baecher, L. & Stewart, M. (2020). Study Abroad for Critical Multilingual Language Awareness Development in ESL and Bilingual Teacher Candidates. *The Electronic Journal for English as a Second Language, 23(4).* http://www.tesl-ej.org/pdf/ej92/a5.pdf

Linder, S., & McGaha, J. (2013). Building on successes: Reflections from two approaches to study abroad for undergraduate and graduate students, *The Educational Forum, 77*(3), 379–389. https://doi.org/10.1080/00131725.2013.792900

National Academies of Sciences, Engineering, and Medicine (2017). *Promoting the educational success of children and youth learning English: Promising futures.* The National Academies Press. https://doi.org/10.17226/24677

Palpacuer Lee, C., Curtis, J. H., & Curran, M. (2017). Shaping the vision for service-learning in language education. *Foreign Language Annals, 51*, 169–184. https://doi.org/10.1111/flan.12329

Santoro, N., & Major, J. (2012). Learning to be a culturally responsive teacher through international study trips: transformation or tourism?, *Teaching Education, 23*(3), 309–322. https://doi.org/10.1080/10476210.2012.685068

Shaw, J. M., Lyon, E. G., Stoddart, T., Mosqueda, E., & Menon, P. (2014). Improving science and literacy learning for English language learners: Evidence from a pre-service teacher preparation intervention. *Elementary Science Teacher Education, 25,* 621–643. https://doi.org/10.1007/s10972-013-9376-6

Stake, R. (1995). *The art of case-study research.* Sage.

Walqui, A., & Heritage, M. (2018). Meaningful classroom talk: Supporting English learners' oral language development. *American Educator, Fall,* 18-39. https://www.aft.org/ae/fall2018/walqui_heritage

Wright, W. (2016). Let them talk! *Educational Leadership, February,* 24–29. http://www.ascd.org/publications/educational-leadership/feb16/vol73/num05/Let-Them-Talk!.aspx

York-Barr, J., Ghere, G., & Sommerness, J. (2007). Collaborative teaching to increase ELL student learning: A three-year urban elementary case study. *Journal of Education for Students Placed at Risk, 12*(3), 301–335. https://doi.org/10.1080/10824660701601290

Yuan, H. (2018). Preparing teachers for diversity: A literature review and implications from community-based teacher education. *Higher Education Studies, 8*(1), 9–17. https://doi.org/10.5539/hes.v8n1p9

Zwiers, J. (2014). *Building academic language: Meeting Common Core Standards across disciplines.* (2nd ed.). Jossey-Bass.

14 From Problematic to Powerful

The Critical Role of Teacher Education Faculty During Teacher Study Abroad

Danielle M. Carrier

Introduction

What may we learn about international student teaching from the following comments made by a student teacher during an interview regarding her time in Ecuador?

SABINE: It was also interesting that we had to be there at 7:30, but school didn't start until 9 and school gets out at 2 and can't leave until 3:30, so it was like a solid three hours of like *nothing* [emphasis added].

INTERVIEWER: Uh hum….

SABINE: And then also their specials, which is another hour, so it's four hours out of your day that I was just sitting there and I'm like, I don't know. I just, it was weird.

What to make of all of this extra time Sabine (a pseudonym) had as a student teacher in Ecuador? Did she really just sit there for four hours a day when there was nothing to do? Did she think this extra time was bad and/or unproductive? What opportunities may Sabine have seen with so much unstructured time? Also, how are we to glean what may underlie Sabine's choice of the word "weird" to describe her observations of this extra time?

This chapter is my attempt as a novice teacher education researcher to analyze and provide multiple interpretations toward paradoxical aspects of my interview with Sabine. Based on my interpretations, I posit various design possibilities for teacher study abroad that may lead to developing intentionally conscious, critically minded teacher candidates (TCs). I also provide various examples of how teacher education faculty can conceptualize their role scaffolding TCs' learning through a trusting and authentic relationship aimed at TC (and faculty) transformation.

My analysis uses one interview transcript of one TC to allow for an indepth inquiry that unpacks, illuminates, and interprets my interview transcript as a literary and social text. Drawing on literary analysis, poststructural theory, and critical theory to make meaning of Sabine's international student teaching experience, my argument echoes Tobin (2000) in that there is no simple or unproblematic way to make sense of the meaning of interview transcripts.

I apply poststructural theories of Russian literary critic Mikhail Bakhtin (1981) to my analysis. According to Bakhtin (1981), Sabine and other TC attitudes are reflective of an entire community's ideological beliefs. Sabine, in Bakhtin's eyes, is thus representative of her society's ideologies and tensions. Later in the chapter, I posit possibilities for antiracist work that may translate to TCs' future teaching careers built on ideas of critical whiteness scholar, Robin DiAngelo (2018). As a former US and international elementary school teacher of 14 years and a doctoral student interested in the impact of education abroad within the context of teacher preparation, Sabine's interview helped me dig deeper into my curiosity around teacher study abroad. As one of four TCs I interviewed for a larger exploratory study, Sabine's insights helped me to better understand how international student teaching may affect TCs' conceptions of what it means to teach. In the next section, I provide background information about the program in which Sabine participated.

Background

Sabine was an undergraduate early childhood education TC in a Southeastern, US university-based teacher preparation program. She applied and was accepted to the Consortium for Overseas Student Teaching (COST) in Fall 2018. The COST program is a consortium of 16 colleges and universities in the United States that provides TCs with an international student teaching opportunity as an option for study abroad during their teacher preparation program. TCs who apply and are accepted to COST are placed at a public or private elementary, middle, or high school in various locations around the globe. TCs may choose their top four host country sites from around a dozen available countries. International student teaching placements range from 6–15 weeks after TCs have typically completed the first half of their student teaching semester in the United States. Most COST participants complete pertinent student teaching certification requirements (in accordance with TCs' specific university) prior to travel. For example, Sabine's university student teaching seminars and edTPA portfolio were completed before she departed for Ecuador.

Collaboration between the US university and Ecuadorian COST coordinators determined both Sabine's Ecuadorian host family and school placement at an International Baccalaureate (IB) PreK-12 private school. Pre- and post- departure meetings were conducted by the US COST coordinator to communicate travel logistics, aspects of culture, and to debrief lessons learned upon TCs' return to the United States.

The role teacher education faculty play in TCs' COST experience is generally limited.

US faculty supervise both TCs' US and international placements. When TCs arrive to their international placement, student teaching duties vary depending on the host country school and mentor teacher. Typically, host country schools receive TCs from more than one US college or university affiliated with COST, allowing the opportunity for US TCs to meet and form supportive relationships at the same host country school. During Sabine's time at the Ecuadorian private school, she met and became friends with TCs from other US universities affiliated with COST. At the end of the Ecuadorian student teaching experience, Sabine had fulfilled the early childhood education program requirements and was recommended for her state teaching certification. I interviewed Sabine about her student teaching experience in Ecuador the semester after she returned to the United States and was in process of completing her Master's degree.

Transforming Dominant Ideology

Sitting together at a local southeastern coffee shop one brisk February morning in 2019, Sabine excitedly shared about her student teaching experience in Ecuador. Possibly aided by the hot chocolate, our conversation generally felt pleasurable and easy. A bulk of the questions I asked Sabine, approved by the university's institutional review board (IRB), were in reference to what she perceived she gained as a result of student teaching in Ecuador. Sabine's answers reiterated many previous scholarly findings in this area of research: increased independence; increased self-confidence; exposure to different pedagogies; increased cultural awareness; and so on (see Cushner, 2007; Malewski & Phillion, 2009; Pence and Macgillivray, 2008; Stachowski & Brantmeier, 2002; Stachowski & Sparks, 2007). As it is well documented that study abroad in teacher education provides numerous benefits to TCs who engage in this type of experience, I also wondered, are there any negative impacts associated with TC study abroad? Can expanding one's perspective of the world through international travel in any way be harmful to a TC's growth?

Based on Sabine's interview transcript, I argue that there is risk inherent in teacher study abroad programs that if not thoughtfully planned, may inadvertently replicate TCs' dominant ideologies. Sabine, for instance, could be seen as representative of the approximately 80% white majority of US teachers (DiAngelo, 2018; Nasir et al., 2016; National Center for Education Statistics, 2017; Walters et al., 2009). Simultaneously, out of an abundance of caution toward essentializing Sabine's experience and perspective as representative of *all* white, middle-class teachers, I employ what Tobin (2000) describes as a *Bakhtinian interpretive approach* to my analysis of Sabine's interview transcript. According to Bakhtin (1981), Sabine's utterances may be seen as reflecting the *hybridity and heterogeneity* (what Bakhtin defines as the "heteroglossia") of voices and ideological positions present in our larger society. Take for example the following exchange:

SABINE: Sometimes they would do extra things like planning, like for later on. And like getting things ready. But it was nothing that I could do so I thought that was strange where I was like, gosh! I would text my friends who were also in the school and I'd be like, "Guys" heh, "We're not doing *anything* [emphasis added] right now".

INTERVIEWER: Wow. What did they say to you?

SABINE: They, yeah, they also weren't doing anything.

INTERVIEWER: So there wasn't any planned time of teachers meeting? Did they have to [plan] on their own?

SABINE: I think there would sometimes be planned time. But it wasn't every-day. And they were like, "Right now it's not crazy, we like these blocks of time when we have things to do". But when I was there, they didn't have so much to do.

What can we make of this claim that nothing was going on in these class-rooms and Sabine's above quoted statement that her day includes "three hours of nothing"? I suggest several possibilities. One is that Sabine is citing/repeat-ing a discourse she has overheard from the school's teachers, that they were being compelled by their principal to do meaningless busy work before and after the students were present. Or Sabine might be suggesting that this plan-ning time was meaningful for the Ecuadorian teachers, but not for her and her fellow US student teachers. Sabine's statement, "but it was nothing that I could do", can be read as double-voiced, a combination of her feeling she had nothing to contribute to planning and her Ecuadorian mentor teacher telling her, "There's nothing you can do".

Another interpretation of these statements is that they reflect Sabine's pro-jection onto her Ecuadorian classroom of US discourses around teacher plan-ning time. Her pre-service experiences in classes and field placements in the US may have exposed her to notions of teachers outside of their hours of instruction being busily engaged in such tasks as reading and grading student work, writing reports, meeting with parents and colleagues, and preparing the next day's lessons. Sabine may have heard her mentor teachers in the US complaining about the countless hours they spend working after school, in the evenings, and on weekends, leading to Sabine's puzzled utterances about her Ecuadorian host teacher who "didn't have so much to do". When I asked Sabine what she meant by the abundance of free planning time, she stated that she felt the Ecuadorian teachers did not seem stressed out. Sabine explained that it seemed the Ecuadorian teachers did not have the same amount of administrative tasks that she observed required of US teachers. Sabine clar-ified that the Ecuadorian teachers were typically working during planning time and she never had anything to do during that time, also noting a grade difference: Pre-K (Ecuadorian placement) and upper elementary grades (US placement).

Sabine's questioning of time usage thus reveals an authoritative US dis-course that Bakhtin (1981) would argue holds "the authority of religious dogma, or of acknowledged scientific truth or of a currently fashionable book" (pp. 342–343). Currently in the United States, teachers experience a frequent pressure to plan and teach highly scripted lessons around content that is intended to be measured by a high stakes standardized assessment (Nasir et al., 2016). Though scripted teaching provides an easy frame for US state agencies and administrators to track teaching and learning, the emphasis placed on teaching to the test has become an authoritative discourse with consequences. According to Carver-Thomas & Darling-Hammond (2017), 8% of US educators voluntarily leave the profession citing dissatisfaction around testing and accountability, unhappiness with school administration, and dissatisfaction with the teaching career.

Juxtaposing the US teacher accountability discourse with which Sabine is familiar to the new discourse Sabine encounters at her Ecuadorian school produces a dissonance in Sabine's conception of what it means to teach. Sabine comments later in the interview about aspects of her student teaching experience that she perceived as problematic:

SABINE: I mean there wasn't much teaching. You know, teaching teaching. I did get a lot of experience which when I look back I was like, oh, I was doing things. At the time, I just felt that I'm just sitting there.

INTERVIEWER: And what was your mentor, was she teaching during that time?

SABINE: She was always helping. I just felt like, you know sometimes the kids at my table knew what they were doing and I was just sitting there. It just didn't feel like what you think it should because when I did my first half of student teaching here [US] I was at the front of the classroom, like I did not sit down. But there [Ecuador], I'd pull up a chair and sit there.

INTERVIEWER: Do you prefer any way?

SABINE: Yeah, no, I would prefer I mean being with them. I don't know if I prefer being at the front.

The dissonance Sabine describes between "helping" and "teaching" positions "helping" as less desirable (Luttrell, 2013) and "teaching" as a commonsense act that deliberately and obviously controls classroom discourse. Her comments, "It just didn't feel like what you think [teaching] should" may stem from discourses Sabine carried with her from the US to Ecuador. By shifting student teaching contexts to Ecuador, Sabine experienced conflict and tension when encountering new discourses about teaching. Bakhtin's (1981) writings are helpful in this interpretation of Sabine's comments in thinking about his notion of an "ideological becoming" (p. 342). Put another way, Sabine's potential for developing new ways of viewing the world and systems of ideas are a part of her ideological becoming. Bakhtin writes that contexts containing a diversity of voices create exciting opportunities and possibilities for expanding one's worldview.

Faculty/supervisors at this important juncture in the study abroad experience play an essential role in guiding TCs through a cycle of critical reflection for transformative learning (Liu & Ball, 2019). Had Sabine's supervisor led Sabine through an examination of her assumptions and used this examination as a scaffold for Sabine's critical reflections in the Ecuadorian context, Sabine may have had the opportunity to deepen her ideological becoming. In lieu of face-to-face supervision, Sabine documented her experience in the Ecuadorian classroom through weekly written reflections. Sabine's reflections described day-to-day occurrences rather than deep, critical analyses of her background in relation to traveling from global north to global south. Her reflections were then electronically submitted to her US student teaching supervisor. Due to the way in which COST supervision was structured, Sabine was unable to engage in mutual dialogue in real time with her supervisor that may have helped her process some of the perplexing and insightful observations that she made.

Perhaps independently Sabine would have added the new Ecuadorian discourse of flexible time to her developing knowledge of teaching. However, it is not likely that exposure to new discourses alone will result in the transformative learning that would directly benefit Sabine and her future students. With scaffolded faculty dialogue that helps Sabine critically self-reflect with regard to the new and familiar discourses around time, Sabine's pedagogical tool kit is more likely to expand after deeply analyzing the potentialities of the new discourse she encounters.

The Case for Transformative Dialogue

Since Sabine's transcript serves as the foundation upon which I build my arguments, I run the risk of reading meanings into her words. Offering speculative interpretations in any study implies that researchers may project their own meanings onto their informants (Tobin, 2000). This issue applies not only to researchers, but to psychologists, teachers, and to interpersonal relationships in general. To understand another person, we use intuition, empathy, and imagination. To make meaning of another person's statements—spoken, written, or painted—we must read the statement not only to decode, but to also interpret. Making meaning of Sabine's utterances about her international student teaching experience therefore requires that I respond intuitively, imaginatively, and generously to her words. To do so is to treat Sabine's speech with the care, dignity, and benefit of the doubt we accord to artists, writers, and scholars. To make sense of Sabine's transcript, I have also read something of myself as a former international schoolteacher and participant in three study abroad programs—one as an undergraduate and two focused on teaching as a graduate student—along with years of teaching experience into Sabine's comments. I will never know exactly what Sabine feels and what she means, but I can listen empathetically, think about what she has said to me, and attempt to make sense of her words similar to processes used in literary studies and psychoanalytic interpretation. Take for example another excerpt from our interview:

INTERVIEWER: Seeing [differences between gender, race, and social class] did you look and reflect on anything differently here in the United States?

Or the same? Do you find [issues of race, gender, social class] similar there to here?

SABINE: Yeah. That's what happens in a lot of places unfortunately. And I just hated it because the kids weren't seeing diversity. And I'm like that's not how you should be growing up, but I mean most of my kids were from Ecuador and so there was one girl, her mom was from Mexico—light skin, blonde hair so it was very interesting cause I didn't realize that that's how it was there, I just figured everyone was darker skin, brown hair, brown eyes. I was like, "There's not a cultural divide there", but there is. Like a really big one. Venezuelans are also looked down upon there as well, because Venezuela is having so many political issues. They're fleeing to Ecuador. And so a lot of them don't have jobs which is like pretty much how it is with the United States and Mexico to where people will come here and sometimes, you know typically they get jobs I feel like, but yeah so it was a big, like cultural divide as well.

There are many perspectives shared in this section of the interview transcript that pertain to issues of race, class, and gender in an attempt to interrogate the ways in which these characteristics affect our lives. Along with discussing ideological content, referring to "the body of ideas reflecting the social needs and aspirations of an individual, group, class, or culture" (*American Heritage Dictionary*, 2000), Sabine broaches issues that in the US context remain typically tough to discuss. A dialogical engagement similar to Freire's (1970/1993) call to develop *conscientização*, or critical consciousness through naming, love, humility, faith in people, mutual trust, hope, and critical thinking is a perspective Sabine's supervisor, working within a more hands-on structure toward international supervision, could have taken. Acknowledging the complexity of individual personal histories and perspectives coupled with dialogue between "people who are attempting, together, to learn more than they know now" (Freire, 1970/1993, p. 71) creates the possibility for transformational learning.

Knowing Sabine did not have the opportunity to engage in critical dialogue with her university supervisor, I can only speculate as to what her words may mean. One interpretation toward the thoughts Sabine offers around diversity and culture is that she possesses a justice-oriented perspective, recognizing the importance of *everyone's* humanity (Belle, 2019). Her comment, "I just hated it because the kids weren't seeing diversity" reflects an understanding that physical differences are impactful to one's experience in the world. Her use of the words "unfortunately" and "cultural divide" speak to her knowledge that certain privileges are afforded to individuals or groups which possess lighter skin (DiAngelo, 2018).

Another interpretation some may find is that Sabine possesses a hierarchical, racist worldview. The tacit definition Sabine uses to define diversity— a group of individuals with different skin and hair color— implies that dark skin and hair is inferior. The mom Sabine describes from Mexico with light skin and blonde hair signifies the divide Sabine observes between light/dark. Sabine's binary identification serves as way of uncovering one side of a phenomenon that she valorizes juxtaposed to an opposing side that she constructs as inferior, i.e., light skin (valued)/dark skin (inferior). Sabine then uses Venezuela to elucidate Ecuador's cultural divide in that it's not just dark people that "are looked down upon", but also the Venezuelan refugees. Later on in the interview, Sabine comments in regards to the Venezuelan immigration issue that the problem "might be because I guess the people who are coming over are typically darker". From Sabine's observations, dark skin causes problems.

One last, though not exhaustive, Bakhtinian interpretation of Sabine's words is that she is repeating discourses from the United States that she's heard in her teacher preparation program, on the news, or in conversation with her friends and family. Her comment, "That's not how you should be growing up" may be a discourse Sabine heard in a teacher preparation program that is committed to social justice. When Sabine says, "it was very interesting cause I didn't realize that that's how it was there, I just figured everyone was darker skin, brown hair, brown eyes", she is surprised. As Sabine is fair-skinned with blonde hair, she assumes that traveling to Latin America means that she will encounter a culture with people that do not look like her. When most of Sabine's students in her Ecuadorian school have light skin, she questions the perceived "cultural divide" she assumes did not exist in Ecuador. Gleaned from everyday observations in Ecuador, Sabine encounters what Bakhtin (1981) terms "internal persuasiveness". As a discourse, internal persuasiveness is "denied all privilege, backed by no authority at all, and is frequently not even acknowledged in society" (p. 342). Sabine arrives at the crux of what she encounters as internally persuasive—the racial hierarchy she observes in Ecuador is wrong.

From Problematic to Powerful

Whatever the meaning regarding Sabine's observations of Ecuadorian culture, we see that study abroad in teacher education can have a variety of effects on its participants. My careful reading of Sabine's interview transcript uncovers the possibility that some of these effects may be negative. Take for instance, Sabine's stance on immigration.

INTERVIEWER: And that's in the signs?

SABINE: Yeah. It's if you're Ecuadorian, you get on this line, if you're not, this line. There were churches we'd go into and if you want to go in if you want to go to the top, you pay 10 cents if you're Ecuadorian. If you want to go to the top and you're not Ecuadorian, $2. It was just like, "Why?" Me and my friends were saying if we did that in the States, if we said, "If you don't have a US citizenship, you have to pay more".

INTERVIEWER: Could you imagine that?

SABINE: Oh my gosh it'd be insane, so I just wonder, you know I guess they just get by with it because first of all, typically, people don't think of Ecuador, like in the States, like people, I feel like people don't think like "Let's go down to Ecuador" so people don't *know* that and I think people from the States are the only people that would bring it up cause we're like, you know, "Everyone should be treated the same", which like yes, but like I feel like a lot of other countries do see that divide differently than we do. I guess [I don't know] I just thought it was really weird and like interesting [...] I think the only issue would be with Venezuela, if the Venezuelans start causing an issue, being like, "We deserve to stay here" or people in Ecuador start saying, "Oh they do deserve to stay here" and it becomes an issue between people there. I think what's happening here [in the US], it's an issue between our people, pretty much. Our citizens saying either people should be able to come in or people should not. I think they're [Ecuadorians] just not having an issue yet of so many people in their country having an issue [with immigrants].

INTERVIEWER: So can you see the issue here from multiple lenses because you've been there?

SABINE: Yeah, but it's also like I can't take a stance on it all the time where I'm like, I want to, I can see both sides though, like I get it.

Sabine waffles back and forth between perspectives, seemingly wanting to take a stance, but cannot. At one point Sabine begins with "Oh my gosh it'd be insane" to end her statement with, "I guess [I don't know] I just thought it was really weird and like interesting". The problematic aspect of Sabine's confusion is the absence of time and space during her study abroad experience to work through her paradoxical thoughts together with her supervisor. As I talked with Sabine, it was the first time she engaged in conversation around race, gender, and social class with a university affiliate in relation to student teaching abroad. Identifying and articulating (i.e., in Freirean terms, "naming") her observations is a first step toward engaging issues of social justice that have the potential to inspire learning beyond superficial, vicarious ways. A critical, scaffolded exploration of the assumptions Sabine may have brought with her to Ecuador directed by thoughtful, trusted study abroad faculty could help Sabine avoid a hardening of ideas or misconceptions through ongoing reflections and dialogue.

For example, Sabine's supervisor could provide Sabine with a series of critical reflection prompts while she is in Ecuador. One prompt could elicit Sabine's observations of Ecuadorian society. In a simultaneous prompt, Sabine could engage in a self-examination of her own experience in Ecuador. Using her thoughts from both prompts, Sabine could read, reflect, and weave together possible ties/connections she's making between her observations of and in Ecuador and the United States. In tandem with dialogue and support provided from trusted university faculty, Sabine's reflective writing can become a catalyst for faculty and Sabine (and potentially the other COST

TCs at the same school) to critically examine Sabine's thoughts in connection to Ecuador's larger socio-political context and that of the United States.

Absent the reflective writing and critical dialogue, we see some of the possible assumptions Sabine may possess. One of these assumptions is that Sabine may see me as representative of her university-based teacher preparation program and feels that she cannot be entirely truthful because her stance on political issues may not mirror mine. She says, "It's also like I can't take a stance on it all the time where I'm like, I want to, I can see both sides though, like I get it" after she tells me that she can see immigration issues from multiple lenses. Had the opportunity been built into Sabine's study abroad experience for a trusted relationship with university faculty replete with ongoing dialogue around complex societal issues, Sabine may have gained more confidence asserting a stance on immigration. However, in the attempt to build the trust and authenticity needed to inspire transformative learning, faculty must model this vulnerable process in order to move problematic moments to powerful potentialities.

Another assumption Sabine may have brought with her to Ecuador is encapsulated in the phrase "West knows best" (Zajda, 2015). When interpreting this part of the transcript through Bakhtinian interpretive analysis, one can see various Eurocentric discourses present in Sabine's life. Growing up in the Southeastern Unites States in a white, middle class family, Sabine was afforded opportunities to travel on mission trips to Honduras during summers. Sabine's mom was nervous when Sabine traveled to Honduras and Costa Rica because, as Sabine attributes, her mom noticed Sabine would typically return home ill with parasites and other sicknesses. Out of three other top host country choices— Ireland, the Netherlands, and New Zealand— Ecuador ranked last on Sabine's list. Had the worries and discourses her mother shared with Sabine filtered into Sabine's beliefs about desirable countries in which to student teach abroad? Taking up the Eurocentric discourse including her understanding of charging foreigners more money to visit cultural sites (not realizing that this "gringo tax" is intended to neutralize the inordinate spending power of foreigners to allow nationals the chance to afford their country's attractions) the discourses with which Sabine grew up may have heavily colored her sense-making of Ecuadorian society.

Possibilities for Antiracist Transformative Work

While not all study abroad programs in teacher education expose white TCs to non-white students, Sabine taught students that were racially different than her. Sabine's observation of race in Ecuador held the potential to help her identify her own racial privileges afforded in the United States. The following excerpt shares a few of Sabine's thoughts around race in the Ecuadorian context:

INTERVIEWER: …Did you notice any differences between gender, race, and social class?

SABINE: Yes.

INTERVIEWER: What did you notice?

SABINE: We talked about it.

INTERVIEWER: Really.

SABINE: Me and my friends who were there. We talked about it a lot because we're like, so all the kids there are light-skinned. So all of the families they come from are light-skinned. There's like a lot of them are *blonde* [emphasis added]. It's so interesting. And then most of all, the teachers are typically light-skinned, there's some that are a little darker-skinned. But not dark. But most of the people who worked there, like people who did cleaning up and kitchen work and things that were darker-skinned type jobs.

INTERVIEWER: Wow…

SABINE: And so it was very interesting. We were like, "That's not great". And we were talking, we don't ever think we saw a kid who was dark-skinned so there are black people in Ecuador. You, I did not see them at that school.

One way to interpret the transcript points to the words Sabine uses to describe race. Words such as "light-skinned", "blonde", "darker-skinned", "not dark", "darker-skinned type jobs", and "black people" uttered through Sabine's white frame may reinforce racial messages that position whites as superior (Feagin, 2013). Sabine inadvertently describes cleaning up and work in the kitchen as "darker-skinned type jobs", which out of context may sound racist in a simplistic understanding of the term: racists are people who dislike others because of their race (DiAngelo, 2018). Though Sabine is not race prejudice based on the context of our entire interview, the vocabulary she uses takes up connotations that reinforce racist ideology.

Another interpretation framed by Bakhtin's (1981) view is that the individual is a medium through which societal ideologies and tensions are expressed. As mentioned earlier, *heteroglossia* is present in many of Sabine's utterances. Sabine's talk of "darker-skinned jobs" referring to "people who did cleaning up and kitchen work" is a phenomenon of which DiAngelo (2018) writes in her book, *White Fragility: Why It's So Hard for White People to Talk About Racism*. DiAngelo (2018) explains that her white parents were more likely to receive a higher caliber of care than would people of color after years of gathering research demonstrating racial discrimination in health care:

> Conversely, *the people who cleaned my mother's hospital room, did the laundry, cooked and cleaned the cafeteria, and maintained the facilities* were most likely people of color. The very context in which I entered the world was organized hierarchically by race.
>
> (DiAngelo, 2018, p. 52, emphasis is mine)

It is apparent through DiAngelo's own personal story that Sabine is not alone in her construction of white-framed racial views. When translating white-framed views to teaching contexts, white US citizens rarely recognize that it is predominately white, middle class norms that structure most aspects of US schooling (Nasir et al., 2016). As a white student teaching supervisor working at a university with a predominantly white student population, it is critical that other white teacher education faculty and I learn to engage our TCs in deconstructing *race talk*. Termed and explicated by Toni Morrison (1993), *race talk* refers to "the explicit insertion into everyday life of racial signs and symbols that have no meaning other than positioning African Americans into the lowest level of the racial hierarchy" (p. 45). Our white TCs' racial language use may appear innocent; however, this is precisely why white teacher educators have a responsibility to dialogue about race with their TCs. Interrupting the forces of racism begins with unsettling the racial status quo, which Sabine was willing to engage by sharing her observations. Sabine quietly observed an Ecuadorian societal tension that may have been particularly difficult to discuss at her school in Ecuador due in part to the Ecuadorian state's legacy of making African descendants absent (Walsh & Salazar, 2015).

A first step toward facilitating a productive conversation around observed racial disparities in Ecuador, building off Sabine's willingness to engage issues of race, would be to affirm Sabine's perspective before faculty shares theirs (DiAngelo, 2018). Faculty could say, "Sabine I'm hearing that you've noticed a racial disparity in the enrollment of students in your school. You've noticed that this disparity is not good. I understand that perspective. I'm wondering if you've also thought about what you and I might assume about a school that does not have any black students? I can think through that with you and maybe together we can come up with some ideas". My acknowledgement of Sabine's observations and my willingness to work with her to dig deeper into her assumptions leads us to dialogue together about ways in which many school sites (for example, in Ecuador) may fail to see the many assets black students bring to school. We talk about the ways in which white supremacy tacitly structures "elite" schools, reasons why this might happen, and the reasons and ways Sabine may be able to challenge this status quo. Through research together, we learn that Afro-Ecuadorians were identified as "peoples" with collective rights just 12 years ago through the Constitution of Ecuador. We also learn of the ongoing challenges that Afro-Ecuadorian communities face (Walsh & Salazar, 2015). After this research, I engage in further dialogue with Sabine asking questions such as, "Knowing Afro-Ecuadorians have been systematically excluded and seeing the manifestations of this exclusion at play in your school, have you observed similar exclusionary practices in the United States?" If Sabine makes a connection to systematic racism in the United States, I could ask, "If your future class includes black students, can you think of ways you might include the perspectives of your future students and families into your teaching? How might including students' and families' voices into your teaching practice transform your teaching?"

As the answers to the preceding questions will vary, Yolanda Sealy-Ruiz (2020), founder and faculty sponsor of the *Racial Literacy Roundtable Series* at Columbia University Teachers College, suggests that faculty lead TCs on an "Archeology of the Self" as a way of engaging in personal reflection about racial beliefs. A helpful step in Dr. Sealy-Ruiz's "model of the Archeology of the Self" (Sealy-Ruiz, 2020) for faculty working with TCs is critical humility. Critical humility is achieved through further dialogue that, in my case, would help both Sabine and I acknowledge that we are not all-knowing beings, that issues of race live within us, and that understanding the limits of our own worldviews will eventually allow us identify and disrupt notions of white supremacy or Eurocentrism. In our imagined dialogue, I share some of my own missteps in upholding white supremacist structures that purposefully ignore the assets black students bring with them to school. I share experiences I've had working with people of color and their perspectives of white people discussing race. I acknowledge that my own continual antiracist work as a teacher educator to interrupt internalized superiority (DiAngelo, 2018) is tough and constant. I share through my own archeology of self (Acosta, 2019) that the deep excavation and exploration of my beliefs, biases, and ideas that have shaped me have also helped me realize my complicity in a white-supremacist-cis-hetero-ableist society (Carter-Andrews et al., 2019).

As was evident that Sabine knew the importance to become an antiracist teacher, another prompt faculty could ask to help Sabine clarify her beliefs is, "How may focusing on the various layers of your privileged and marginalized identities affect your work as a teacher? How may you rely on your self-work in your future classroom to control a troubling moment in the most positive and productive way?" Leading TCs to connect their lives to a contextual awareness of the historical forces that shape the particular communities in which TCs work, faculty can help TCs gain this critical skill for use in multiple teaching contexts.

Other probes faculty might use to engage TCs such as Sabine traveling from global north to global south include: "In what ways do you observe operations of power and oppression at the interpersonal, institutional, and structural level? How does your identity shape your understanding of your observations? How may the understanding of your observations change through the perspective of someone with multiple intersecting identities (i.e., the Venezuelan "immigrants" in Ecuador)? Why may it be important to engage in complex conversations about white supremacy and its manifestations in your international context?" What Sabine, or any TC engaged in teacher study abroad, should leave their host country deeply understanding is that *all* students of any race, gender, social class are deserving of a quality education that embraces who they are and the communities from which they come. Engaging in vulnerable, nuanced, tough dialogue around race, centered in a process of self-discovery, is one way to turn problematic observations during a study abroad experience into opportunities for powerful, transformational learning.

Final Thoughts

Through my multifaceted analysis of Sabine's experience in Ecuador, the reader may see aspects of study abroad in teacher education that may be problematic. Though Sabine's discourse is just one example out of many TCs that study abroad, her discourse illuminates the risk of faculty's failure to engage TCs in critical dialogue. Sabine frequently mentioned her efforts to engage in dialogue with her friends stating, "I would text my friends", "We talked about it", and "We talked about it a lot". Sabine's seeming preoccupation with communication gives us a glimpse into the role dialogue played in helping her cope and manage her experience in Ecuador. Building upon this desire for communication, teacher educators are well positioned to purposefully engage TCs in critical dialogue that leads to transformative learning. By helping TCs dig deeper into the discourses they bring with them abroad, faculty may help TCs (and themselves) engage in rich, critical learning that has the potential to disrupt hierarchical worldviews and the inequities perpetuated by them.

References

Acosta, A. (Host). (2019, October 15). Healing through the archeology of self with Dr. Yolanda Sealy-Ruiz (No. 1) [Audio podcast episode]. In NYC Healing Collective. https://soundcloud.com/nychealingcollective

American Heritage dictionary of the English language, fourth edition. (2000). Houghton Mifflin Company.

Bakhtin, M. M., & Holquist, M. (1981). *The dialogic imagination: Four essays.* University of Texas Press.

Belle, C. (2019). What is social justice education anyway? *Education Week (38)*19, pp. 18–19.

Carter-Andrews, D. J., Brown, T., Castillo, B. M., Jackson, D., Vellanki, V. (2019). Beyond damage-centered education: Humanizing pedagogy for teacher educators and preservice teachers. *Teachers College Record, 121*(4), p. 1–28.

Carver-Thomas, D. & Darling-Hammond, L. (2017). *Teacher turnover: Why it matters and what we can do about it.* Learning Policy Institute.

Cushner, K. (2007). The role of experience in the making of internationally-minded teachers. *Teacher Education Quarterly, 34*(1), 27–39.

DiAngelo, R. (2018). *White fragility: Why it's so hard for white people to talk about racism.* Beacon Press.

Feagin, J. (2013). *The white racial frame: Centuries of racial framing and counter-framing.* Routledge.

Freire, P. (1970/1993). *Pedagogy of the oppressed* (M.B. Ramos, Trans.; 20th anniversary ed.). Continuum. (Original work published 1970).

Liu, K. & Ball, A. F. (2019). Critical reflection and generativity: Toward a framework of transformative teacher education for diverse learners. *Review of Research in Education, 43*, 68-105.

Luttrell, W. (2013). Children's counter-narratives of care: Towards educational justice. *Children & Society, (27)*4, pp. 295-308. DOI:10.1111/chso.12033

Malewski, E., & Phillion, J. (2009). International field experiences: The impact of class, gender and race on the perceptions and experiences of preservice teachers. *Teaching and Teacher Education, 25*(1), 52–60.

Morrison, T. (1993, December 2). On the backs of blacks. *Time Magazine.* Retrieved from http://content.time.com/time/magazine/article/0,9171,979736,00.html

Nasir, N., Scott, J., Trujillo, T. & Hernández, L. (2016). The sociopolitical context of teaching. In D. Gitomer & C. Bell (Eds). *Handbook of research on teaching* (5th ed., pp. 349–390). American Educational Research Association.

National Center for Education Statistics, U.S. Department of Education. (2017). Elementary and secondary education. In *Digest of education statistics: 2017*(chap. 2). Retrieved from https://nces.ed.gov/programs/digest/d17/ch_2.asp

Pence, H. M., & Macgillivray, I. K. (2008). The impact of an international field experience on preservice teachers. *Teaching and Teacher Education, 24*(1), 14–25. doi:10.1016/j.tate.2007.01.003

Sealy-Ruiz, Y. (2020). *Arch of self, LLC.* Yolanda-Sealy-Ruiz. https://www.yolandasealeyruiz.com/

Stachowski, L. L. & Brantmeier, E. J. (2002). *Understanding self through the other: Changes in student teacher perceptions of home culture from immersion in Navajoland and overseas.* Paper presented at the Annual Meeting of the Association of Teacher Educators, Denver, Colorado.

Stachowski, L. L. & Sparks, T. (2007). Thirty years and 2,000 student teachers later: An overseas student teaching project that is popular, successful, and replicable. *Teacher Education Quarterly, 34*(1), 115–132.

Tobin, J. (2000). *"Good guys don't wear hats": Children's talk about the media.* Teachers College Press.

Walsh, C. & Salazar, J. G. (2015). (W)riting collective memory (de)spite state: Decolonial practices of existence in Ecuador. In J. C. Branche (Ed.), *Black writing, culture, and the state in Latin America* (p. 253–266). Vanderbilt University Press.

Walters, L. M., Garii, B., & Walters, T. (2009). Learning Globally, Teaching Locally: Incorporating International Exchange and Intercultural Learning into Pre-service Teacher Training. *Intercultural Education, 20*(sup1), S158. doi:10.1080/14675980903371050

Zajda, J. (2015). Globalisation and its impact on education and policy. In *Second International Handbook on Globalisation, Education and Policy Research* (pp. 105–125). Springer.

Section 3

Innovation in Teacher Study Abroad

15 Thinking Locally in a Global Context

Principles for Designing a Shared Community-Engaged Study Abroad Program

Zuzana Tomaš, Amie Van Horn-Gabel, and Silvija Marniković

Introduction

Study Abroad (SA) has long been considered a high impact practice in higher education, and specifically within teacher education where the ability to communicate across cultural divides is an essential competence teachers' draw upon daily. Despite its high impact, some scholars have raised concerns over the value of SA programs, especially short-term programs that are designed around visits to iconic landmarks with few authentic interactions with the locals (e.g., Douglas, 2015). At best, such delocalized SA programs perpetuate the superficial understanding of culture, and, at worst, they can help "create ghettos in which participants avoid interacting with the local culture and develop ethnocentric attitudes". (Boyer, 1994, p. 48).

In the ongoing debate over the necessary length of the SA sojourn, many argue that even relatively short programs can have a positive impact on participating teacher candidates, as long as they are localized in a community whose stakeholders are invested in interacting with the Study Abroad participants (e.g., Lindahl et al., 2020; Tarrant et al., 2014; Vatalaro et al., 2015). Additionally, short-term Community-Engaged Study Abroad (CESA) can also positively impact community stakeholders (Sherraden et al., 2013; Tomaš et al., 2020).

In this chapter, we make a case that community-engaged, service-learning pedagogy is an effective innovation for teacher education programs wishing to develop or improve their study abroad offerings. First, we provide an overview of what community-engaged learning means in the international context. We then discuss five key principles for designing a CESA program in TESOL, as well as illustrate how we developed and implemented this innovative, locally focused experience in Montenegro. Using qualitative research data described in a larger project (see Tomaš et. al., 2020), we highlight how focusing on the community at both the program and day-to-day activity levels, not only supported teacher candidates in thinking locally in global contexts, but further increased a sense of mutuality and allowed participating youth to explore personal agency.

Principles for Developing Community-Engaged Study Abroad Programs

Community-Engaged Learning (CEL) rests on the belief that collaborations between institutions of higher education and broader communities can foster mutually beneficial exchange of knowledge and resources, thus increasing participants' commitment to public good through active citizenship. Much like critical service-learning, CEL amplifies an asset-based view of communities and argues for a democratic distribution of agency and power in university-community partnerships. While many use the terms service-learning (SL) and CEL interchangeably, increasingly, CEL has been preferred over service-learning in an effort to avoid the problematic service-servee relationships implied in "service-learning" and to democratize contributions of collaborating partners (Haddix, 2015).

Regardless of terminology, we believe that CESA programs that genuinely recognize and leverage the partner capacity have the potential to positively impact the skill and identity development in participating in- and pre-service teachers while contributing to the growth of all involved stakeholders. With that, we are guided by our definition of a CESA program (see Tomaš, et al., 2020) that foregrounds the role of the host community in partnerships abroad, defining CESA as:

> ...a meaningful, reciprocal, structured international experience that expands the assets of both university and community-based participants and cultivates agency among collaborating partners. In such partnerships, both sets of participants work together to leverage resources and engage in developing, sharing, and critically reflecting on personal, academic, and/or professional experiences. This helps to expand participants' awareness of intercultural and social justice issues which, in turn, fosters a shared communal yet global mindset. The main purpose of SLSA is to help create authentic, synergistic spaces wherein program goals are collectively pursued in ways that honor and privilege the host community while contributing to the growth of all involved.

How can interested teacher educators design meaningful community-focused international SA programs that share power among partners and foster agency? In what follows, we explain five principles that guided our own collaborative partnership. We find principles rather than steps more appropriate because CESA program development originates from different entry points and evolves organically rather than following a predictable pattern. To illustrate, our CESA in Montenegro would not have happened if Silvija, a teacher from Montenegro and co-author of this chapter, did not come to our university on a Fulbright exchange, or, if she did not have the kinds of trusting relationships at her school that allowed her administration to embrace the innovative program, or if Zuzana, the faculty member had not been co-awarded a sizable grant that allowed in-service teachers to more easily participate in the SA program. While steps taken may differ significantly depending on particular circumstances or personal contacts, principles can broadly shape CESA program development.

Principle 1: Partners Discuss Assets and Needs and Agree on Goals, Roles, and Outcomes

As our afore-mentioned definition indicates, a necessary guiding principle for a successful partnership must involve partners coming together to agree on overarching goals with meaningfully aligned outcomes, while gaining clarity on their respective roles. This initial planning discussion also presumes openness about available resources and is contextualized through identified assets and needs for both partners. In the case of our Montenegrin program, we discussed the assets of the US participants, namely, the creativity and enthusiasm of our US-based pre- and in-service teachers. We also considered their needs to expand intercultural competence and experience teaching in engaging meaningful ways in a context where most learners are just beginning English language development. From the perspective of Montenegrin participants, namely the EFL learners, we identified local knowledge, motivation to learn English, intercultural communication, and multilingualism as the main assets. In terms of Montenegrin partner needs, we recognized the desire for an affordable summer program for kids and the want for improved visibility of the school as a way of addressing decreasing enrollment.

Our vision for the Montenegrin CESA program was to engage all stakeholders in a valuable, positive, community-oriented intercultural learning and teaching experience. The goals for the US participants were included in the course syllabi and revolved largely around skills relevant to effective pedagogy of oral English and cultural issues in teaching English, including Global Englishes. In line with community-engaged pedagogy, the TESOL course objectives extended to include an expanded view of citizenship and social justice. The goals for the participating Montenegrin EFL learners centered on improving oral English skills and confidence in using English. The aim for the Montenegrin EFL teacher participants involved developing mentorship skills, while the high school teaching assistants learned basic teaching and professional skills.

It was important to us that everyone involved was willing to take on both expert and learner roles. US pre- and in-service teachers taught, but were also challenged to learn a few basic Albanian or Montenegrin words, and were prompted to notice a range of cultural differences. EFL participants were expected to be "learners," but through project-oriented tasks, many also acted as teachers explaining their projects and inspiring others to contribute to them. Montenegrin teachers, pre-service teachers, and high school assistants were developing new pedagogical skills while simultaneously acting in the role of mentors and cultural consultants to the US participants.

From the start, we were mindful of some constraints and challenges, such as the short-term character of our program and differences in cultural, experiential, and linguistic background of the US and the Montenegrin participants. We agreed to set fairly modest expectations in the first year of the program and put in place a protocol for soliciting daily and end-of-the-program feedback from the participants. We were pleased to find overwhelmingly positive outcomes for all involved participants in both years of the program (for further discussion see Tomaš et al., 2020).

Principle 2: Partners Share Power, Ownership, and Resources

Traditional approaches to service-learning have been said to privilege the university student over the local participants (Fisher & Grettenberger, 2015). The *student* gains a broader worldview, the *student* learns to become an active citizen, the *student* develops stronger communication skills. In the community-engaged service-learning model, all participants benefit. Shared power among varied participants is embedded in the partnership structure. Ideally, hierarchy is reduced, and *all* stakeholders are actively engaged in decision-making and resource sharing.

To cultivate the culture of equity and shared power in our CESA, we thoughtfully included the viewpoint of varied stakeholders. Rather than acting as the sole director of the program, the CESA university leader invited a community representative and teacher at the school to act as a co-director and a graduate student with considerable international experiences as a co-facilitator of the program. The principal of the school and other staff also shared an important role in developing the CESA. Working closely with the US-based counterparts, they provided insights as to existing and lacking resources. They strategically leveraged the new program to secure AC units, computer projectors, and teaching materials to create space conducive to learning during the summer break. On a daily basis, the school staff and local families offered transportation to the nearby town for the US teachers to help them offset costs. Local teachers who participated in professional development workshops alongside US pre- and in-service teachers provided pedagogical and cultural knowledge. These partners also worked together to pool logistical resources, such as reserving rooms, serving refreshments, and supporting technology. Additionally, the Montenegrin partners ensured that translated information about program events was distributed to local families, and even the local and national media.

The most notable shifts in balancing power came in the second and third year of the partnership. In the second year, we invited three Montenegrin pre- and in-service teachers and five high school youth (who participated as students in the program in Year 1) to assist alongside the US pre- and in-service teachers. Through daily classroom assistance, reflective feedback in debriefing sessions, and participation in offered professional development sessions, these integral Montenegrin participants shared knowledge and expertise as an invaluable local resource. This "co-learning" approach purported by Fisher and Grettenberger (2015) posits host participants as co-creators who actively engage in the learning community. Consequently, the local participants are put in the role of experts providing valuable contributions while at the same time benefiting from skill development. In the upcoming third year, three former CESA program participants from the United States chose to return to Montenegro, this time as university alumni, traveling to what is now endeared as a home-away-from-home. While COVID19 halted these plans, these past CESA participants hope to return in the future and assist in the third intensive summer English institute by the Montenegrin community of EFL teachers, pre-service teachers, and high school students who wish to sustain the program. This includes sought-out free accommodation by the local Tourist Office—something that would not have been possible without the goodwill built over the first two years of the program.

Principle 3: Partners Prioritize Open Communication, Facilitate Rich Interactions, and Mediate Cultural and Linguistic Differences

Open communication is often predicated on the commitment from the key stakeholders, in our case, the Montenegrin administrative staff and the US university study abroad office. A signed memorandum of understanding (MOU) attested to the desire to collaborate and specified key commitments and responsibilities of both partners. Next, both the US-based program leaders as well as the host school administration and its teachers made sure to establish their "visibility" and availability to all participants throughout the CESA duration, allowing for vital information to be communicated effectively. Once US participants committed to the CESA program, the faculty member offered several meetings and communicated the information received from the Montenegrin partner, such as student enrollment details. The Montenegrin partner contacted local families about the program dates, times, and the registration process and navigated the process of reserving accommodation, airport transfers, and other in-country logistics. Once the program started, the Montenegrin school administrators were an ever-present support to the students, families, and US cohort.

In our intention to create an authentic and synergistic space where needs and interests of both partners were considered, daily meetings with representatives from both sides were included in the program's agenda. After the teaching sessions, participants were provided with a chance to reflect on the connections between course content and their experiences in the classroom, as well as on broader cultural and civic issues. While in Year 1 these sessions only included the participating US pre- and in-service teachers, in Year 2 we decided to invite local teachers and assistants, which greatly enhanced feedback about the program. In addition to such formal meetings, we also strove to create opportunities for less formal interactions among the participants, be it during a 20 minute daily recess, chatting in the teacher's lounge over börek and Turkish coffee, evening get togethers at the local beach, or a field trip to a nearby museum.

It is important to acknowledge that while this communication-focused principle guided our daily efforts, language barriers and differences in inter-cultural communication at times challenged participants in achieving their communicative goals. US participants who were best able to overcome these communication challenges were usually the in-service teachers with expe-rience interacting with newcomers and EL families in the United States. One such teacher reported using strategies such as learning a few words in Montenegrin and Albanian, speaking slowly, and even using charades and drawings to communicate. Another experienced teacher recollected a situa-tion where she was driving to a nearby town with the school principal who did not speak English yet by relying on her handful of Albanian words and gestures, she was able to "have a lovely conversation" about places to visit. Another participating US in-service teacher reflected on grappling with ped-agogical choices in order to address a classroom dynamic that involved the sole adult male student dominating conversation time.

Open and clear communication is key in any community-based partner-ship and ideally, it is characterized by the absence of hierarchical, paternalistic protocols that can undermine programs striving for equity and shared power. An added caveat in the CESA context is the importance of awareness and mediation of possible linguistic and cultural differences. Community part-ners must work together to support all participants in navigating these com-munication challenges in ways that celebrate rather than cause apprehension.

Principle 4: Partners Work Collaboratively to Monitor and Evaluate the Program

Monitoring and evaluating any educational enterprise is crucial to its success, and when enhanced with community participation in an international con-text it becomes even more important. This is because each partner's context adds to the programmatic layers of complexity that when managed well, can be enriching, but when mismanaged, can quickly become a source of frus-tration for all involved. As Fisher and Grettenberger (2015) noted, listening to the community voices and collecting feedback from the host community about the program is a "rule of thumb" for adding to the successes of a study abroad program for both partners.

Planning for monitoring and feedback solicitation in CESA programs ought to occur in the early stages so as to account for necessary actions, such as translation or piloting of program evaluation instruments. Partners ought to agree on whose responsibility it is to monitor the day-to-day communi-ty-based activities, draft feedback instruments, and process the data. Together, they should also reflect on the findings in order to analyze the attainment of outcomes to make future improvements. This can happen in the final days of the CESA, immediately following the program, and with a delay to allow time for a more complete digestion of the experience.

To illustrate, in our collaborative project, each partner was responsible for drafting an evaluation survey for the respective stakeholders—Zuzana, the US-based study abroad faculty member, prepared the survey for the US participants and Silvija, the Montenegrin EFL teacher, for the Montenegrin participants. Feedback solicited from the 26 participating US pre- and in-service teachers was overwhelmingly positive; the majority reported attaining or exceeding course objectives and experiencing meaningful professional and personal growth. Similarly, of the 118 Montenegrin English learners surveyed, an overwhelming majority rated the program as effective or highly effective in terms of English language improvement and of having more positive views of English as a result of the program. Benefits acquired from collecting additional qualitative data, namely, observations, reflections, interviews, and a focus group, extended beyond general satisfaction in the involved stakeholders. The CESA enabled participating US-based K-12 and Montenegrin EFL teachers and assistants to expand their professional profiles and the school administrator credited the program to stabilized enrollment, increased school visibility, and even educational prestige in the region (for a more detailed discussion of the research methodology and results see Tomaš, et al., 2020).

The findings from the program assessment and stakeholders' reflections in Year 1, guided the program improvements in Year 2 in a number of ways. First, as mentioned previously, we invited local teachers, pre-service teachers, and interested highschoolers to participate as mentors and cultural informants, which allowed for increased intercultural engagement and more balanced power sharing between US and Montenegrin participants. Second, we responded to the needs of the Montenegrin Association of English Language Teachers (ELTAM) by participating at its annual conference and by allowing three of the Year 2 US participants to spend part of the CESA at the ELTAM and US Embassy Podgorica co-sponsored summer English camp. Lastly, we chose an informal setting for the final celebration, allowing for more organic opportunities for the local families and US teachers to interact, even enjoying a potluck dinner showcasing a variety of local dishes. Our post Year 2 improvement plans involve increased collaboration between stakeholders with increased community leadership. Our experience highlights that when stakeholders work together to utilize the results of evaluative tools to drive improvement, CESA programs are greatly enhanced, furthering their sustainability.

Principle 5: Partners Value Mutual Trust, Respectful Relationships, and Commitment to Sustainability

CESA programs are neither easy nor straightforward to develop, especially in the first year when stakeholders rely solely on the possibilities that the partnership might create. Oftentimes, commitments to the community are made before it is certain that the number of recruited university participants will allow the program to run since study abroad budgets are predicated upon strict financial bottom lines. Similarly, community partners often have to navigate a range of bureaucratic or logistical roadblocks and relate any concerns of the host community about the proposed program to the collaborative partner. Being open about these uncertainties and keeping the community partner informed on relevant updates is the first key to developing a trusting relationship.

While trust may take time to develop, respect must be present in the collaboration from the initiation of the very first conversation, and a constant throughout the partnership. This may be obvious to the university faculty who often launch CESA programs, but it may be less clear to university students, especially those with limited intercultural experience. This is because respect is often conceptualized differently across cultures. For instance, in some cultures it is a sign of reverence to greet elders first and a failure to do so would be considered highly disrespectful. An offer of an alcoholic beverage during working hours was quite surprising to one of our CESA participants, but from the perspective of the host community, this was a gesture of hospitality. Faculty leading CESA programs should make students aware of any cultural differences relevant to how respect may be exhibited in the host community while promoting widely-accepted practices familiar to the western university participants (e.g., end-of-program thank you notes) that can further foster a positive, respectful environment during a partnership.

One common criticism of service-learning, community-based programs is that they are often restricted to a semester or, in the case of a short-term SA program, to just a few weeks (e.g., Fisher & Grettenberger, 2015). When not handled sensitively, departure of university students from the community may leave behind a sense of a lack of commitment, even feelings of exploitation. In the SA context, there is greater potential for such assumptions as it may not be possible to recruit a sufficient number of university students or ensure that faculty can participate on an annual basis. In our case, we were determined to find a way for the summer institute to sustain itself regardless of the extent to which the US university students were involved (see description of shifted power balance described in Principle 2). What greatly contributed to our sustainability goal was the return of several US participants to the Montenegrin community in subsequent years.

How can we best avoid a service-servee model in CESA programs? How can we ensure shared community relationships? If we aim for meaningful partnerships, then we must begin with meaningful planning. The principles outlined here offer insights as to what this looks like in practice. Duarte's (2016) Six Standards of Practice provides additional considerations which may apply to other CESA programs, such as discussion of marketing and environmental factors. The goal for Duarte, which we share, is "more than mutually and privately beneficial, this improved approach is reciprocally and publicly beneficial". While these five principles show our commitment to various stages and characteristics of a multi-year CESA program, our unique approach in the day-to-day implementation further highlights its emphasis on community engagement.

Enacting Principled Community Engaged Pedagogy on the Ground

Because the community-engaged pedagogy was the cornerstone of this SA program, another goal was that it also be enacted on the ground through community-engaged instructional approaches in the intensive English summer institute. We believed that promoting this important theme, both at the program and day-to-day levels, could bring all the participants from different classes together and result in an increased sense of community. In what follows, we draw upon additional research data from a larger project published elsewhere (see Tomaš et al., 2020) to illustrate the value of extending community-focused principles to day-to-day CESA activities that involve interactions between US teachers and Montenegrin learners. Specifically, we exemplify this through a discussion of one specific project that was implemented during our first CESA, including the voices of teachers and learners from reflections, interviews, and surveys.

The community-oriented project, The Ulcinj Kindness Rock Project, aimed to cultivate positivity and to inspire others through simple acts of kindness, while simultaneously developing confidence and oral language skills in English. Eighth and ninth graders organized and implemented the school-wide system for the project, which involved devising project steps and responsibilities in team-based discussions and providing bilingual presentations to each grade-level that guided students—including some of the parents—to create a Kindness Rock. This extensive project resulted in two formal Kindness Rock Gardens: one at the school, the other in a downtown park. Video clips and photos document their journey, culminating in a student-produced video.

In reflecting on the project, Jill, a US in-service teacher, described the initial difficulties in "getting students to work together." Jill's hypothesis was that "the kids just never worked on any type of group project before" and "had difficulties being good communicators with one another." This was corroborated by all nine Montenegrin EFL teachers who attended the professional development sessions; experiential learning is not commonly used in Montenegro, reportedly due to curricular constraints. To address students' reluctance to work together, Jill and her co-teacher Shelby implemented various team building activities such as the Human Knot "to show [the EFL learners] how to work together." For Mery, a participating Montenegrin EFL teacher, seeing team-building activities in action was impactful; she stated that it was the single most important thing she was going to take away from the program. She explained:

> We miss community building in our country, in our educational system. In this program, we worked a lot on that community building, we had

to help each student, and not to work with good ones, successful ones, and put the others apart. We have to help them and make them feel safe and comfortable. And American teachers did that and I'm so grateful to be reminded of that.

The increased trust and commitment that resulted from the team building activities made students more invested in working together and more curious about the project. They were able to focus on tasks at hand, working in specialized committees that reflected their strengths to accomplish self-determined goals. Throughout the process, students considered choices and made decisions in their teams. In the words of one of the Montenegrin students, "it was such a great experience, it was all about teamwork, new ideas, we were not used to that way of learning here. It's so much more involvement and fun, in this whole project, everybody has a part to do, and that makes you proud". Both the process and ultimately the final outcomes (two rock gardens) of The Kindness Rock project inspired not only achievement but pride among the eighth and ninth graders, which extended to the entire school community who contributed their own kindness rock. As one of the US teachers commented, "the project helped everyone "to become a community at the school so fast" and how it "helped bring us together".

Beyond an increased sense of pride and achievement, typical of successful community-focused project-based learning, this and several other projects that were embedded in the Montenegrin CESA program appeared to cultivate the participating youths' sense of personal agency. After a mini-lesson about "taking the kindness project further into their individual lives", students returned to the classroom after the weekend reporting making connections with homeless people they had previously ignored, greeting strangers on the street, and expressing gratitude to their family members. One student shared with her teacher photos of a self-designed "kindness sticky notes" project that involved mounting a poster board with twelve affirming messages written on sticky notes in the town center. The student proudly announced that by the end of the day only three of the twelve sticky notes remained on the board! Two students who participated in Year 1 of the program brought the Kindness Rock project to their own high school later that year where they convinced their teachers and administrator to engage the whole school in creating their own rock garden during a schoolwide antidiscrimination event!

In sum, we are hard pressed to imagine our CESA program being as successful without a community-focus at the level of the programmatic principles that guided our partnership as well as the day-to-day activity level, which transcended traditional classroom learning into meaningful, human interactions that simply happened to be in English. It does not mean that important aspects of the English language were not taught or practiced. Rather, aligned with the tenets of project-based learning, the US teachers allowed their Montenegrin students' interests and strengths to guide language instruction. Instead of designing lessons around pre-planned, discrete language skills that would have solely helped learners improve language competence, it was important to both SA partners to engage everyone in community-engaged collaboration, therefore cultivating our sense of mutuality.

Conclusion

From its inception, our CESA fostered community engagement with a joint ownership over the program. Our approach to a shared power that respected and gave voice to all participants—host school staff, US university faculty and teacher participants, Montenegrin teachers and learners—resulted in a new learning community. The result wasn't one community coming to another community, but a new community working as one.

It is our hope that our model and experiences outlined in this chapter can help guide teacher educators to engage teacher candidates with thinking locally in global communities. This can be achieved while simultaneously promoting equity and agency through intentional practices that privilege host communities and leverage resources to serve the ultimate goals of the CESA programs. Indeed, as Roberts (2003) contends, a "balance of experiential learning and serious interaction in an international arena is an ideal condition for teachers to develop perspective consciousness about the world" (p. 272). This is well exemplified through one of our pre-service teacher's reflection:

> I recognize a greater responsibility to my community and the global community. I hadn't quite yet realized the potential impact I can make as a global citizen. I feel that I have grown socially and emotionally because I have opened my eyes to a whole new way of looking at life. Although I believed I was already good at putting myself in another's shoes, I realized I was not as good as I thought. This trip gave me the ability to have more genuine empathy for people of other cultures. I have a greater desire to be a good global citizen.

In order for CESA programs to have an equally positive and transformative impact on the host community, program leaders can lean on the discussed five principles as they develop their own programs that strive for such dual impact. And if the first reiteration of one's CESA does not produce desired outcomes, program leaders are encouraged to gather community feedback and use the lessons learned as a "primary guidepost for all subsequent work with that same community" (Fisher & Grettenberger, 2015, p. 573). It is, after all, only such prolonged, sustained engagement that can lead to transformative learning at the global scale for all involved.

Acknowledgement

The authors gratefully acknowledge funding from the NPD Grant T365Z160111, awarded by the Office of English Language Acquisition, U.S. Department of Education.

References

Boyer, E. L. (1994). Creating the New American College. *The Chronicle of Higher Education, 40*(27), A48. Retrieved from https://search-proquest-com.ezproxy.emich.edu/docview/214654518?pq-origsite=summon

Douglas, S. R. (2015). Student perspectives on a short-term study abroad experience. In P. Clements, A. Krause, & H. Brown (Eds.), *JALT 2014 Conference Proceedings* (pp. 208–216).

Duarte, G. (2016). What to look for in global service-learning: six standards of practice to guide your decisions. *OCIC, 7.* https://readymag.com/OCIC/iAMvol7/17/

Fisher, C. M., & Grettenberger, S. E. (2015). Community-based participatory study abroad: A proposed model for social work education. *Journal of Social Work Education, 51*(3), 566-58–2.

Haddix, M. (2015). Preparing community-engaged teachers. *Theory Into Practice, 54,* 63–70.

Lindahl, K., Hansen-Thomas, H., Baecher, L., & Stewart, M.A. (2020). Study abroad for critical multilingual language awareness development in teacher candidates. *TESL-EJ, 23*(4).

Roberts, A. (2003). Proposing a broadened view of citizenship: North American teachers' service in rural Costa Rican schools. *Journal of Studies in International Education, 7*(3), 253–276. Retrieved from https://journals.sagepub.com/doi/10.1177/1028315303251398.

Sherraden, M., Bopp, A., & Lough, B. (2013). Students serving abroad: A framework for inquiry. *Journal of Higher Education Outreach & Engagement, 17*(2), 7–42.

Tarrant, M. A., Rubin, D. L., & Stoner L. (2014). The added value of Study Abroad: Fostering a global citizenry. *Journal of Studies in International Education, 18*(2), 141–161. Retrieved from http://citeseerx.ist.psu.edu/viewdoc/download?doi=10.1.1.645.6951&rep=rep1&type=pdf

Tomaš, Z., Van Horn-Gabel, A., & Marniković, S. (2020). Examining the value of a TESOL service-learning study abroad for U.S. pre-and in-service teachers and Montenegrin community stakeholders. *TESL-EJ, 23*(4). Retrieved from http://tesl-ej.org/pdf/ej92/a6.pdf

Vatalaro, A., Szente, J., & Levin, J. (2015). Transformative learning of pre-service teachers during study abroad in Reggio Emilija, Italy: A case study. *Journal of the Scholarship of Teaching and Learning, 15*(2), 42–55.

16 Developing Global-Mindedness in Teacher Education through Virtual and International Intercultural Experiences

Clara Bauler, Xiao-Lei Wang, and Devin Thornburg

Introduction

Teacher education programs across the United States have struggled to systematically implement principles and practices to develop the necessary knowledge and skills to support teacher candidates in working with culturally and linguistically diverse learners (Lucas et al., 2008). One way we have attempted to foster culturally and linguistically-responsive practices in our teacher education program is through designing international collaboration and experiences. Research findings from studies on the impact of study abroad experiences have revealed the development of more culturally-responsive, self-aware, and reflective educators (Colón-Muñiz et al., 2010; Cushner & Mahon, 2009; Freed et al., 2019; Lindahl et al., 2020; Nero, 2009). We have also emphasized the role of intercultural dialogue and study abroad experiences as a pivotal practice in providing authentic spaces for teacher candidates to reflect on how to scaffold teaching and learning for linguistically and culturally diverse learners.

However, similar to many other teacher education programs, we have faced challenges in situating global experiences as a central tenet of our educational goals and practices. Part of the challenge lies in the structural limitations of study abroad programs which have traditionally been implemented within the boundaries of single courses or a specific disciplinary field (Smolcic & Katunich, 2017). Furthermore, study abroad programs tend to be of a short nature as the costs associated with traveling to a foreign country might be considerably high for many teacher candidates (Sachau et al., 2010). Unfortunately, restrictions on traveling imposed by health, economic, and social crises, such as the current global pandemic, have also become a tangible characteristic of our times. These barriers are real and pose significant obstacles to program-wide implementation (Walters et al., 2009).

In this chapter, we provide an alternative framework for developing global-minded teachers that taps into both virtual and international resources in a more cost-effective and sustainable way. We share and describe teacher candidate engagement in international exchange and dialogue through both more traditional study abroad experiences as well as classroom-based, virtual collaborative opportunities, without requiring participants to physically travel abroad. Teacher candidates actively participated in cultural events, interacted with people from different cultures, reflected on issues encountered, and developed an understanding that "we are all connected", beginning to move away from the mindset of "we and the other" to the direction of "we" (Wang & Bernas, 2014). Supported by an analysis of program implementation through pictures, student work, and student comments, we reflect on the possibility of using virtual and international experiences as a promise for a program-wide proposal for preparing global-minded teachers to work with linguistically and culturally diverse learners.

Toward a Framework for Global-Mindedness in Teacher Education

Our practices are grounded within the *medial framework* developed by Phillipe Eberhard and Xiao-lei Wang (Eberhard, 1999; Eberhard & Wang, 2010; Eberhard 2014). The medial framework derives from a grammatical notion of the middle voice found in Ancient Greek. Most modern languages have lost the middle voice, having only kept the active and the passive voices, as in "I educated Susan about Italy" (active voice) and "Susan was educated by me about Italy" (passive voice). In contrast, the middle voice indicates that the action is performed with special reference to the subject and the verb. For example, the Ancient Greek verb *dialegomai* (to engage in dialogue) conjugated in middle voice conveys that in a dialogue, where something happens to language, no single person is in charge or responsible for what happened. The conversation brings us to a different place, we are neither active nor passive but truly medial or middle-voiced.

The medial framework can be used as a lens to think about the process of helping teacher candidates develop a "global mindset". There are four crucial principles involved when applying the media framework in the context of educating global minded teachers: (1) creating guided experience, (2) encouraging constant reflection, (3) developing the "we" concept, and (4) broadening the horizon. These principles interact with each other and form a continuous and systematic process. Each principle is elaborated below.

Experience

The first step in becoming global-minded begins with experiences in a different cultural setting, whether in-person or virtual. However, the crucial aspect of the experience cannot be superficial and must be guided to avoid bias. The guided experience cannot happen in isolation, but occurs in dialogue with peers, teacher educators, and, above all, people from different cultural backgrounds than their own. Participants need guidance as each iteration will be an opportunity to examine pre-conceived values, beliefs, and misconceptions. The action of comparing and contrasting is fundamental for the experience to be meaningful, that is, to debunk one-sided notions that can be detrimental to the development of global mindedness.

Reflection

Experience in itself is not enough. The advantage of medial thinking is that it fosters self-understanding by looking at our role in the global society and our place in it, despite what our current understanding is. Self-understanding requires us to first self-reflect and negotiate with "others" who hold different views. A crucial part of the process of educating global minded-teacher candidates is that our actions are not ours alone; although we carry them out, we are also encompassed by them. The medial framework involves teacher candidates in critically engaging themselves in differences, constantly to question their own beliefs and positioning. This process leads them to cultivate openness habitually. It is a process that just like learning is never fully achieved. It is always in the making and always at its beginning (Andreotti et al., 2012).

We

Through experience and reflection, the medial framework helps teacher candidates move toward a more inclusive both-and-more way of thinking of the new culture that they encounter. In other words, teacher candidates begin to form a mindset that tends to avoid thinking of the new culture as "the other". Instead, teacher candidates begin to develop the ability to articulate a plural subject in the concept of "we" (i.e., the "other" and teacher candidates themselves together) in the processes of interaction.

Horizon

As teacher candidates are in interactions with people, processes, and practices of diverse cultures, they have the opportunity to broaden their horizons, progressively seeing more than before. To put medial thinking visually, the image of the horizon is apt because being able to see the horizon does not mean that we are determined by it; instead, we can change it and change ourselves in the process. The fascinating aspect of the horizon metaphor is that it moves as we move and that it changes us as we change it. Cultivating our horizon also involves cultivating our understanding and ultimately our self-understanding. The medial framework reminds us that we are part of the horizon. We are not in charge of it, yet not at its mercy either. Hence, we are able to impact and change our reality directly and actively. For teacher educators, that means having direct influence on actions, interactions, and relationships with students and communities.

The medial framework helps guide all types of intercultural experiences, be they international or virtual. It encourages teacher candidates to cultivate their horizon in the ongoing process of being and becoming a global citizen. These are important values, knowledge, and skills to work with, across and within cultural and linguistic diversity. In the remaining part of the chapter, we will elaborate on our pedagogical practices to integrate global-mindedness in various stages of our teacher education program. We have attempted to create a pathway to expose teacher candidates to linguistic and cultural diversity via the four basic principles derived from the medial framework.

Virtual and International Intercultural Experiences

Our university is a moderately-sized higher education institution in New York state. The focus of our efforts thus far to develop global-minded teachers has been through our five-year combined Bachelors/Masters degrees in one of the following areas: Childhood, Adolescence, Special Education, and Teachers of English to Speakers of Other Languages. Over the years we have designed practices to engage teacher candidates in authentic intercultural experiences because we saw a need to develop a more critical and reflective stance toward linguistic and cultural diversity. These practices involved traveling to cultural sites as well as virtual collaboration and dialogue with international faculty and students. In this section, we outline the implementation of pedagogical practices embodied in four different intercultural experiences. Teacher candidates engaged in the medial process of creating experiences, practicing reflection, developing a "we" concept, and broadening their horizon.

Virtual Intercultural Experiences

Co-Teaching with International Educators

We collaborated with a Spanish college professor of media and communications from the University of Sevilla for two semesters co-teaching one Educational Foundations and one Sociolinguistics course. These courses were part of the initial coursework for our five-year BA/MA program in Childhood Education. He was hired as a consultant to bring greater international awareness to the program. In the first semester, he joined synchronously via Skype every week, contributing presentations to the entire class during its regular class times on such topics as Pierre Bourdieu's (1974) notions of cultural capital in schools and schooling. He would also beam in to co-facilitate discussions in smaller groups of teacher candidates from the class, comparing Spanish and US education systems, or offer feedback on debates about such topics as high-stakes testing in both countries undertaken by the candidates.

The following semester, online experiences became part of the course planning for Sociolinguistics. The work with the Spanish professor entailed online interaction and language learning with school-aged students in Spain, where he also worked as an educator, paralleling the experiences teacher candidates were gaining with local multilingual learners in US schools during their fieldwork. For example, one of the synchronous meeting was about ways of greeting across different languages and cultures. The meeting included teacher candidates and fifth-grade students from highly diverse backgrounds, including eight different countries. The fifth-grade students and teacher candidates in the United States discussed cultural greetings and created lessons. The cultural diversity of the Spanish school, with 54 countries represented, also led to reflective writing by the teacher candidates about the implications for teaching multicultural populations in the United States.

Designing a Collaborative Arts Festival

Several teacher candidates in our university were part of a global arts and human rights class as a liberal arts course, co-taught by professors in Art Education, Special Education and Childhood Education. The professors had learned about the Western Sahara, a disputed region within Morocco, where education offerings were limited because of economic hardships. The one advanced college-level program was for Sahrawis who sought to become artists and educators. For the Sahwaris, the main source of revenue for the region, populated by 250,000 people on campus, was their art. Teacher candidates from the United States and Western Sahara collaborated and interacted via online synchronous and asynchronous exchange to learn and discuss the struggles and successes of the use of art to both represent their efforts for independence and to bring revenue in creating an educational system. By having this educational and cultural exchange, the goal was to foster greater understanding between the United States and the Western Sahara while offering our teacher candidates an opportunity to engage in dialogue. The political and economic challenges of the Sahrawi people became a focus on a broadening of the students' understanding and interest in international relations, diplomacy and cultural and linguistic influences.

At the end of the semester, there was a web-based festival open to our entire university community. The festival took place in university spaces for a half-day. Through the use of technology the reach became international. Figure 16.1 below demonstrates the interconnectedness among and across cultures with the use of guitars and Latin rhythms as a representation of cultural blending and influences.

Figure 16.2 below depicts US teacher candidates doing a cultural Latin dance performance for the Western Saharan audience. The virtual interactions allowed both groups to reflect about their previous notions of art and culture in both countries and how one country influenced the other culturally.

Reflecting Critically about Social Media and Human Rights

The course involved a series of projects after reading about and discussing areas where social media had been instrumental in representing or leading to social change. The course was offered to students who sought to enter

Figure 16.1 Arts festival in the Western Sahara with Arts and Education teacher candidates performing

Figure 16.2 Arts festival in the United States with teacher candidates performing

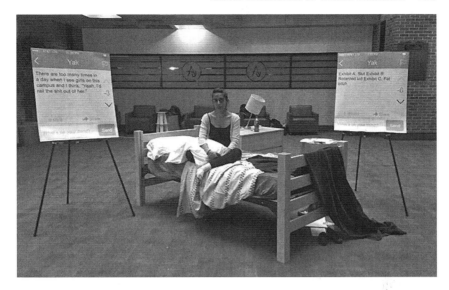

Figure 16.3 Event at the University Center at our US institution

the five-year BA/MA program as part of their first year experience at the university. Their professor has developed collaborations with educators in other countries through faculty development seminars abroad, leading to collaborative projects such as this. Two events during the course included synchronous Skype conversations with high school and college students from other countries, such as Norway, the Netherlands, Spain, Morocco, South Africa, the Philippines, India, and Argentina, about the role of the arts in highlighting the importance and challenges in human rights related to race and language differences.

Figure 16.3 demonstrates an art-making project where our teacher candidates took on social media bullying and gender violence with an event in the University Center depicting virtual and physical places as well as victims. The teacher candidate in the picture represents an abused college student who was a victim of date rape. The posters include a social media platform that did not monitor violence, which became a site for bullying and gender-related abuse.

International Intercultural Experiences

Considering Alternative Perspectives in Cuba

In January 2016, two of our faculty designed a course to take teacher candidates to Cuba to learn about the educational system there. The course was over a two-week period, intensively exposing candidates to educational experiences in schools and cultural programs in the areas of Havana and Pinar del Río.

Teacher candidates were to visit schools and classrooms to observe, exchange information with teachers and school leaders about curriculum, and design curriculum for US students. One of the challenges that were faced, however, was that the Cuban government sought to support tours to educational sites that were carefully screened for Western contact and many of the scheduled schools were either closed or with limited students and teachers available during the visits. However, the teacher candidates were able to gather significant information and experiences about what might be considered more alternative forms of education (e.g., community arts programming), as Cuba is filled with such engaging projects, offered to populations typically less able to participate in formal schooling because of disability.

Each day that the teacher candidates were in Cuba, they were gathered together in the late afternoon before dinner to reflect on their experiences. Throughout many of the entries, particularly as the latter part of the trip ended in Pinar del Río (a smaller city in Cuba), the teacher candidates wrote about experiences where they noted how they felt a part of the country as expressed in the journal entry below:

> One of the main points that I would "teach" to others about Cuba is that just because a country is poor and in bad condition in terms of infrastructure and available resources, doesn't mean that the spirits and the minds of these people are in as bad a condition as their surroundings. While I am in no way at all glorifying the poverty of the island, I want to point out the spirits of the people despite their situation. The Cuban people have some of the most positive attitudes of anyone I've come across. The culture is simply one that is inviting and shockingly looking out for each other. This would be the first thing I would tell people coming here.

Exploring Alternative Pedagogies in Italy

Our most recent study abroad experience involved bringing teacher candidates to Italy to visit Italian cultural relics, listen to lectures provided by Italian educational experts, and visit Italian schools. Teacher candidates inquired into the similarities and differences between Italian classrooms and US classrooms, early Roman education, the Montessori curriculum and the Reggio Emilia approach, and ways the Italian educational system has responded to immigrant students. Teacher candidates visited sites in Rome, Tuscany, and Florence. In the last two sites, they were able to observe, interact, and/or teach in six different Italian schools. To reflect on their experiences, teacher candidates wrote seven online dialogic journals through which they shared and participated in back and forth conversations with their peers. Teacher candidates also utilized photographic images as an integral part of their reflections. Figure 16.4 is an example of this dialogic reflection, where Teacher Candidate A wrote the entry and to which Teacher Candidate B commented as displayed in Figure 16.5.

Things I learned...

    1. The teacher stays with their group of students throughout their elementary school learning.

    2. The teacher has a strong leading role and connection to the students.

    3. The students were very familiar with the English language they even had the understanding of the tenses.

Readings...

    1. Michael Agar stresses that in order to know another language we have to go beyond the grammar and focus on the vocabulary.

    2. To effectively communicate with one another we have to understand one's culture.

Question...

    1. Are students who don't speak English or Italian accommodated?

Figure 16.4 Dialogic reflection online post

The online dialogue above demonstrates Teacher Candidate A's dynamic perceptions on the most memorable things she learned from the experience. The picture she took highlights a new type of classroom group structure where the teacher remains with students throughout their elementary years, a cultural practice that differs from most US schools, where students switch teachers when they move to different grades. Teacher Candidate A's notes also emphasize the idea that language learning is intimately connected to culture, an understanding that comes from several attempts and continuous observations during interaction and communication with people from other cultures. Finally, her journal poses a remaining question about the education of immigrant children in Italy in comparison to the United States. Teacher Candidate B's comment stresses the differences and learning from the pedagogical practices they were a part of in Italy. The dialogical journal allowed teacher candidates to not only read each other's posts, but compare and contrast their own and

Re: Re: Journal 7 - Individual Contributions due and Comments due Wednesday, 1/22 at midnight
by   Monday, January 20, 2020, 6:55 PM

Hi   ! I enjoyed reading your response. Similar to yours, my most memorable moments in the trip were the school visits that took place in Florence. These visits will always remain in the back of my head and how the strategies used in the classroom are so different from New York in so many ways. It is extremely important for us, as future educators, to think from a global perspective when viewing these cultural practices, so I completely agree with you! I am intrigued by your question about if students who don't speak English or Italian are accommodated, because this is extremely important.

Sum of ratings:10 (1) 10   Permalink   Show parent   Edit   Delete   Reply

Figure 16.5 Dialogic reflection online comment

their peers' experiences. The peer sharing through the online dialogical journal became a resource for furthering candidates' reflection and sensitivity about the issues being discussed during the intercultural experience (Bauler & Gordon, 2018).

Connections to the Medial Framework

The four principles of the medial framework helped us analyze the outcomes of international and virtual experiences through pictures, student work, and comments. Regarding virtual intercultural experiences, a sense of shared responsibility began to grow in our teacher candidates. This was visible when teacher candidates designed lessons with the Spanish professor, discussed cultural practices with K-12 students in Sevilla, and considered how refugee status might affect students in their own classrooms with peers from Western Sahara. In directly engaging with each other, teacher candidates, K-12 students, and international and domestic professors developed a "we" concept toward the role of global educators of linguistically, racially and culturally diverse learners. The festival and virtual collaboration afforded teacher candidates to engage in common planning and sharing of ideas, broadening their horizons about common cultural influences and ideas, such as the different ways children learn how to say "hello", the presence of Muslims in the Iberia Peninsula and Latin America as well as the growing significance of Latino/a music and artistic expression in the United States. The opportunity to directly see, talk, and reflect virtually with peers across the globe created a bridge between the teacher candidates' lived experiences and preconceived ideas. The development of a "we" concept grew organically as a result of the joint planning and execution of the various events.

Regarding international intercultural experiences, a sense of "we" began to increase especially in teacher candidate's daily reflections. In Cuba, for example, the notion of time that had initially been perceived as different and contradictory in the beginning of the trip started to become "our" time by the middle of the trip. A new notion of community was added and problematized through discussions and cultural comparisons. In Italy, teacher candidates' dialogical reflections reflected the important role direct interactions with local students and teachers played in mediating the process of moving from memorable experiences, which related to "self", to cultural comparisons among diverse pedagogical and social practices between the United States and Italy schools, which entailed a "we". This new added educational perspective helped broaden teacher candidates' horizons toward new methodologies and pedagogies. Teacher candidates were then driven to pose even more questions about the education of linguistically diverse students in both countries, a process that made visible the incomplete nature of becoming a global educator.

Lessons Learned

In our complex world, affording all teacher candidates the opportunity to reflect, dialogue, and engage with cultural and linguistic diversity should be at the heart of teacher preparation, not at the margins. Informed by the lens of the medial framework, we have gained insights about program-wide implementation from multiple experiences in globalizing our coursework. Specifically, it was impactful to integrate virtual collaborations into early parts of the teacher education curriculum. In contrast with organizing early foundations courses solely on theoretical levels of learning, virtual international interactions helped us ground ideas of culture, language, and learning through concrete experiences. Varied forms of international collaborations illuminated how the medial framework can yield a more developmental approach to a more culturally and linguistically-responsive curriculum in teacher education. In other words, in adopting the medial framework, we can use international and virtual intercultural experiences as complementary pedagogical practices to place authentic intercultural dialogue as a foundation for preparing global-minded teachers.

Given the lessons we learned, we offer three suggestions to program-wide implementation. First, the timing of experience was crucial as teacher candidates needed to be exposed to as well as engaged in international and global topics or exchanges earlier in their program than at the end. In other words, instead of aiming at a culminating experience with student teaching or a single course at the end of their program, engaging in intercultural dialogue and reflection at any point of their teacher preparation journey was in itself conducive to a more encompassing notion of a shared "we". Teacher candidate reflections made visible indications of the broadening of horizon; that is, through all types of intercultural experience, teacher candidates were able to reflect by considering perspectives that were different than their own. These findings also point to the need for carefully designed activities that consider the pre, during and post of a global interaction (Nero, 2009). Rather than focusing on the experience only, reflecting before, during and after intercultural dialogue should also be an integral aspect of the pedagogical practice.

Along with timing, the right materials, interactions, and contexts were invaluable elements to help teacher candidates develop a global mindset. The role of the teacher educator in prompting and guiding reflection for critical awareness was indispensable (Lindahl et al., 2020; Vatalaro et al., 2015). Without the teacher educators acting as a "more capable guide", teacher candidates might not have seen beyond the limits of their own self and experience (Vygotsky, 1978). The scaffolding was evidenced in the dialogue with peers during the study abroad experiences, with international students, as well as with international professors virtually through synchronous meetings. These pedagogical spaces were all intentionally designed by the teacher educators, who acted in concerted ways to prompt, facilitate and propel conversations that involved reflective opportunities for cultural comparisons. These intentional opportunities for dialogue were in themselves the sites for medial thinking as teacher candidates were able to reflect about others with others, ultimately broadening their horizons by adding novel perspectives.

Above all, experience was at the heart of success (Cushner, 2007, 2011). Teacher candidates engaged *directly* with people, places, and activities in international and virtual experiences. Teacher candidates were not merely learning *about* linguistic and cultural diversity; they were *in* direct contact and interaction with linguistic and cultural diversity. All intercultural experiences provided opportunities for teacher candidates to not only reflect, but also take part in the complexities entailed in working with linguistically and culturally diverse groups of students (Hilliker, 2020; Landa et al., 2017; Morley et al., 2019). Particularly during times of global disasters, such as the COVID-2019 pandemic that led to social isolation and travel bans, drawing on the power of virtual connectedness becomes critical in efforts to continue culturally and linguistically-responsive educational practices. The value of intercultural dialogue and collaboration goes beyond the medium and physical space. Independent of being abroad or online, the ability to cultivate relationships and consider alternative perspectives is what allows educators to widen their horizons and move toward becoming global-minded teachers.

References

Andreotti, V. D. O. & de Souza, L. M. T. (2012). Introduction: (Toward) Global citizenship education 'otherwise'. In *Postcolonial perspectives on global citizenship education* (pp. 13–18). London: Routledge.

Bauler, C. V. & Gordon, D. M. (2018). Developing linguistic and cultural awareness for working with ELLs: Activities for beginning teacher preparation. In P. B. Swanson & S. A. Hildebrandt (Eds.), *Researching edTPA problems and promises: Perspectives from ESOL, English, and WL teacher education* (pp. 87–115). Charlotte, NC: Information Age.

Bourdieu, P. (1974). Avenir de classe et causalité du probable. Revue française de sociologie, 3–42.

Colón-Muñiz, A., SooHoo, S., & Brignoni, E. G. (2010). Language, culture and dissonance: A study course for globally minded teachers with possibilities for catalytic transformation. *Teaching Education, 21*(1), 61–74.

Cushner, K. (2007). The role of experience in the making of internationally-minded teachers. *Teacher Education Quarterly, 34*(1), 27–39.

Cushner, K., & Mahon, J. (2009). Intercultural competence in teacher education. *The SAGE handbook of intercultural competence*, 304–320.

Cushner, K. (2011). Intercultural research in teacher education: An essential intersection in the preparation of globally competent teachers. *Action in Teacher Education, 33*(5–6), 601–614.

Eberhard, P. (1999). The mediality of our condition: A Christian interpretation: *Journal of the American Academy of Religion*, 67 (2), 411–434.

Freed, A., Benavides, A., & Huffling, L. (2019). Teaching, Reflecting and Learning: Exploring Teacher Education Study Abroad Programs as Transformational Learning Opportunities. In Pedagogy in Basic and Higher Education-Current Developments and Challenges. *IntechOpen*. DOI: 10.5772/intechopen.88578.

Hilliker, S. (2020). Virtual exchange as a study abroad alternative to foster language and culture exchange in TESOL Teacher Education. *TESL-EJ, 23*(4).

Landa, M., Odòna-Holm, J., & Shi, L. (2017). Education abroad and domestic cultural immersion: A comparative study of cultural competence among teacher candidates. *The Teacher Educator, 52*(3), 250–267.

Lindahl, K., Hansen-Thomas, H., Baecher, L., & Stewart, M. A. (2020). Study abroad for critical multilingual language awareness development in teacher candidates. *TESL-EJ, 23*(4).

Lucas, T., Villegas, A. M., & Freedson-Gonzalez, M. (2008). Linguistically responsive teacher education: Preparing classroom teachers to teach English language learners. *Journal of Teacher Education, 59*(4), 361–373.

Morley, A., Braun, A. M., Rohrer, L., & Lamb, D. (2019). Study abroad for preservice teachers. *Global Education Review*, 6(3), 4–29.

Nero, S. (2009). Inhabiting the other's world: Language and cultural immersion for US-based teachers in the Dominican Republic. *Language, Culture and Curriculum, 22*(3), 175–194.

Sachau, D., Brasher, N., & Fee, S. (2010). Three models for short-term study abroad. *Journal of Management Education, 34*(5), 645–670.

Smolcic, E., & Katunich, J. (2017). Teachers crossing borders: A review of the research into cultural immersion field experience for teachers. *Teaching and Teacher Education, 62*, 47–59.

Vatalaro, A., Szente, J., & Levin, J. (2015). Transformative learning of pre-service teachers during study abroad in Reggio Emilia, Italy: A case study. *Journal of the Scholarship of Teaching and Learning, 15*(2), 42–55.

Vygotsky, L. (1978). Interaction between learning and development. In *Mind and Society*, pp. 79–91. Cambridge, MA: Harvard University Press.

Wang, X.-L. & Bernas, R. (2014). *People without borders: Becoming members of global communities*. Untested Ideas Research Center.

Walters, L. M., Garii, B., & Walters, T. (2009). Learning globally, teaching locally: incorporating international exchange and intercultural learning into pre-service teacher training. *Intercultural Education, 20*(1), S151–S158.

17 Transforming Language Teacher Education

Utilizing Virtual Exchange as an Alternative to Study Abroad

Shannon M. Hilliker, Barbara Loranc-Paszylk, and Chesla Ann Lenkaitis

Introduction

Field experiences as well as student teaching experiences are essential to teacher candidates as they slowly are introduced into the classroom environment and begin to lead instruction of a class. For example, Baecher (2012) studied novice teachers in a Teaching English to Speakers of Other Languages (TESOL) program and provided teacher candidates' responses on what could strengthen their teacher education program to help them in their future teaching positions. Participants in the study ranked their practicum course second in the curriculum as the experience that had most prepared them for their teaching job. In addition, 72% of the teachers in the study agreed or strongly agreed that their field experiences prior to practicum "greatly enriched their courses" (Baecher, 2012, p. 585). This study shows the importance of teacher candidates' opportunities to interact with students and participate in clinically rich experiences in their teacher education curriculum. Study abroad is a viable option for teachers to participate in clinical experiences that can transform classroom practices (Allen, 2010), however there is little research that shows how study abroad can impact teacher development in TESOL programs.

Since virtual exchange "involves the engagement of groups of learners in extended periods of online intercultural interaction and collaboration with partners from other cultural contexts or geographical locations as an integrated part of their educational programs and under the guidance of educators and/ or expert facilitators," (O'Dowd, 2018, p. 5) it can be used as an alternative to study abroad (Hilliker, 2020). This trend has been recognized by educational policy-makers and institutions (European Commission, 2017; Navracsics, 2016) because of factors such as demanding courses, scheduling issues and the increased costs of travel (Lewis & Niesenbaum, 2005; NAFSA, 2003). Health concerns are another deterrent, especially given the recent worldwide pandemic. Shorter-term study abroad trips have shown to be an alternative to a semester or year-long one (Lenkaitis, 2019a). It is especially important to note that intercultural learning can occur when virtual exchange is employed in teacher education because it can add a clinically rich component to all classes in a program. In this way, through technological means, teacher candidates are afforded access to other teacher candidates in their content area so they can practice the concepts they are learning in their coursework. In addition, they are gaining intercultural competence (Guth & Helm, 2011) and technology skills (Lenkaitis, 2019b) that are imperative in the 21st century classroom.

Due to the authors' recent research that has shown that virtual exchange is a viable way for language teacher candidates to develop in such areas as inter-cultural competence (Hilliker et al., 2020), global awareness (Lenkaitis et al., 2019), reflection (Lenkaitis, 2020a), learner autonomy (Lenkaitis, 2020b), peer assessment and teaching expertise (Loranc-Paszylk, 2016, 2018) and in order to add to the growing body of research of using virtual exchange as an alter-native to study abroad (Hilliker, 2020), this chapter will report on a virtual study abroad where teacher candidates from the United States were paired with teacher candidates from Poland to discuss weekly topics as they related to their coursework to pedagogical content knowledge.

Literature Review

Transformative Learning

Transformative learning takes place when a significant experience impacts a learner and changes his/her perspective through discourse and social inter-action (Mezirow, 1997). Because of this, transformative learning theory calls for educators to include activities for learners aimed to challenge student assumptions and beliefs and expose them to different points of view in a trusting environment (Cranton, 2002; Taylor, 2000).

There are four levels of transformative learning that are framed in ethnocen-trism and in order to change a person's view they must be in contact with ideas different from our own over time (Mezirow, 1997). According to Mezirow (1997), "(w)e do not make transformative changes in the way we learn as long as what we learn fits comfortably in our existing frames of reference" (p. 7). Therefore, so that learners have the opportunity to have experiences outside these existing frames, the following four learning goals of Mezirow's (1997) framework build on one another: (1) to expand on an existing point of view, (2) to establish a new point of view, (3) to transform a point of view, and (4) to become aware and critically reflective of points other than our own (Mezirow, 1997, p. 7). Boling (2007) and Curran and Murray (2008) also have conducted studies on transformative learning in teacher education, however, there has been little attention given to studies that pair teacher candidates with coun-terparts in a different country to explore topics from a cultural point of view.

Study Abroad

Currently, topics such as teacher candidates' reflection (Trilokekar & Kukar, 2011), multicultural competencies (Sharma et al., 2011), and critical aware-ness (Palmer & Menard-Warwick, 2012) dominate the study abroad research that spotlights teacher education. Pre-service teachers' language proficiency and cultural perspectives (Allen, 2010) are the focus of study abroad with more seasoned professionals. This literature suggests that study abroad, even as short as five days (Lenkaitis, 2019a), has a positive impact on developing teacher candidates as they participate in classrooms in another country (Baecher, & Chung, 2019; Lindahl, et al., 2020; Tomaš et al., 2020). Study abroad develops teacher candidates' consciousness of different cultures and perspectives (Hilliker, 2020; Palmer & Menard-Warwick, 2012; Phillion, et al., 2001; Sharma, et al., 2011; Trilokekar & Kukar, 2011).

TESOL is an obvious field in which teacher candidates should have a study abroad experience in order to better understand how language is acquired and cultural aspects that can impact teaching and learning. Studies have shown growth in pre-service TESOL teacher candidates as a result of study abroad experiences (Hyesun & Peter, 2019). Hyesun and Peter (2019) reported on interaction with peers as well as the experience of living in another culture as important to a teachers' time abroad. Although attention is given to teacher candidates being in a different country while they learn, it is also possible to also acquire similar skills via a virtual study abroad experience which gives participants contact with those from different countries and supports focused tasks relevant to the curriculum. In addition, study abroad can be a place to develop the language skills of non-native speaking teachers (Faez & Karas, 2019). In an article on study abroad, Faez and Karas (2019) reported that participants had the opportunity to increase their knowledge about teaching and learning and also improved language proficiency in the process. Comparable results have been seen when language teacher candidates have been partnered with other teacher candidates and language learners through virtual exchange (Hilliker et al., 2020; Lenkaitis, 2019d; Lenkaitis & Loranc-Paszylk, 2019).

Virtual Exchange

Virtual exchange is a viable way to replace a study abroad experience in teacher education courses while also benefiting the students on the other end of the exchange (Hilliker, 2020). A body of research on virtual exchange has grown in recent years that focuses on teacher education and virtual exchange (Dooley & Sadler, 2013; Fuchs et al., 2012; Lenkaitis, 2020a; Zhang et al., 2016). When teacher candidates are partnered together they can learn from one another about technology integration in the second language classroom (Dooley & Sadler, 2013; The EVALUATE Group, 2019), plan and discuss lessons together (Chen, 2012; Loranc-Paszylk, 2018), and practice and reflect on theory (Turunen & Tuovila, 2012; Yuan, 2018).

Global awareness and identity (Lenkaitis et al., 2019; Helm & Guth, 2010) and intercultural competence (Lenkaitis, 2019a; Sanchez-Hernandez & Alcón-Soler, 2018) are both important benefits for teacher candidates that participate in virtual exchanges. Virtual study abroad utilizes virtual exchange as an innovative instructional approach in higher education that can mimic a clinical study abroad experience (Hilliker, 2020). Language teacher development research has proven that such skills such as pragmatics (Cunningham, 2017), technological skills (Zhang, et al., 2016), and language competence (Perez Cañado, 2010) have improved with virtual exchange.

Dooley and Sadler (2013) examine the effect a two-year exchange project had on teacher education through focus on student language teachers living abroad in Spain and the United States. Over the course of both years, the language teacher candidates in this study communicated with each other online. This type of exchange offered different opportunities and resulted in increased skills because of contact with counterparts in a different country (Dooley & Sadler, 2013). The most recent study published by The EVALUATE Group (2019) partnered 1,018 teacher candidates from 34 different institutions across 25 virtual exchange projects. The findings of this study suggest that participants, because of their interaction the virtual exchange tasks, developed their pedagogical and language competence. Hilliker's (2020) study found that when TESOL teacher candidates were paired with students from Mexico via teleconference the TESOL teacher candidates were positively influenced by their participation in a virtual study abroad. This research described the ways virtual study abroad supported teacher candidates' learning as they interacted with English as a foreign language students and categorized the benefits of virtual study abroad for giving teachers more clinically rich and practical experiences.

Pedagogical Content Knowledge

Teacher education programs begin to support teacher candidates when they develop pedagogical content knowledge as they take subject knowledge and work to convey ideas to students (Shulman, 2013). In order for teachers to move from novice to expert they need a variety of interactions with students to practice (Clift & Brady, 2005), as well as opportunities for professional development that is sustainable, situated in authentic teaching contexts, and challenges their ideas about teaching (Gess-Newsome et al., 2017). Pedagogical content knowledge has been explored in a number of domains, but researchers have indicated how different foreign language teaching is from other subject teaching (Borg, 2006) due to the concurrent requirement of linguistic medium and content (Freeman, 2016). In other words, the foreign language teacher needs to possess both the expertise in the pedagogical and linguistic background, and at the same time should possess the adequate level of fluency in this language to function as a model for foreign language use.

Research Question

Due to research that has shown that virtual exchange is a viable way for language teacher candidates to professionally develop (Loranc-Paszylk, 2018; Lenkaitis, 2020a) and in order to add to the growing body of research of using virtual study abroad (Hilliker, 2020), this chapter will answer the following the research question: In what ways does participation in a virtual study abroad, via online exchange, transform teacher candidates' perspectives while taking a course focused on pedagogical content knowledge?

Methodology

Participants

After the authors met at a computer assisted language learning conference, students from each of their universities were partnered because they are all studying to become second language teachers. Participants from a university in the United States were partnered with participants at a university in Poland in a 6-week virtual study abroad. All participants were TESOL teacher candidates and were partnered with at least one international partner based on availability to meet synchronously through video conference. Their meetings were an additional course component that allowed them to have a virtual study abroad experience through interaction with those from a different culture. There were a total of 28 participants: 9 from the United States and 19 from Poland. Teacher candidates collaborated in one of the thirteen 2–3 person groups on the basis of their availability outside of the classroom.

Procedures

Participants used Zoom (https://zoom.us) to virtually meet. Apart from the Week 1 introductions and Week 6 for a culminating activity, participants met to discuss weekly topics during Weeks 2–5. For all synchronous sessions, although participants were instructed to meet for at least 15 minutes each week at a time that was convenient for the group (Lenkaitis et al., 2019), throughout the exchange; groups met for a combined total of 36 hours, 19 minutes, 9 seconds. Therefore, each of the thirteen groups met for approximately 3 hours over the course of the six synchronous sessions.

Common weekly topics were chosen so that everyone would be able to have the opportunity to have a transformative learning experience (Mezirow, 1997). Just as a traditional study abroad entails exploring intercultural themes/ differences, the following topics were chosen for this virtual study abroad to allow the participant the opportunity to engage with the culture of their partner(s): sports and patriotism (Week 2), advertising (Week 3), crime (Week 4), and natural disasters (Week 5). Researchers on both sides of the exchange selected photos of these topics that were relevant to their countries' current events. The photos were piloted prior to being used by English language students and teacher candidates not in the study to gauge their relevance and potential for discussion. The photos acted as stimulus for the weekly discussion. The societal macro topics (Lenkaitis & Loranc-Paszylk, 2019) were selected to give teachers prompts that would elicit discussions that they might encounter outside of the classroom in a face-to-face study abroad situation.

In addition to that, the choice of the topics was dictated by the need to assure the participants could hold discussions as ambassadors of their own culture and to eliminate unevenness resulting from the fact that native speakers of English interacted with non-native speakers.

During Weeks 2–5, participants completed a pre-survey and post-survey regarding the weekly topic in order to investigate the development of the teacher candidates' perceptions of selected topics and approaches to virtual study abroad. Each survey had the same two questions:

1 Using the scale (1 - being not relevant at all to 7 - extremely relevant), how relevant is this week's topic to your virtual study abroad?
2 Please explain your answer to the question above.

Results

The authors of this study was on Weeks 2–5. Therefore, the data that were analyzed were the pre- and post-surveys from each of these weeks. Quantitative analyses, which included descriptive statistics and t-tests were carried out with the Likert-scale questions on IBM SPSS Statistics 25.0. When comparing means, t-tests did not show significant differences. However, the means for each Likert-scale question from pre- to post-survey did show some fluctuation. Standard deviations values were larger due to the small number of participants and the range of their ratings. Also, due to this total number of participants, data from both groups were combined in order to view the virtual exchange holistically. Table 17.1 details these quantitative results.

Qualitative analyses on open-ended responses were completed via NVivo 12 for Windows. Word frequencies informed the following researcher-created coding categories. In addition to building on those used in Hilliker (2020), the following categories emerged from the word frequencies completed via Nvivo:

1 Facilitate communication with teacher candidates from another country
2 Connections made between culture and language

Table 17.1 Descriptive Statistics from Pre- and Post-Survey Questions

Survey	Mean	Standard Deviation
Pre - Week 2	4.88	1.67
Post - Week 2	4.50	2.03
Pre - Week 3	4.50	1.71
Post - Week 3	4.59	1.79
Pre - Week 4	4.54	1.72
Post - Week 4	4.38	2.02
Pre - Week 5	4.59	2.09
Post - Week 5	4.73	2.23

3 Application of course knowledge
4 Recognition of stereotypes
5 Uncertain about connection

These categories coincided with participants discussing the weekly topics of their virtual study abroad, which allowed them to focus on the intercultural communication with their partners and their awareness of their partners' country and university. Two coders worked independently to code the data and reached a 91.7% agreement (Kappa = 0.62). To reconcile differences, both coders worked together to reach a 100% agreement. Table 17.2 illustrates each coding category definition and the number of coded instances for each category during Weeks 2–5 while Table 17.3 lists representative examples of each coding category. The authors looked at results holistically so did not separate by United States or Poland.

Table 17.2 Definitions of Coding Categories and Coding Breakdown

Coding Category	Definition	Number of Coded Instances - Week 2		Number of Coded Instances - Week 3		Number of Coded Instances - Week 4		Number of Coded Instances - Week 5		Total Number
		Pre	Post	Pre	Post	Pre	Post	Pre	Post	
Facilitate communication with teacher candidates from another country	Using own knowledge to compare and relate to other teacher candidates	9	5	9	11	7	6	5	6	58
Connections made between culture and language	Effective communication involves both language and culture	5	3	12	3	7	9	11	10	60
Application of course knowledge	Course material and concepts are related to teaching and learning	4	3	6	4	2	1	3	1	24
Recognition of stereotypes	Typical similarities and differences teacher candidates may have about others	3	2	0	1	5	1	0	1	13
No explanation	Unable to or did not explain rating	7	15	1	9	7	11	9	10	69

Table 17.3 Examples of Coded Instances

Coding Category	Examples
Facilitate communication with teacher candidates from another country	• We have to be aware of what is happening in the world. • I can compare opinions with my international partner and also get to know something new about the topic. • Being aware of struggles countries go through can allow others to empathize with them.
Connections made between culture and language	• This topic affects everyone differently but does affect everyone regardless of their culture. • Communication is part of the coursework, and communication is key to dealing with preparation and the aftermath of a natural disaster. • Understanding people's advertisements and how other countries are similar or different is a part of communication. • I think advertising and the way companies in other countries in particular choose to advertise is telling. You learn more about what is important in the advertiser's eyes, what information or product do they want you to focus on, what is the message that they are trying to send, and how do they view the average human and/or citizen in a country based on the information and message presented in the advertisement?
Application of course knowledge	• Patriotism is a huge issue in todays [sic] world, and because of mass media and the way information is shared, paired with how sports are presented in the media cycle; they seemed to be tied. I do not see how sports play a role. I understand the pride a person has over a team or an athlete. • Natural disasters are a fairly important topic related to the course work. Natural disasters allow group members to understand climate differences and comparisons as well as how communities get together during disasters.
Recognition of stereotypes	• I consider this week's topic relevant enough to the coursework because the crime exists all over the world and it is worth exchanging the experience pertinent the situation in a given country. I can assume that in this are [sic] we find many differences. • Sports exist in every culture throughout any language. Patriotism varies with individuals.
No explanation	• I'm unsure of the connection to the coursework • Not sure how it relates

Discussion

Based on this study's qualitative results, it can be suggested that virtual study abroad was a viable option to transform teacher candidates' perspectives while taking courses focused on pedagogical content knowledge as they need opportunities to develop their language teaching expertise (Shulman, 2013). The results of this virtual exchange as a possible alternative to study abroad showed a connection to pedagogical content knowledge that teacher candidates were learning in class to interactions with their peers from another country. These types of experiences allowed language teacher candidates to consider different cultural viewpoints in order to transform their perspectives on pedagogical content knowledge (Cranton, 2002; Taylor, 2000). The teacher candidates engaged in a virtual exchange environment in which their ideas about intercultural, societal macro topics were discussed weekly with their partners. In these synchronous sessions, participants gained insight about these topics through the expertise of their partner and home country. Because of this, participants were able to gain a unique perspective on their coursework beyond what they could gain in the classroom and learn about how topics were similar and different across both countries. As a result, this international experience, a virtual study abroad, gave participants the opportunity to transform their perceptions about intercultural, societal macro topics while working with international partners. Even though there were a number of coded instances in the "No explanation" category, this does not imply that teacher candidates were trying to figure out why they were given these weekly topics. Rather, this suggests that teacher candidates were starting the conversation about these topics in their intercultural partnerships, but simply did not know how to articulate their ideas. With more time, participants would be able to become aware and critically reflective of points other than their own (Mezirow, 1997).

Within the categorization that has been developed for this study, based on codes from a previous study abroad via virtual exchange article by Hilliker (2020), qualitative data demonstrated that language teacher candidates have been able to (1) expand on an existing point of view, (2) establish a new point of view, and (3) transform a point of view, based on the theoretical underpinnings of transformative learning (Mezirow, 1997). Drawing on the participants' accounts of the gaps they have noticed in their knowledge, it can be speculated that in the future a virtual study abroad can be designed to encourage language teacher candidates to become aware and critically reflective of points other than our own (Mezirow, 1997).

Therefore, virtual exchange can be an alternative for a study abroad as it shows development of the participants' perspectives on their pedagogical knowledge and teacher education curriculum as a result of their interactions with peers from another culture. This resonates with the previous literature about study abroad (Hilliker, 2020; Lenkaitis, 2019a; Palmer & Menard-Warwick, 2012; Sharma et al., 2011; Trilokekar & Kukar, 2011). Although there is fluctuation shown in some of the participants' pre- and post-survey answers from initial weeks to final weeks, there was an increase in the first two weeks, but then in the final weeks more students seemed to recognize the relevance of the course content to the intercultural learning (Lenkaitis, 2019a; Sanchez-Hernandez & Alcón-Soler, 2018).

The language teacher candidates realized the complexity of issues related to intercultural learning, while interacting with their international peers and performing the virtual exchange tasks, the participants had a chance to confront several issues through a perspective of their international peers. As a result of the contact with their partners, language teacher candidates realized the sophistication of issues related to intercultural dimensions of pedagogical content knowledge and engaged more in their coursework with representatives of different cultures. By drawing on their experiences, teacher candidates realized complex cultural issues related to coursework and showed evidence of epistemological humility (Hilliker et al.; Ess, 2007; Pegrum, 2011) as they expressed gaps in their area of expertise. However, regardless of these gaps, teacher candidates noticed the importance of having a virtual study abroad, via virtual exchange, as a key to facilitate communication with teacher candidates from another country.

Limitations

Since the data were self-reported, some participants may have not expressed all of their perspectives regarding their virtual study abroad, via virtual exchange, which in turn could have impacted their pre- and post-survey answers. Regardless, coding was completed by two independent coders in order to find commonalities among answers. In addition, they worked together to choose the most representative examples when analyzing the data. Furthermore, since transformative learning needs to be over time, collecting data from a virtual study abroad, via virtual exchange, for more than six weeks would be beneficial to investigate additional viewpoints and have teacher candidates become aware and critically reflective of points other than their own (Mezirow, 1997). For example, with more time, the weekly topics may lend themselves to increased cultural discussion related to pedagogical content knowledge versus a number of coded instances in the No explanation category. Since this exchange was focused on sharing cultural information, the teacher candidates were not given shared course content as they were assumed to be experts in their respective language and culture. However, future iterations of a similar virtual study abroad could focus on weekly topics that are directly correlated to course content and pedagogical practice.

Conclusion

One of the goals of a teacher education program is to provide teacher candidates opportunities to practice the craft they are learning in clinically rich environments. Field work and practicum experiences are typically attached to coursework, which often can be difficult to find through local teachers, classrooms, and schools. With available technology, specifically virtual exchange, teacher candidates can be connected to different classrooms around the state, country, and world and discuss topics that coincide with program and university goals. In the case of teachers, more specifically language teachers, being connected to another country and a group of teachers through a virtual study abroad, via virtual exchange, provides a clinically rich experience that they would not have had otherwise. Not only did this virtual study abroad transform teacher candidates' learning by expanding, establishing, and transforming their viewpoints (Mezirow, 1997), but it also led to better understanding of their pedagogical content knowledge. We are not dismissing the value traditional study abroad can afford participants, but when travel opportunities are limited virtual study abroad can be a viable alternative to include as part of language teacher preparation programs.

References

Allen, L. Q. (2010). The impact of study abroad on the professional lives of world language teachers. *Foreign Language Annals*, *43*(1), 93–104. https://doi.org/10.1111/j.1944-9720.2010.01062.x

Baecher, L. (2012). Feedback from the field: What novice preK-12 ESL teachers want to tell TESOL teacher educators. *TESOL Quarterly*, *46*(3), 578–588. https://www.jstor.org/stable/41576069

Baecher, L. & Chung, S. (2019). Transformative professional development for in-service teachers through international service learning. *Teacher Development*, *24*(1), 33–51. https://doi.org/10.1080/13664530.2019.1682033

Boling, E. C. (2007). Linking technology, learning, and stories: Implications from research on hypermedia video-cases. *Teaching and Teacher Education*, *23*(2), 189–200. https://doi.org/10.1016/j.tate.2006.04.015

Borg, S. (2006). The distinctive characteristics of foreign language teachers. *Language Teaching Research*, *10*, 3–31. https://doi.org/10.1191/1362168806lr182oa

Chen, W.-C. (2012). Professional growth during cyber collaboration between pre-service and in-service teachers. *Teaching and Teacher Education*, *28*(2), 218–228. doi:10.1016/j.tate.2011.09.010

Clift, R. T., & Brady, P. (2005). Research on methods courses and field experiences. In M. Cochran-Smith & K. M. Zeichner (Eds.), *Studying teacher education. The report of the AERA Panel on Research and Teacher Education* (pp. 309–424). Mahwah, NJ: Lawrence Erlbaum.

Cranton, P. (2002). Teaching for transformation. *New Directions for Adult and Continuing Education*, *93*, 63–71. https://doi.org/10.1002/ace.50

Cunningham, D. J. (2017). Methodological innovation for the study of request production in telecollaboration. *Language Learning & Technology*, *21*(1), 75–98. https://dx.doi.org/10125/44596

Curran, E., & Murray, M. (2008). Transformative learning in teacher education: Building competencies and changing dispositions. *Journal of the Scholarship of Teaching and Learning*, 103–118. Retrieved from https://scholarworks.iu.edu/journals/index.php/josotl/article/download/1704/1702

Dooley, M. & Sadler, R. (2013). Filling in the gaps: Linking theory and practice through telecollaboration in teacher education. *ReCALL*, *25*(1), 4–29. doi:10.1017/S0958344012000237

Ess, C. (2007). Liberal arts and distance education: Can Socratic virtue (αρετυ) and Confucius' exemplary person (junzi) be taught online? In J. Lockard & M. Pegrum (Eds.), *Brave new classrooms: Democratic education and the internet* (pp. 189–212). New York: Peter Lang.

European Commission. (2017). Study on the feasibility of an Erasmus+ virtual exchange initiative: Final report. Retrieved from https://ec.europa.eu/education/sites/education/files/erasmus-virtual-exchangestudy_en.pdf

Faez, F., & Karas, M. (2019). Language proficiency development of non-native English-Speaking teachers (NNESTs) in an MA TESOL program: A case study. *TESL-EJ*, *22*(4). https://eric.ed.gov/?id=EJ1204612

Freeman, D. (2016). *Educating second language teachers: 'The same things done differently.'* Oxford: Oxford University Press.

Fuchs, C., Hauck, M., and Müller-Hartmann, A. (2012). Promoting learner autonomy through multiliteracy skills development in cross-institutional exchanges. *Language Learning & Technology, 16*(3), 82–102.

Gess-Newsome, J., Taylor, J. A., Carlson, J., Gardner, A. L., Wilson, C. D., & Stuhlsatz, M. A. M. (2017). Teacher pedagogical content knowledge, practice, and student achievement. *International Journal of Science Education*, 1–20. doi:10.1080/09500693.2016.1265158

Guth, S. & Helm, F. (2011). Developing multiliteracies in ELT through telecollaboration. *ELT Journal, 66*(1), 42–51. https://doi.org/10.1093/elt/ccr027

Helm, F. and Guth, S. (2010). The multifarious goals of telecollaboration 2.0: Theoretical and practical implications. In S. Guth and F. Helm (Eds.) *Telecollaboration 2.0: Language, Literacies, and Intercultural Learning in the 21st Century* (pp. 69–106). New York: Peter Lang. doi: 10.3726/978-3-0351-0013-6

Hilliker, S. (2020) Virtual exchange as a study abroad alternative to foster language and culture exchange in TESOL teacher education. *The Electronic Journal for English as a Second Language 23*(4), 1–13. Retrieved from http://www.tesl-ej.org/wordpress/issues/volume23/ej92/ej92a7/

Hilliker, S. M., Lenkaitis, C. A., & Bouhafa, Y. (2020). The role of intercultural virtual exchanges in developing pragmatic awareness. In C-C. Lin & C. Zaccarini (Eds.). *Internationalization in Action: Leveraging Diversity and Inclusion in Globalized Classrooms.* Bern, Switzerland: Peter Lang.

Hyesun, C., and Peter, L. (2019). Taking the TESOL practicum abroad: Opportunities for critical awareness and community-building among preservice teachers. In M. Khosrow-Pour (Ed.). *Pre-Service and In-Service Teacher Education: Concepts, Methodologies, Tools, and Applications*, pp. 737-759. Hershey, PA: IGI Global.

Lenkaitis, C. A. (2019a). Rethinking study abroad and intercultural competence. In B. Loranc-Paszylk (Ed.) *Rethinking Directions in Language Learning at University Level* (p. 137–163). Research-publishing.net. https://doi.org/10.14705/rpnet.2019.31.895

Lenkaitis, C. A. (2019b). Valuing technology in the L2 classroom: Student and teacher perceptions, preferences, and digital identity. In M. Montebello (Ed.) *Embracing Digital Learners in an Age of Global Educational Change and Rapid Technological Advancements* (p. 173–189). Hershey, PA: IGI Global doi: 10.4018/978-1-5225-9304-1.ch011

Lenkaitis, C. A. (2019c). Rethinking virtual exchange: Partnering EFL learners with TESOL teacher candidates. *NYS TESOL Journal 6*(2), 3–15. Available at http://journal.nystesol.org

Lenkaitis, C. A. (2020a). Teacher candidate reflection: Benefits of using a synchronous computer-mediated communication-based virtual exchange. *Teaching and Teacher Education 92.* https://doi.org/10.1016/j.tate.2020.103041

Lenkaitis, C. A. (2020b). Technology as a mediating tool: videoconferencing, L2 learning, and learner autonomy. *Computer Assisted Language Learning*, 33(5-6), 483–509. https://doi.org/10.1080/09588221.2019.1572018.

Lenkaitis, C. A., & Loranc-Paszylk, B. (2019). Facilitating global citizenship development in lingua franca virtual exchanges. *Language Teaching Research*, 1–18. doi: 10.1177/1362168819877371

Lenkaitis, C. A., Loranc-Paszylk, B., & Hilliker, S. (2019). Global awareness and global identity development among foreign language learners: The impact of virtual exchanges. *MEXTESOL Journal 43*(4), 1–11.

Lenkaitis, C. A., Calo, S., & Venegas Escobar, S. (2019). Exploring the intersection of language and culture via telecollaboration: Utilizing Zoom for intercultural competence development. *International Multilingual Research Journal, 13*(2), 102–115. doi: 10.1080/19313152.2019.1570772

Lewis, T. L., & Niesenbaum, R. A. (2005). Extending the stay: using community-based research and service learning to enhance short-term study abroad. *Journal of Studies in International Education, 9*(3), 251–264. https://doi.org/10.1177/1028315305277682

Lindahl, K., Hansen-Thomas, H., Baecher, L., & Stewart, M. A. (2020). Study abroad for critical multilingual language awareness development in ESL and bilingual teacher candidates. *TESL-EJ, 23*(4). Retrieved from http://www.tesl-ej.org/wordpress/issues/volume23/ej92/ej92a5/

Loranc-Paszylk, B. (2016). *Incorporating cross-cultural video conferencing to enhance Content and Language Integrated Learning (CLIL) at the tertiary level.* New directions in telecollaborative research and practice: Selected papers from the second conference on Telecollaboration in Higher Education. https://doi.org/10.14705/rpnet.2016.telecollab2016.499

Loranc-Paszylk, B. (2018). Marking the difference – use of peer assessment in a cross-cultural telecollaborative project involving EFL teacher trainees. In J. Pitura, S. Sauro (Eds.) *CALL for Mobility* (pp. 13–28). Bern, Switzerland: Peter Lang.

Mezirow, J. (1997). Transformative learning: Theory to practice. *New Directions for Adult and Continuing Education, (74)*, 5–12. https://doi.org/10.1002/ace.7401

NAFSA. (2003). *Securing America's future: global education for a global age. Report of the strategic task force on education abroad.* Association of International Educators. http://www.nafsa.org/Policy_and_Advocacy/Policy_Resources/Policy_Reports/Securing_America_s_Future/

Navracsics, T. (2016). *Engage – why we need to open up education more than ever.* Third dialogue with Southern Mediterranean countries on Higher Education. Brussels. Speech cited in Study on the feasibility of an erasmus+ virtual exchange initiative: final report (p. 24). European Commission. https://ec.europa.eu/education/sites/education/files/erasmus-virtual-exchange-study_en.pdf

O'Dowd, R. (2018). From telecollaboration to virtual exchange: state-of-the-art and the role of UNICollaboration in moving forward. *Journal of Virtual Exchange, 1*, 1–23. Research-publishing.net. https://doi.org/10.14705/rpnet.2018.jve.1

Palmer, D. K., & Menard-Warwick, J. (2012). Short-term study abroad for Texas preservice teachers: On the road from empathy to critical awareness. *Multicultural Education, 19*(3), 17–26. Retrieved from https://eric.ed.gov/?id=EJ1001531

Pegrum M. (2011). Modified, multiplied, and (re-)mixed: Social media and digital literacies. In M. Thomas (Ed.), *Digital Education* (pp. 9–35). Digital Education and Learning series. New York: Palgrave Macmillan. https://doi.org/10.1057/9780230118003_2

Perez Cañado, M. L. (2010). Using virtual learning environments and computer-mediated communication to enhance the lexical competence of pre-service English teachers: A quantitative and qualitative study. *Computer Assisted Language Learning, 23*(2), 129–150. https://doi.org/10.1080/09588221003666222

Phillion, J., Malewski, E. L., Sharma, S., & Wang, Y. (2009). Reimagining the curriculum: Future teachers and study abroad. *Frontiers: The Interdisciplinary Journal of Study Abroad, 18*, 323–339. Retrieved from https://eric.ed.gov/?id=EJ883706

Sánchez-Hernández, A., & Alcón-Soler, E. (2018). Pragmatic gains in the study abroad context: Learners' experiences and recognition of pragmatic routines. *Journal of Pragmatics.* https://doi.org/10.1016/j.pragma.2018.08.006

Sharma, S., Phillion, J., & Malewski, E. (2011). Examining the practice of critical reflection for developing pre-service teachers' multicultural competencies: Findings from a study abroad program in Honduras. *Issues in Teacher Education, 20*(2), 9–22. Retrieved from https://eric.ed.gov/?id=EJ954551

Shulman, L. S. (2013). Those who understand: Knowledge growth in teaching. *Educational Researcher, 15*(2), 4–31. Retrieved from https://journals.sagepub.com/doi/pdf/10.1177/002205741319300302

Taylor, E. W. (2000). Analyzing research on transformative learning theory. In J. Mezirow and Associates (Eds.), *Learning as transformation: Critical perspectives on a theory in progress.* San Francisco: Jossey-Bass.

The EVALUATE Group. (2019). *Evaluating the impact of virtual exchange on initial teacher education: A European policy experiment.* Research-publishing.net. https://doi.org/10.14705/rpnet.2019.29.9782490057337

Tomaš, Z., & Horn-Gabel, V., Marnikovic, S. (2020). Examining the value of a TESOL service-learning study abroad for US pre- and in-service teachers and Montenegrin community stakeholders. *TESL-EJ, 23*(4). Retrieved from http://www.tesl-ej.org/wordpress/issues/volume23/ej92/ej92a6/

Trilokekar, R. D., & Kukar, P. (2011). Disorienting experiences during study abroad: Reflections of pre-service teacher candidates. *Teaching and Teacher Education, 27*(7), 1141–1150 .https://doi.org/10.1016/j.tate.2011.06.002

Turunen, T. A., & Tuovila, S. (2012). Mind the gap. Combining theory and practice in a field experience. *Teaching Education, 23*(2), 115–130. Doi: https://doi.org/10.1080/10476210.2012.669751

Yuan, R. (2018). "Practice what I preach": Exploring an experienced EFL teacher educator's modeling practice. *TESOL Quarterly, 52*(2), 1–12. doi: 10.1002/tesq.419

Zhang, Z., Li, J., Liu, F., & Miao, Z. (2016). Hong Kong and Canadian students experiences a new participatory culture: A teacher professional training project undergirded by new media literacies. *Teaching and Teacher Education, 59*, 146–158. Doi: http://dx.doi.org/10.1016/j.tate.2016.05.017

18 Representation and Reciprocity in Early Childhood Education

Cross Cultural Field Insights in an Anishinaabe Context

Lucinda G. Heimer, Dennis R. White,
Lynell Caya, and Paige Lancaster

Introduction

> In 1971 when I heard that the National Teacher Corps was recruiting students to teach in Indigenous communities, I was thrilled and sought out the recruiter somewhere in an ivory tower on Bascom Hill. She was happy to accept my application, but I was floored when the young Black woman told me that I was the first Indigenous person she had ever met even though she was recruiting for the Wisconsin Indian Teacher Corps. I wanted to teach and was able to interview. I was told I was not accepted because with a degree in Mathematics I would not be able to relate to Indigenous children at the elementary level, though it may have had something to do with my long hair worn in braids, tied with red ribbons.
>
> (Dennis White, Lakeland Anishinaabe faculty)

This recollection hints at the pronounced and personal impact of colonization and race relations in the United States. The Teacher Corps was created as part of the Higher Education Act of 1965 to address the need for teachers in predominantly low-income areas (Woodcock & Alawiye, 2001). Yet, as the quote suggests, a tribal member, the Lakeland faculty instructor, was barred from teaching in his own community, one considered low-income. This illustrates how assimilationist history and colonization changed over time from more explicit oppression (e.g., boarding schools) to the illogical nature of credentialing policy in the Teacher Corps. Today, the opportunity gap compels us to consider alternate approaches and pedagogies for meeting each child's needs (National Center for Education Statistics, 2019). The disparity between the demographics of the children who are not meeting expected academic standards and those of the teaching staff suggest the need to better prepare teachers for under-represented communities (Brayboy et al., 2012). Creating pathways in Indigenous communities to teacher credentialing is a part of the larger partnership between the University of the Midwest (UM) and the Lakeland Anishinaabe community. We use pseudonyms for people, places, and agencies in our research.

As Indigenous and non-Indigenous educators working and writing together with early childhood education (ECE) teacher candidates at UM, we explore the experiences of teacher candidates crossing cultural contexts in an international field experience *within* the United States. The term Indigenous is used in reference to Native American Peoples, First Peoples of the United States, and specific tribes in the United States. The choice of the term Anishinaabe is intentional as it refers to a group of culturally related Indigenous people, including tribes within the United States and Canada (Treuer, 2012). Through the use of a more global term, we seek to protect the privacy of the tribe. However, we acknowledge the importance of using tribal names as too often unique and varied lived experiences are generalized or erased through the use of labels such as Native American, American Indian, First Nations and Indigenous. The impact of colonization, specifically as it relates to the sovereign status of an Indigenous community, was explored throughout the field experience by the teacher candidate researchers, the UM faculty, and the Lakeland instructor serving as both participants and authors. This is an uncommon practice in research on experiential learning and strengthens our practical insights. The UM faculty and teacher candidates all identify as white women and the Lakeland instructor as an Anishinaabe man. Visiting a nation within a nation and unpacking the policy, law, and governance as it relates to early education provides possibilities for cultural border crossing. We propose that critical reflection on historical impact provides insight for how lived experience and racial awareness influences the teaching of children by teacher candidates.

Context

International Field Work in ECE

Research on teacher education that addresses diverse student populations has suggested the need for teacher candidates to critically define and explore the histories and lived experiences of children and families (Auld et al., 2016; Nieto, 2010). Urgency for this work is partially fueled by the continuing demographic disparity between educators (predominantly white middle class) and the populations they teach (children of color) (Ladson-Billings, 2005).

International fieldwork literature has focused on short-term global experiences where faculty have investigated student interest, involvement, and insights (Madrid et al., 2016; Moss & Marx, 2011). In teacher education, field experiences in diverse settings offer teacher candidates opportunities to step out of their familiar contexts. However, the quality of such experiences has been critiqued, with suggestions of potentially detrimental impacts as these experiences may fail to provide support for deep internalization of self-awareness in a new cultural context (Auld et al., 2016; Madrid et al., 2016). In some instances, contrary to intended program goals, Western ethnocentrism, biases, and colonial mentality are actually reinforced (Cushner & Chang, 2015; Smolcic & Katunich, 2017). Current research includes few experiences within the United States, working with Indigenous populations exploring the effects field experiences have on teacher candidates or the Indigenous communities. The notion that international work can be conducted within the borders of the United States warrants further consideration as nations within a nation (Sumida Huaman et al., 2019).

Sovereignty

International field experiences with Indigenous communities in the United States require a basic understanding of the historical and political foundations of tribal sovereignty and the survival of Anishinaabe people. In the United States, there are currently over five hundred Indigenous nations of approximately three million people (Dunbar-Ortiz, 2015). However, the US education system regularly fails to teach how the United States came to exist and how these sovereign nations were created (Dunbar-Ortiz, 2015). Tribes were moved through colonization into "retained portions of their original land" often called reservations (Treuer, 2012). Despite the strength of early Indigenous governance, the move to reservations changed governance to a new model. Tribal nations had jurisdiction over land and tribal members. However, dimensions of those nations fell under separate state and federal mandates (e.g., gaming, taxation, criminal law), compromising the governance and authority of those sovereignties. The legacy of trauma caused by the effects of colonization and removal continues. One example of the intergenerational impact of these policies began through the creation of boarding schools in 1860 (Treuer, 2012). These schools, established by Christian missionaries, were an attempt to assimilate Indigenous children and youth into the Euro-American culture during the late 19th and early 20th centuries (Archuleta et al., 2000). Not until the Indian Child Welfare Act (1978) were Indigenous parents given the right to deny this form of education for their children (US Department of the Interior, 2020). The influence of colonization, and specifically the residential boarding school experience, has had mental health consequences for current tribal community members (Bombay et al., 2014; Centers for Disease Control, n.d.).

> The most devastating changes in the lives of Indigenous people were made by the federally run boarding schools or the mission schools. Children were rounded up like cattle, and taken away from their homes, their language, and their culture for most of the school year. I recall an elder telling me that he never spoke the language again after being punished for speaking Ojibwe to other Anishinaabe. His punishment was lye soap in his mouth with a wet towel wrapped around his head. The burns to his mouth healed but the scars to his psyche did not.
>
> (Dennis White, Lakeland Anishinaabe Faculty)

Placing teacher candidates in a context where historical trauma continues to play out allows for greater awareness of trauma's impact in their future work with children. Our study acknowledges the impact of intergenerational trauma and colonization in education settings (Bombay et al., 2014; Brave Heart, 2007; Smith, 2012).

Field Placements in Indigenous Communities

Indigenous populations in off-reservation public schools are growing, making Indigenous students less likely to have Indigenous teachers or teachers with "Indigenous cultural competency" (McCarty & Lee, 2014). Consideration of historical trauma and teaching children in ways that seek to reclaim and recreate an authentic Indigenous identity are not infused in the classroom (Bombay et al., 2014; Brave Heart, 2007). As such, the educational experiences of children from Indigenous communities with sovereign status reveal a history deserving attention.

> While I feel that our own Indigenous teachers, knowledgeable in the culture, ways, traditions, and language of our people, are the best ones to teach our future generations of strong, healthy Anishinaabe, there is hope through positive impact of changing the viewpoint of only a few future non-Anishinaabe teachers. While we provide pathways for Indigenous community members to teach in their home communities, we must consider how many generations have passed with very few Indigenous teachers. As a reflection of the beautiful symmetry inherent in mathematics, which frames my worldview, to provide a reversal of the situation must necessarily take several generations.
>
> (Dennis White, Lakeland Anishinaabe Faculty)

As an administrator in the community, Dennis acknowledges that the field experience is a beginning step in a process to provide culturally relevant teaching. The host context and history of interactions among individuals, communities, and institutions in the host and home are often not explored fully in internationalization efforts (Sumida Huaman et al., 2019). University programs that address a deeper understanding of colonization, racism, and oppression increase teacher candidates' awareness of equity issues as they take positions supporting children in classrooms (Nieto, 2010; Sleeter, 2001). International field placements provide visiting teacher candidates culturally based knowledge of the host community. Through student teaching, both university students and host community members learn about student teaching, one step in the credentialing process.

Theoretical Framing

Smith (2012) suggests that colonization is evident in Western notions of truth, and calls for deconstructing the power inherent in research practices, questioning whose interests are being served. Through our participatory nature, we situate ourselves within decolonizing work which considers intergenerational trauma and historical legacy as part of the analysis (Swadener & Mutua, 2008). In the internationalization of education there is a need to address issues of power, equity and representation as these relate to the purpose and development of knowledge, questioning who is served in the process (Sumida Huaman et al., 2019).

Reflective practice allows access to concepts of power and privilege connecting with insider/outsider identities. Through the use of critical reflection, frames of reference are opened, ways of thinking are adapted, and new perspectives are formed (Trilokekar & Kukar, 2011). Self-reflection and critical engagement challenges limited views of diversity by connecting context and identity (social class, race, ability etc.) with privilege and oppression (Kim & Kim, 2017). Reflective practice suggests that learning is more easily applied to the future if the learner is able to have a concrete experience, observe and reflect, and analyze the process (Kolb, 1984). The teacher candidates in our initiative engaged in the reflective process throughout the short-term field experience as participants, researchers, authors, and presenters (Schön, 1987). This builds on traditional approaches to reflection by adding an iterative layer. The process required (a) preparation for, engagement in, and reflection on fieldwork; (b) revisiting and discussing the reflections through coding and analysis; (c) writing about the discussion of the reflection; and (d) sharing insights through presentations with other teacher candidates and researchers at conferences. This, along with inclusion of the faculty mentors representing both communities in the writing process, provided an important foundation for our work, helping us to address "settler innocence" and opening a space for critical sharing (Tuck & Yang, 2012).

Methods

This study is part of a larger collaborative effort between UM and the Lakeland Anishinaabe community. The goal at the center of the larger partnership is to create a pathway for Anishinaabe community members to complete degrees and licensing credentials with the option to stay in their community and teach. This smaller study focused on the cross-cultural aspects of the work as experienced by teacher candidates who identified as white women between the ages of 21 and 39.

The UM Context

It is notable that this field study was recognized as an international program at UM's Global Studies Center, especially given that travel was within the borders of the state. This experience raised awareness of the meaning and power of sovereign nation status. The teacher candidates were enrolled as ECE undergraduate majors in the UM dual licensure program (Birth-3rd Grade/Special Education). The Lakeland field experience was not required, though it was desirable as it offered a short timeframe and low financial commitment, while focusing on cross-cultural learning in early childhood education. Seven practica and two required semesters of the *Identity, Culture, and Social Justice in Education* seminar were completed prior to the Lakeland Anishinaabe field placement.

In multiple ECE classes, concepts regarding identity, power, oppression, privilege, race, and historical trauma were explored through readings, discussion, guest speakers, and assignments. Students examined the social construction of race and applied tenets of Racial Identity Development (RID) theory developed by Janet Helms (Thomas, 2011). Situated in psychology, this theory includes six stages of development for people who are white/dominant culture: (1) contact, (2) disintegration, (3) reintegration, (4) pseudo-independence, (5) immersion/emersion, and (6) autonomy. Using this theory, among others, students applied the concept of race as a measure for insider/outsider status.

The Lakeland Anishinaabe Context

The field placement included pre-trip meetings, the *Introduction to Anishinaabe Culture* course at the Lakeland Anishinaabe community college with the faculty instructor and co-author, field placements in PreK-3rd grade classrooms in the PreK-12 Lakeland Community School, cultural events, and post-trip monthly meetings. The Lakeland community was 75% American Indian, 20% White, and 5% two or more races; contrasting with UM's reported statistics of 1% American Indian, 84% White, 6% Hispanic, 5% African American, 2% Asian, and 1% Southeast Asian. Though members of a dominant culture, teacher candidates were living and working in a new context with a dramatically different racial demographic.

The four teacher candidates lived together in a renovated boarding house within the borders of the community, approximately 300 miles from the UM campus, yet three miles from tribal school campuses. The owner of the home lived onsite and had children who attended one of the schools where they were working. The time in the community, split equally between the Lakeland College and Lakeland Community PreK-12 school, spanned three weeks.

Introduction to Anishinaabe Culture Course

Teacher candidates were enrolled in a three-credit *Introduction to Anishinaabe Culture* course at Lakeland Community College along with one local Anishinaabe student, Mindy. In addition to course readings and discussions, teacher candidates read and spoke the language, learned basic vocabulary, visited community sites, foraged for wild foods, and participated in ceremonies.

> It is important to read or talk about how Indigenous people respect nature or have ceremonies ... but if you, as an outsider to the Indigenous

community, can be a part of ... ceremonies, that experience will provide a deeper knowledge of the Indigenous people. We had a tobacco ceremony the first day... On the second day of class we participated in a feast blessing eagle feathers which we were giving to Indigenous graduates... The ceremonies are so much a part of daily events as to be almost indistinguishable from other events of the day.

(Dennis White, Lakeland Anishinaabe Faculty)

PreK-3 Community School Classroom

At the Lakeland PreK-12 tribal community school, teacher candidates met with an Anishinaabe school administrator, who provided an overview of sovereignty and governance, the history of the community and traditions, funding, and the influence of historical trauma. Time in the school included (a) writing and teaching lessons, (b) helping with lesson preparation and paperwork for assessments, (c) addressing behavior needs of children, (d) packing up the classrooms and celebrations at year end and, (e) multiple field trips.

Data Collection and Analysis

Ethnographic in nature, this qualitative case study focused on reflective insights (Stake, 1995). The research question—How does a cross-cultural field experience affect teacher candidates' understanding of self in relation to cross-cultural teaching?—guided the inquiry. Data included daily reflective passages and faculty feedback posted online throughout the three-week experience. Reflective prompts were offered at each level of engagement. Initial prompts asking for insights, concerns, and questions were extended to include coursework connections. Final prompts referenced content from student reflections and encouraged teacher candidates to question assumptions and dig deeply into differences (e.g., school governance structure, cultural norms). Each of the teacher candidates participated in the data collection, coding, and analysis process (Miles et al., 2013). Teacher candidates wrote reflections while in the field, reviewed journals post experience, presented these insights and continued to critique and reflect during the writing process.

Assigned codes were applied initially as *tourist, relevance* (to future teaching), and *barriers* (to understanding difference). Once teacher candidates coded their own reflections, they read across their own and the reflections of others, and made comments on intersections and insights within the work. With co-researchers, the emergent codes were cross-checked against the data. Insights were compiled and reviewed for convergences. Journaling during the three-week field experience, followed by monthly meetings that included coding, analyzing, discussing, and writing were integral aspects of the methodology. In this process, the UM faculty mentor facilitated data analysis with the teacher candidates.

The research identified several findings related to the teacher candidates: (1) the need to extend beyond their comfort zones as insiders/outsiders, (2) the importance of highlighting strengths versus deficits when working in communities new to them, and (3) the role of education in historically marginalized communities (Heimer et al., 2019). The Lakeland course instructor (Dennis White) served as a participant observer and wrote reflections on his experiences as an integral part of the process. Using the central tenets of ethnography, the insights and analysis of the Lakeland faculty instructor reframed the original research findings to highlight the impact of insider/ outsider identities.

Finding: Insider/Outsider

Fluid Nature of Roles

Each teacher candidate grappled with the shift from insider to outsider in her own way while still recognizing her "temporary" otherness. The ability to regulate was supported by the fact they all came back to the same house within the Lakeland community. They were living in the community, yet they were separate, coming together daily to decompress. This initial impact of seeing self as "other" jolted them into the disintegration stage of a racial experience as they were confronted with the segregation of the Anishinaabe community from the surrounding communities (Thomas, 2011). In this stage, there is an increased awareness of racism and white privilege based on personal experience. As students continued to recognize their position, they realized the risk and discomfort they had chosen.

> It is easy to be myself and put down all of my guards when I am with the people who know me best and share my background, ideas, and values. I don't have to worry about being under scrutiny and I can ask questions without worrying about offending anyone...I'm not used to being outside of my comfort zone.
>
> (Lynell, May 31, 2016)

These worries were raised while students were in the Lakeland community. Later, through reflective research-based discussions, this was unpacked further. Teacher candidates shared that they tend to surround themselves with those who share their backgrounds, ideas, values, etc. on a daily basis, and asked how they could continuously reflect on the discomfort once back in their home settings. They acknowledged the privilege and ease of "sticking with what we know" and appreciated there is effort required when one is seen as unique by the dominant culture. This played out as they considered new ways of thinking through the strengths and deficits of their new context.

Assets Approach

Teacher candidates had a great deal of "practice" through coursework and seven other field placements to use a "strengths-based" approach rather than defaulting to deficit assumptions (Solorzano & Yosso, 2001). This field experience provided concrete examples of strengths-based thinking that made their previously abstract understanding more relevant.

> We took strawberries from the feast to eat later and because the food from the feast was blessed, we couldn't just throw the strawberry tops in the garbage – they either had to be buried, burned, or put in flowing water. On our way back from dinner, we stopped at the river and dumped our cup of strawberry tops in. At first, I thought it wouldn't be that important or interesting, but actually when we did it, it felt really powerful and it was a really great experience. I can't explain how or why it felt that way, but I think following tradition and following through with what we had learned felt good.
>
> (Paige, May 17, 2016)

> I wanted the outside students to know that many aspects of our culture are indeed alive. When UM students attended a community feast in the ceremonial hall, as the officiant of the ceremony, I wanted to make sure that I could invite the students. I asked those sponsoring the feast for explicit approval. When UM students arrived, some elementary students knew them already, providing them a genuine experience.
>
> (Dennis White, Lakeland Anishinaabe Faculty)

Teacher candidates recognized their inability to "join" the community but wanted to connect in meaningful ways. Though temporary, this offered an opportunity for students to relate to the tension of a borderland experience. Anzaldua (2012) uses the term *borderland* when speaking of groups of people who live on an invisible border and have learned to live in both cultural worlds. The cross-community connections (college, PreK-12 school, and community ceremonies) provided a way for students to more fully engage in the activity on the "border" through new relationships (students) crossing contexts (community). Abiding by the cultural rules of both worlds was challenging. The UM teacher candidates only had a glimpse of this challenge but expressed a deeper awareness of the desire for community members to preserve their heritage, culture, and traditions.

Historical Trauma

Teacher candidates applied earlier structures of theory (e.g., racial identity development) to better understand their reactions. They recognized the inability to "have it all figured out" or the idea that biases are absolved through seemingly supportive actions. This stage of pseudo-independence, in which they understood the unfairness of white privilege, was short lived as they realized the depth, breadth, and fluid nature of power. With consideration of trauma, the role of the settler became apparent.

> I felt overwhelmed with all I had learned and saw….it was overwhelming to know that this whole community (and others like it) are so affected by historical trauma issues and it's a long road of healing and working through those issues.
>
> (Paige, May 16, 2016)

> It felt uncomfortable for me for this white guy to be telling the kids about their own culture and history and, in a sense, glorifying what the Europeans brought to America.
>
> (Paige, May 25, 2016)

The excerpts in this section illustrate the dilemma faced by teacher candidates: how to acknowledge the trauma of the past as it survives in hurtful ways today and at the same time honor the joy for the cultural and linguistic richness.

> We are always walking in two worlds. We are always out of our comfort zone when we are away from our homes, our community or our school. I recall some time I spent helping with a seventh-grade art class. The art teacher, a non-Indigenous, wanted to teach the art of yarn bag weaving… One of the traumas, perhaps triumphs amidst tragedies, is that young students must face tragedies. Students were free to sit at the art tables as they felt comfortable to sit. During one span of several weeks, three girls would all sit together, competing yet encouraging each other. At first, I did not realize that the three students shared a trauma. They had all lost their fathers due to some tragic event, one in a boating accident during spearing season, one to a traffic accident involving alcohol, and the other to an overdose. I still consider these girls affected by historical trauma.
>
> (Dennis White, Lakeland Anishinaabe Faculty)

These insights on intergenerational trauma were available through interaction with "translators", consisting of the instructor (Dennis White), the Lakeland student, and community school administration. It was through discussion and listening, with these vital community members, that the UM students were able to internalize these insights.

Translation at the Border

The term translator is commonly used to refer to translation of the language but rarely includes the culture. In our interactions the translation was multifaceted.

We spent the first two hours asking questions and discussing traditions and spirituality. I am glad Mindy (Lakeland Anishinaabe student) is in the class with us because she is able to give us the perspective of a student and young adult. She does not sugarcoat the realities that the young people face and I appreciate her honesty.

(Lynell, May 16, 2016)

Mindy provided the connection at the border for a more complete understanding of the lived experience at Lakeland. She was a translator, not only in terms of the Indigenous language, but also translating her culture to the outside world, at least to four non-Indigenous future teachers. Mindy was able to connect with UM students as they shared status as college students and assist crossing the cultural divide to recognize the privilege and oppression attached to their cultural roles. In the example below the insider/outsider divide is harder to cross.

We, as Indigenous people, are often thrust from one role to the other, mostly in expected situations but sometimes in unexpected ways. We may go to certain stores in town and expect a clerk or the owner to follow us around. Many stores we do not go into for that reason. We feel comfortable when we see other Indigenous people shopping or see an Indigenous clerk at the cash register. We know we can joke and smile with them.

(Dennis White, Lakeland Anishinaabe Faculty)

This illustrates the pervasive nature of settler influence. The student reflections trace beginning understanding of the settler mentality; however, it was the process of coding, analysis, and discussion that reveals the tenacity of the settler identity for students. In the immersion/emersion stage students recognized the need to engage other anti-racist dominant culture members and redefine their understanding of Whiteness. As they were troubled by their initial insights, we discussed and worked together using additional readings in research meetings to make sense of these complicated insights on the power and continuing nature of colonization. Through this process, students were able to indicate a desire to honor the past, acknowledge the "long road" of trauma, and build on cultural strengths advocating for and teaching communities similar to and different from their lived experiences (Brave Heart, 2007). This reflective process, following the visit, supported their continued growth.

Indigenous and non-Indigenous educators of Indigenous students must seek more experiences for each side of the two groups to respond to each other in situations within the scope of Indigenous experience. What was a natural occurrence for the student from Lakeland, including the offering of tobacco or picking wild foods, could be explained from her standpoint to the UM students. That transfer of information…validates to the Lakeland student her own experiences in ways that no lecture or reading could. While I agree the field study brings insight for the UM students that may be more difficult to reach without their experience within the Indigenous community, I feel that the flow of positive experience can be in both directions…When the Indigenous student can teach someone else, the Indigenous student also learns better and more deeply.

(Dennis White, Lakeland Anishinaabe Faculty)

As students and teachers, community members and visitors, we move among the varied contexts and simultaneously shift our roles from insider to outsider. The bi-directional learning allows for Indigenous and non-Indigenous students to grow in confidence and find a sense of self and pride when sharing experiences. Avoiding a burden on historically marginalized community members to teach dominant culture members is crucial. It must be a reciprocal relationship.

Implications

The Lakeland Anishinaabe field experience provided the opportunity for teacher candidates to explore the ongoing effects of historical trauma without minimizing, othering, over-identifying through settler nativism, or explaining away through "settler moves to innocence" (Tuck & Yang, 2012). This deepened insight was influenced by the foundational context and practice before the journey. The dialogic journaling and reflection throughout kept the field experience from becoming easily summarized and, therefore, packed away like a souvenir. Our finding of insider/outsider status revealed that teacher candidates demonstrated a deeper, understanding of the impact of trauma on children and families, and an understanding of historical legacy and colonization beyond a false history (Trilokekar & Kukar, 2011). Through the writing and editing process of the research there is continued reflection and ongoing application of this experience. Our findings supplement recommendations from tribal communities to support Indigenous youth that call for (a) cultural competence training, (b) information for access and equity awareness, and (c) curriculum and pedagogy that recognizes culture, tradition and language (Best et al., 2013; US Department of Education, 2015).

UM cohorts participating in Lakeland field experiences after this study included students who identified as Latina and offered new ways to connect across oppressive systems. Our communities are becoming more diverse and understanding varied histories of oppression, power and privilege helps to honor each child. Successful international partnerships include:

- home community ceremony, language and cultural activities;
- previous domestic field experiences;
- application of critical and ecological theory;
- projects exploring identity and context;

- courses with a focus on social justice, systemic privilege and oppression;
- processes for critical questioning and reflection and
- a willingness of participants to engage.

Given this list, the support and patience of the members of the Anishinaabe community were paramount as we struggled to recognize, own, and process the reality of our nation's history in today's educational settings. Visiting a nation within a nation deepens understanding that schools are an extension of the community; therefore, we need to be a part of the community, not just a part of the educational institution. The importance of reciprocity was clear.

Partnerships with Indigenous communities can be brief and superficial, with researchers following funding sources to new communities. Leaders and researchers need to be committed to the promise of cross-cultural work despite the pain. Educators are complicit in perpetuating a false history if we fail to acknowledge the generational impact of erasure and segregation. Almost 50 years ago, policy was created "for the establishment and operation of exemplary and innovative educational programs and centers, involving new educational approaches, methods, and techniques designed to enrich programs of elementary and secondary education for Indian children" (Indian Education Act, 1972, p. 340). Yet, the population of Lakeland's neighboring public high school consists of 28% Native American, 64% White students, and graduates only 57% Native American versus 93% White students. Through our research we suggest that the intersection of home and school contexts must shift so that the teaching workforce more accurately reflects the varied cultural and linguistic lives of children in classrooms, representation matters.

> Bumping along these roads, Dennis recounts childhood memories and gratitude washes over me. Crossing 20 years of connection, I listen now as he shares and jokes with our ECE university students. His eloquence juxtaposes the challenge and beauty in his life. He suggests we stop to explore the trillium more closely. I attempt to capture the image, but similar to this intersection of lived experience and time, it remains elusive, yet powerful. *Weweni sa naa.*
>
> (Lucy Heimer, UM ECE Faculty, Coordinator of
> the Field Experience)

> The steps to Indigenous success are incremental; yet as in any growth, or decay, of a living organism, that growth is more fractal than linear. The growth is exponential with sudden growth in spurts and unexplained leaps at times.
>
> (Dennis White, Lakeland Anishinaabe Faculty)

This chapter is adapted from: Heimer, L., Caya, L., Lancaster, P., Saxon, L. & Wildman, C. (2019). Nations within a nation: Cross-cultural field insights in an Anishinaabe context. *Global Education Review*, 6 (3). 65-83. https://ger.mercy.edu/index.php/ger/article/view/518

References

Anzaldua, G. (2012). *Borderlands: La frontera*. San Francisco, CA: Aunt Lute Books.

Archuleta, M., Child, B., & Lomawaima, T. (2000). *Away from home: American Indian boarding school experiences*. Phoenix: Heard Museum.

Auld, G., Dyer, J., & Charles, C. (2016). Dangerous practices: The practicum experiences of non-Indigenous pre-service teachers in remote communities. *Australian Journal of Teacher Education, 41*(6), 165–179. http://ro.ecu.edu.au/ajte/vol41/iss6/9

Best, J., Dunlap, A., Fredericks, L., & Nelson, S. (2013). *Culturally-based education for Indigenous language and culture. A national forum to establish priorities for future research.* Rapid City, SD: Regional Educational Laboratory Retrieved from https://www.acf.hhs.gov/sites/default/files/ana/cbeforindigenouslanguageforum.pdf

Bombay, A., Matheson, K., & Anisman, H. (2014). The intergenerational effects of Indian residential schools: Implications for the concept of historical trauma. *Transcultural Psychiatry, 51*(3), 320–338. http://doi:10.1177/1363461513503380

Brave Heart, M. Y. H. (2007). The impact of historical trauma: The example of the Native community. In M. Bussey & J. B. Wise (Eds.), *Trauma transformed: An empowerment response* (pp. 176–193). New York, NY: Columbia University Press.

Brayboy, B. J., Fann, A., Castagno, A. E., & Solyom, J. A. (2012). *Postsecondary education for American Indian and Alaska natives: Higher education for nation building and self-determination.* San Francisco, CA: Jossey-Bass.

Centers for Disease Control. (n.d.). Retrieved from https://www.cdc.gov/tribal/data-resources/

Cushner, K., & Chang, C. (2015). Developing intercultural competence through overseas student teaching: Checking our assumptions. *Intercultural Education 26*(3), 165–178. https://doi.org/10.1080/14675986.2015.1040326

Dunbar-Ortiz, R. (2015). *An Indigenous peoples' history of the United States: For young people*. Boston, MA: Beacon Press.

Heimer, L., Caya, L., Lancaster, P., Saxon, L., & Wildman, C. (2019). Nations within a nation: Cross- cultural field insights in an Anishinaabe context. *Global Education Review, 6*(3). 65–83. https://ger.mercy.edu/index.php/ger/article/view/518

Indian Education Act of 1972, Pub. L. No. 92-318, title IV, 86 Stat. 334-345 (1972).

Kim, K. & Kim, J. (2017). Going beyond the gap between theory and practice: Rethinking teacher reflection with post-structural insights, *Journal of Early Childhood Teacher Education, 38*(4), 293–307. https://doi.org/10.1080/10901027.2017.1388307

Kolb, D. A. (1984). *Experiential learning: Experience as the source of learning and development* (Vol. 1). Englewood Cliffs, NJ: Prentice-Hall.

Ladson-Billings, G.J. (2005). Is the team all right? Diversity and teacher education. *Journal of Teacher Education, 56*(2), 229–234. https://doi.org/10.1177/0022487105275917

Madrid, S., Baldwin, N., & Belbase, S. (2016). Feeling culture: The emotional experience of six early childhood educators in a cross-cultural context. *Global Studies of Childhood, 8*(3), 1–16. https://doi.org/10.1177/2043610616664622

McCarty, T. L. & Lee, T. S. (2014). Critical culturally sustaining/revitalizing pedagogy and Indigenous education sovereignty. *Harvard Educational Review, 84*(1), 101–124. https://doi.org/10.17763/haer.84.1.q83746nl5pj34216

Miles, M. B., Huberman, A. M., & Saldaña, J. (2013). *Qualitative data analysis: A methods sourcebook* (3rd ed.). Thousand Oaks, CA: Sage Publications.

Moss, H., & Marx, H. (2011). Please mind the culture gap: Intercultural development during a teacher education study abroad program. *Journal of Teacher Education, 62*(1), 35–47. https://doi: 10.1177/0022487110381998

National Center for Education Statistics. (2019). *Status and Trends in the Education of Racial and Ethnic Groups 2018*. Retrieved from https://nces.ed.gov/pubs2019/2019038.pdf

Nieto, S. (2010). *The light in their eyes: Creating multicultural learning communities*. New York, NY: Teachers College Press.

Schön, D. (1987). *Educating the reflective practitioner*. San Francisco, CA: Jossey-Bass.

Sleeter, C. E. (2001). Preparing teachers for culturally diverse schools: Research and the overwhelming presence of whiteness. *Journal of Teacher Education, 52*(2), 94–106. https://doi.org/10.1177/0022487101052002002

Smith, L. T. (2012). *Decolonizing methodologies: Research and Indigenous peoples*. London, UK: Zed Books.

Smolcic, E., & Katunich, J. (2017). Teachers crossing borders: A review of the research into cultural immersion field experience for teachers. *Teaching and Teacher Education, 62*, 47–59. https://doi:10.1016/j.tate.2016.11.002

Solorzano, D. G., & Yosso, T. J. (2001). From racial stereotyping and deficit discourse toward a critical race theory in teacher education. *Multicultural Education, 9*(1), 2–8 https://eric.ed.gov/?id=EJ634009

Stake, R. E. (1995). *The art of case study research*. Thousand Oaks, CA: Sage.

Sumida Huaman, E., Chiu, B., & Billy, C. (2019). Indigenous internationalization: Indigenous worldviews, higher education, and tribal colleges and universities. *Education Policy Analysis Archives, 27*(101), 1-29. https://doi: https://doi.org/10.14507/epaa.27.4366

Swadener, B. B., & Mutua, K. (2008). Decolonizing performances: Deconstructing the global postcolonial. In N. K. Denzin, Y. S. Lincoln, & L. T. Smith. (Eds.), *Handbook of critical and Indigenous methodologies* (pp. 31–43). Thousand Oaks, CA: Sage.

Thomas, U. (2011). *Culture or chaos in the village.* New York, NY: Rowman and Littlefield.

Treuer, A. (2012). *Everything you wanted to know about Indians but were afraid to ask.* St. Paul, MN: Borealis Books.

Trilokekar, R., & Kukar, P. (2011). Disorienting experiences during study abroad: Reflections of pre-service teacher candidates. *Teaching and Teacher Education, 27*(7), 1141–1150. https://doi: 10.1016/j.tate.2011.06.002

Tuck, E. & Yang, K. W. (2012). Decolonization is not a metaphor. *Decolonization: Indigeneity, Education and Society, 1*(1), 1–40. https://jps.library.utoronto.ca/index.php/des/article/view/18630

US Department of Education. (2015). *White house initiative on American Indian and Alaska Native education school environment listening sessions final report.* Retrieved from http://sites.ed.gov/whiaiane/

US Department of the Interior. (2020). *Indian Child Welfare Act of 1978.* Retrieved from https://www.ssa.gov/OP_Home/comp2/F095-608.html

Woodcock, D. B., & Alawiye, O. (2001). The antecedents of failure and emerging hope: American Indians & public higher education. *Education, 121*(4), 810.

Index